2 Spas, St. Lucia

Resorts such as Calabash Cove, Body Holiday, and Sandals Grande St. Lucian have gorgeous spas that make the most of their tropical island setting. *(Ch. 3)*

3 Mount Gay Rum Tour & Tasting, Barbados

Established in 1703, Mount Gay Rum is the world's oldest rum company. They take great pride in their history, offering fascinating tours with plenty of samples. *(Ch. 2)*

4 Diamond Falls, St. Lucia

Brilliant flowers and towering trees line the pathways that lead to the splendid Diamond Falls and mineral baths deep within botanical gardens. *(Ch. 3)*

5 Sailing, St. Lucia

A sailing excursion along the lovely west coast is the best way to get from Rodney Bay to Soufrière. Most trips include a snorkeling stop at a secluded beach. *(Ch. 3)*

6 Rainforest Hike, St. Lucia

Edmund Forest Reserve has an abundance of exotic flowers and rare birds such as the bright Jacquot parrot. A trek through this lush landscape also offers spectacular views of mountains, valleys, and the sea. *(Ch. 3)*

7 The Pitons, St. Lucia

Rising above Soufrière Bay, these distinctive peaks are the symbol of St. Lucia. Stay right between them at Viceroy's Sugar Beach resort, climb them with a guide, or simply marvel at their beauty. *(Ch. 3)*

8 Swim with the Turtles, Barbados

The waters off Barbados are home to adorable hawksbill and leatherback sea turtles. To spot them, book a dive with Barbados Blue in the Carlisle Bay Marine Park, snorkel from Dottins Reef, or just swim from the Treasure Beach Hotel. *(Ch. 2)*

9 Dance to Island Music, Barbados

Barbados nightclubs often feature great local bands. In Holetown and on the narrow waterfront byway known as "The Gap" on the south coast, you can hear live reggae, soca, pop, and jazz at various venues. *(Ch. 2)*

10 Golf at Sandy Lane, Barbados

On an island with spectacular courses, Sandy Lane Resort has three of the best. The famous Green Monkey Course is reserved for guests, but the Old Nine and Country Club courses are open to everyone. *(Ch. 2)*

11 Scuba and Snorkeling, St. Lucia

Anse Chastanet, just around the bend from the Pitons, has a colorful coral-lined wall that drops to more than 140 feet. Other great diving and snorkeling spots are at Anse Cochon and points along the western shore. *(Ch. 3)*

12 Sunbury Plantation House, Barbados

Period furnishings, old prints, and horse-drawn carriages create a postcard vision of plantation life in the 18th and 19th centuries. Take a tour, try the restaurant's buffet lunch, or splurge on a five-course dinner. *(Ch. 2)*

13 Harrison's Cave, Barbados

This extensive cave system winds its way through the limestone underneath Barbados. There's even a 40-foot waterfall. It's a very popular sight, so plan your visit around the cruise-ship crowds. *(Ch. 2)*

CONTENTS

1 EXPERIENCE BARBADOS AND ST. LUCIA 13

What's Where 14

Barbados Planner............. 16

St. Lucia Planner.............. 18

If You Like..................... 20

When to Go................... 23

Great Itineraries.............. 24

Weddings and Honeymoons............. 26

Family Travel to Barbados and St. Lucia........ 28

2 BARBADOS 29

Planning 32

Exploring Barbados 35

Beaches....................... 52

Where to Eat.................. 59

Where to Stay 69

Nightlife 87

Shopping...................... 91

Sports and Activities.......... 95

3 ST. LUCIA 105

Planning 107

Exploring St. Lucia 110

Beaches...................... 128

Where to Eat................. 133

Where to Stay 141

Nightlife and Performing Arts.............. 154

Shopping..................... 156

Sports and Activities......... 159

About Our Writer 170

Getting Here and Around 170

Essentials 176

TRAVEL SMART.......... 169

Getting Here and Around 170

Essentials 176

INDEX.................... 185

ABOUT OUR WRITERS... 192

MAPS

Barbados 34

Bridgetown 36

South Coast.................. 39

East Coast, West Coast, and Central Interior........... 47

St. Lawrence Gap 62

Holetown and Vicinity......... 66

St. Lucia...................... 111

Vigie to Cap Estate........... 114

Castries...................... 118

Soufrière and Vicinity 125

Rodney Bay Village 135

ABOUT THIS GUIDE

Fodor's Recommendations

Everything in this guide is worth doing—we don't cover what isn't—but exceptional sights, hotels, and restaurants are recognized with additional accolades. **Fodor's**Choice ★ indicates our top recommendations. Care to nominate a new place? Visit Fodors.com/contact-us.

Trip Costs

We list prices wherever possible to help you budget well. Hotel and restaurant price categories from $ to $$$$ are noted alongside each recommendation. For hotels, we include the lowest cost of a standard double room in high season. For restaurants, we cite the average price of a main course at dinner or, if dinner isn't served, at lunch. For attractions, we always list adult admission fees; discounts are usually available for children, students, and senior citizens.

Hotels

Our local writers vet every hotel to recommend the best overnights in each price category, from budget to expensive. Unless otherwise specified, you can expect private bath, phone, and TV in your room. For expanded hotel reviews visit Fodors.com.

Restaurants

Unless we state otherwise, restaurants are open for lunch and dinner daily. We mention dress code only when there's a specific requirement and reservations only when they're essential or not accepted.

Credit Cards

The hotels and restaurants in this guide typically accept credit cards. If not, we'll say so.

Top Picks
★ **Fodor's**Choice

Listings
⊠ Address
⊠ Branch address
🕮 Mailing address
☎ Telephone
🖷 Fax
⊕ Website
✎ E-mail

🎟 Admission fee
◷ Open/closed times
Ⓜ Subway
✛ Directions or Map coordinates

Hotels & Restaurants
🛏 Hotel
🛏 Number of rooms
🍽 Meal plans

✕ Restaurant
🍴 Reservations
👔 Dress code
🚫 No credit cards
$ Price

Other
⇨ See also
☞ Take note
⛳ Golf facilities

EXPERIENCE BARBADOS AND ST. LUCIA

WHAT'S WHERE

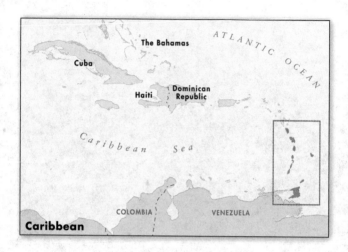

Caribbean

1 Barbados. Broad vistas, sweeping seascapes, craggy cliffs, and acre upon acre of sugarcane make up the island's varied landscape. The warm Bajan hospitality, welcoming hotels and resorts, sophisticated dining, lively nightspots, and, of course, magnificent sunny beaches have forged a long, successful history of tourism.

2 St. Lucia. One of the greenest and most beautiful islands in the Caribbean is, arguably, the most romantic. The scenic southern and central regions are mountainous and lush, with dense rain forest, endless banana plantations, and fascinating natural attractions and historic sites. Along the west coast and in the far north, picturesque and distinctively appealing resorts are interspersed with dozens of delightful inns that appeal to families, lovers, and adventurers.

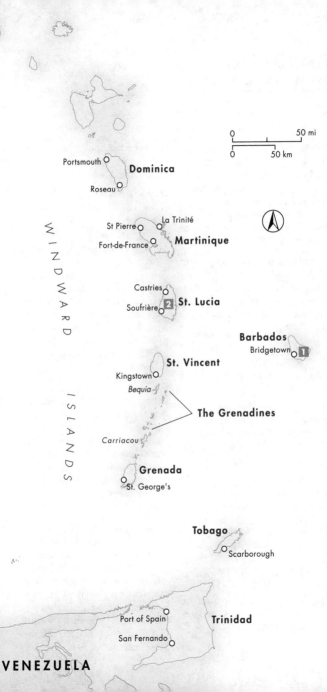

BARBADOS PLANNER

Island Activities

There's always something to do in Barbados, and that's the appeal to most visitors. White-sand **beaches** await your arrival whether you choose to stay among the classy row of resorts on the west coast or on the more affordable south coast.

Exceptional **golf courses** lure a lot of players to the island, but the private courses—notably Royal Westmoreland and Sandy Lane—aren't for anyone with a light wallet.

The island's **restaurant scene** is impressive; you can choose from street-party barbecue to international cuisine that rivals the finest dining on the planet.

Getting out on the water is the favored activity, whether that's on a **snorkeling** day sail, in a **minisub**, on a **deep-sea fishing boat**, or **surfing** at Bathsheba Soup Bowl.

Logistics

Getting to Barbados: Fly nonstop to Barbados from Boston, Fort Lauderdale, Miami, and New York–JFK or connect through any of those cities. Grantley Adams International Airport (BGI) is in Christ Church Parish, about 15 minutes from hotels situated along the south coast, 45 minutes from the west coast, and about 30 minutes from Bridgetown.

Hassle Factor: Low because of frequent nonstop flights from airports in the United States.

On the Ground: Ground transportation is available immediately outside the customs area. Some resorts arrange ground transfers if you make arrangements in advance. Otherwise, you can take a taxi. Airport taxis aren't metered, but fares are regulated (about $38–$40 to Speightstown, $30–$35 to west-coast hotels, $16–$22 to south-coast hotels). Be sure, however, to establish the fare before getting into the taxi and confirm whether the price quoted is in U.S. or Barbadian dollars.

Getting Around on the Island: You may want to rent a car if you're staying in an isolated area, but bus service is good throughout the island—especially between Bridgetown and stops along the west and south coasts. Taxis, of course, are always an option.

Where to Stay

If you stay on either the tony west coast or the action-packed south coast, you'll have access to great beaches. East-coast beaches are not safe for swimming, but you'll find spectacular ocean views. Prices in Barbados increase significantly in high season (December 15–April 15) than during the quieter months. Most hotels include no meals in their rates, but some include breakfast, many offer a meal plan, some require you to purchase the meal plan in the high season, and a few offer all-inclusive packages.

Resorts: Great resorts run the gamut—from unpretentious to knock-your-socks-off—in size, intimacy, amenities, and price. Many are well suited to families.

Villas and Condos: Families and long-term visitors may choose from a variety of condos—from busy time-share resorts to more sedate holiday complexes. Villas and villa complexes range from luxurious to simple.

Small Inns: A few small, cozy inns are located in the east and southeast regions of the island.

Tips for Travelers

The minimum legal drinking age in Barbados is 18.

Electricity in Barbados is 110 volts, just as in the United States. No converters or transformers are needed for U.S. appliances.

A 7.5% government tax is added to all hotel bills, and a 7.5% V.A.T. is imposed on restaurant meals, admissions to attractions, and merchandise sales (other than duty-free items). Prices are often tax-inclusive; if not, the V.A.T. will be added to your bill.

The Barbados dollar is pegged to the U.S. dollar at a rate of Bds$1.98 to US$1. U.S. currency is accepted almost everywhere on the island, so many travelers never change their money into local currency—although change will most often be given in local currency. ATMs are widely available but dispense local currency only.

ST. LUCIA PLANNER

Island Activities

The island's **beaches** are certainly inviting—but St. Lucia is a volcanic island, so you won't find long stretches of fine white sand. Reduit Beach, in the north, is considered the island's best beach with more than a mile of golden sand.

St. Lucia offers excellent **diving**, particularly along its southwest coast near Soufrière. Dive Saint Lucia, in Rodney Bay, is a state-of-the-art facility that offers dive trips, equipment, and instruction. Dive shops located at Anse Chastanet, an upscale resort near the Pitons, and Ti Kaye, farther north at Anse Cochon, specialize in beach-access diving.

A **day sail** on a catamaran is one of the best ways to see the island and perhaps the best way to travel from Castries to Soufrière, or vice versa. And **deep-sea fishing** is also first-rate.

St. Lucia's crown jewel is its well-preserved **rain forest**, which is best explored on a guided hike.

Climbing one of the **Pitons** is a rewarding experience for adventurers, but you must hire a guide.

Logistics

Getting to St. Lucia: Fly nonstop to St. Lucia from Atlanta, Boston, Charlotte, Miami, Newark, and New York–JFK—or connect through any of those cities.

St. Lucia's primary gateway is Hewanorra International Airport (UVF) in Vieux Fort, on the island's southern tip. All large jets land at Hewanorra, which is particularly convenient to resorts in Vieux Fort or the Soufrière area. Regional airlines and small aircraft fly into George F. L. Charles Airport (SLU) in Castries, also referred to as Vigie Airport, which is convenient to resorts in the north. The 40-mile (60-km) drive between Hewanorra and resorts in the north takes about 90 minutes; between Hewanorra and Marigot Bay, about 60 minutes; and between Hewanorra and Soufrière, about 45 minutes.

Hassle Factor: Medium to high due to the long drive from Hewanorra International Airport.

On the Ground: Taxis are available at both airports if transfers are not included in your travel package, but the 90-minute ride to the north from Hewanoorra is expensive ($80–$100 for up to four passengers). The 45-minute ride from Hewanorra to the Soufrière area is $75–$80. A helicopter is available to Castries from Hewanorra; it's a costly ($165 per person) but convenient option, cutting the transfer time to about 12 minutes.

Getting Around: A car may be important if you're staying at a small inn or hotel away from the beach or plan to confine your exploring to the northern part of the island. Driving elsewhere is tricky due to the winding mountain roads and sharp hairpin turns. Taxis are readily available for short trips or all-day excursions.

Where to Stay

Nearly all St. Lucia's resorts and small inns are tucked into lush, secluded coves, unspoiled beaches, or forested hillsides in three primary locations along the calm Caribbean (western) coast: Rodney Bay north to Cap Estate, Castries to Marigot Bay, and in and around Soufrière. Only a pair of sister resorts are in the south at Vieux Fort.

Big Beach Resorts: Most people choose to stay in one of St. Lucia's many beach resorts, the majority of which are upscale and fairly pricey. Several resorts offer an all-inclusive option, including three Sandals resorts and two Sunswept resorts (The Body Holiday and Rendezvous), St. James's Club Morgan Bay Resort & Spa, East Winds Inn, Coconut Bay Beach Resort & Spa and Serenity at Coconut Bay, and Royalton St. Lucia Resort & Spa.

Small Inns: If you want something more intimate and perhaps less expensive, St. Lucia has dozens of small, locally owned inns

and hotels that may or may not be directly on the beach.

Villas: Luxury villa communities and independent private villas are a good alternative for families. Many of these are in the north in or near Cap Estate.

Tips for Travelers

The minimum legal drinking age in St. Lucia is 18.

Electricity in St. Lucia is 220 volts, 50 cycles. U.S. appliances will require a plug adaptor (square, three-pin) and, if they are not dual-voltage, a transformer.

A 10% government V.A.T. is added to all hotel and restaurant bills. A 10% service charge is usually added to restaurant bills; otherwise, tip 10%–15%. Tip bellboys $1 per bag, maids $2 per night, and taxi drivers 10% of the fare.

The Eastern Caribbean dollar is pegged to the U.S. dollar at a rate of EC$2.67 to US$1. U.S. currency is accepted almost everywhere on the island, but you'll get change in local currency. It's helpful to have some local currency if you plan to shop in smaller markets or ride buses.

IF YOU LIKE

A Romantic Rendezvous

Both Barbados and St. Lucia are popular destinations for weddings, honeymoons, second honeymoons, and other intimate getaways.

BARBADOS

The Atlantis Hotel. Blending the historic atmosphere with modern amenities and a cliffside location on the rugged east coast works perfectly—and the food is good.

Cobblers Cove Hotel. Sophisticated and classy, consider splurging on the amazing penthouse suites in this west-coast establishment.

The Crane. While the property is huge and the resort is off the beaten path, the ocean views are spectacular and Crane Beach is one of the island's loveliest beaches.

The House. A candlelit dinner on the beach and spa treatments for two are special treats at this luxurious, adults-only, beachfront enclave.

Sandals Barbados. Everything here is geared for couples and romance. A special indulgence: a personal butler who will even draw a candlelit bubble bath for you, complete with Champagne.

Sweetfield Manor. Perched on a ridge overlooking Carlisle Bay, this restored manse in a garden setting is a delightful bed-and-breakfast inn with seven rooms.

ST. LUCIA

Jade Mountain. The crème de la crème—adjacent to Anse Chastanet—every open-plan "sanctuary" has an infinity pool and views of the Pitons.

Ladera. This sophisticated, elegantly rustic, small inn is perched directly between the Pitons with private plunge pools.

Rendezvous. For couples only, this all-inclusive beachfront resort in Castries offers a variety of accommodations and lots of activities.

Sandals Halcyon. Lots of folks find this couples-only resort—the smallest and most intimate of three Sandals properties on the island—quite romantic.

Serenity at Coconut Bay. At this upscale, adults-only enclave, the luxe accommodations have private garden patios and saltwater plunge pools—and personal butlers care for every need.

Sugar Beach, A Viceroy Resort. Location, location, location. A full-service, upscale, beachfront resort with ultra-stylish villas that spill down the hillside between the Pitons.

Ti Kaye Village. Quiet and remote, your private cottage—each with a garden shower—peeps out of the hillside high above Anse Cochon.

Great Eating

The culinary experience in Barbados ranges from fine gourmet dining to simple local fare—and everything in between. On St. Lucia, most chefs embrace the Creole style with a focus on local produce and spices.

BARBADOS

The Atlantis. Lunch alfresco is the perfect choice when touring the east coast—especially when it's a Bajan buffet.

Daphne's. Seafood and Italian fare are the specialties at this chic beachfront restaurant.

Fish Pot. This seaside restaurant serves fresh seafood and tempting Mediterranean specialties.

Waterfront Café. Try local specialties or old favorites while people-watching along The Careenage.

ST. LUCIA

Boucan. Everything on the menu here features chocolate.

Chateau Mygo. For casual dockside dining with a view, you can't beat this spot on Marigot Bay—one of the prettiest in the Caribbean.

The Cliff at Cap. Diners come to Cap Maison's restaurant for the chef's nouveau French–West Indian cuisine and the dining room's spectacular cliffside setting.

Coal Pot. The delicious meals at this island institution have been sought after since the early 1960s.

Dasheene Restaurant at Ladera. Dinner at this terrace restaurant is memorable, but the close-up view of the Pitons is breathtaking during lunch or the cocktail hour.

Orlando's. Chef Orlando Satchell presents his "Share the Love" style of Caribbean cuisine, which always involves local ingredients.

The Water

Both Barbados and St. Lucia offer a number of ways to enjoy the beautiful Caribbean Sea with either very little or a whole lot of exertion.

BARBADOS

Beaches. South-coast beaches are broad, with white sand and low-to-medium surf; on the west coast, beaches can become quite narrow after autumn storms.

Diving and snorkeling. Divers can explore more than two dozen dive sites, including a number of sunken wrecks; snorkelers especially enjoy the protected reef that stretches along much of the west coast.

Sea excursions. Take a day cruise on a catamaran and snorkel and swim with the turtles, a romantic sunset cruise with dinner and cocktails, or a spirited voyage on a pirate ship.

Sportfishing. Charter fishing trips depart from The Careenage in Bridgetown year-round.

Windsurfing. The island's southern tip is one of the world's prime locations for windsurfing—and its cousin, kitesurfing.

ST. LUCIA

Beaches. Reduit Beach at Rodney Bay is the longest, broadest beach on St. Lucia; but tiny beaches in quiet coves are equally appealing.

Diving and snorkeling. Enjoy the best diving—wall, wreck, reef, and drift—between the Pitons and Anse Cochon; beach-entry sites at Anse Chastanet and Anse Cochon appeal to divers and snorkelers alike.

Sea excursions. A day sail along the coast between Rodney Bay and Soufrière is a perfect way to visit the island's natural attractions and historic sites.

Sportfishing. Generally catch-and-release, the captain may let you bring a fish ashore for you (or the hotel chef) to prepare for your dinner.

Shopping

It's fun to bring home a memento for yourself and souvenirs for your friends and family.

BARBADOS

Art. You can find a broad selection of local art at galleries in Speightstown; adjacent to Earthworks in Edgehill; at the Hilton Barbados near Bridgetown; at The Tides Restaurant on the west coast; and at Champers restaurant in the south.

Bajan souvenirs. Best of Barbados sells items ranging from prints and housewares to arts and crafts—all Bajan made or designed.

Rum, perfume, and more. The departure lounge at Grantley Adams International Airport is a veritable shopping mall of duty-free goods.

ST. LUCIA

Batik and silkscreen. You'll find locally made batik clothing and wall hangings by Caribelle Batik in Morne Fortune and Joan Alexander-Stowe in Soufrière; Bagshaws of St. Lucia creates clothing and table linens in tropical patterns from silk-screened fabric handmade in its La Toc studio.

Sauces, spices, and more. At Castries Market on Saturday morning, buy hot pepper sauce, vanilla extract, chocolate, bags of spices, straw mats, wood carvings, and a zillion other items to bring home.

WHEN TO GO

High season in Barbados and St. Lucia runs from mid-December through mid-April. If you visit in mid-May or June, prices may be 20% to 50% less, particularly in Barbados. The period from mid-August through late November is typically the least busy time in both Barbados and St. Lucia; however, some hotels on Barbados close for several weeks in September and/or October (the slowest months in the off-season) for annual maintenance and staff vacations. Some restaurants close during that time, too.

Temperatures are fairly consistent throughout the year in Barbados and St. Lucia. The "rainy season" (June–November), which coincides with the Atlantic hurricane season, feels hotter because there's more humidity. Hurricanes are rare in Barbados, as they usually pass well to the north, but drenching tropical rainstorms are not unusual in the fall.

Festivals and Events

In Barbados: In late April the popular Barbados Reggae Festival celebrates that infectious music with a week of live performances by both local and international bands. Gospelfest occurs in May, with performances by gospel headliners from around the world. Dating from the 19th century, Crop Over—a monthlong festival similar to Carnival—begins in July and ends on Kadooment Day (a national holiday) to mark the end of the sugarcane harvest. In mid-November the annual Food & Rum Festival attracts international chefs, wine experts, and local rum ambassadors.

In St. Lucia: In April the St. Lucia Golf Open is an amateur tournament held at the St. Lucia Golf Resort & Country Club in Cap Estate. St. Lucia Jazz, featuring international stars, is held at various venues in early May; as it's the year's premier event, finding accommodations during that week may be difficult. St. Lucia's summer Carnival is held in Castries beginning in late June, culminating in two days of music, dancing, and parading in mid-July. The St. Lucia Billfishing Tournament, which attracts anglers from far and wide, is held in October. Also in October, Creole Heritage Month culminates in Jounen Kwéyol Entenasyonnal (International Creole Day)—featuring Creole food, music, games, and folklore performances in Castries and other locales—on the last Sunday of the month.

GREAT ITINERARIES

Barbados

Barbados from Bottom to Top. You must visit Harrison's Cave—a unique natural wonder in the Caribbean. The underground tram ride through the cave will thrill the whole family. Afterward, visit Flower Forest and Orchid World, two beautiful gardens that are nearby and have snack bars where lunch is available. On your way home, stop at Gun Hill Signal Station for a panoramic view of the whole southern half of the island.

A Day in Barbados's Wild Wild East. From Speightstown, head east to Farley Hill and the Barbados Wildlife Reserve before continuing on to St. Nicholas Abbey, a beautifully restored great house that's definitely worth a stop. Nearby, the scenic overlook at Cherry Tree Hill provides a spectacular view of the whole Atlantic coast. Then the ride along the coastal road, which hugs the Atlantic Ocean, is particularly scenic. You may glimpse some daredevil surfers at Bathsheba Soup Bowl! Stop for lunch—perhaps a Bajan buffet—at a cliffside inn before heading back through the center of the island. From south-coast hotels, do the trip in reverse.

A Day at Sea along the West Coast of Barbados. Catamaran party boats—*Tiami* and *Cool Run-*

nings—depart from Bridgetown, near the cruise-ship terminal, for a full day of sailing, snorkeling, and swimming with turtles. It's a unique and fascinating experience for the whole family. Lunch and drinks are included. Alternatively, explore wrecks and reefs 100 to 150 feet underwater without getting wet on an Atlantis Submarine cruise. Day trips on the submarine are fascinating, but on the evening cruise the sub's bright spotlights illuminate interesting sea creatures that only appear at night.

A Day (and Evening) on Barbados's South Coast. Escape the hot sun at the Barbados Museum in the Historic Garrison District, a World Heritage site, and at the nearby George Washington House in Bush Hill—yes, he slept here. Then head for busy St. Lawrence Gap, and choose a place for lunch. Spend the afternoon at one of the easily accessible beaches. If it's Friday night, stick around for the Oistins Fish Fry—a street party where you can buy an inexpensive meal of barbecued fish or chicken, sides, cold drinks, music, and see lots of people—locals and visitors alike.

A Day (and Evening) on Barbados's West Coast. At Mullins Beach, near Speightstown, you can rent watersports equipment and beach chairs and find refreshments at Mullin's

Restaurant. At night, head for 1st and 2nd streets in Holetown. Pick any restaurant—they're all good—and end the day at Duke's or Red Door Lounge.

St. Lucia

A Day in St. Lucia's South. St. Lucia's most interesting natural attractions are in the south—specifically, in and around Soufrière. From Rodney Bay or Castries, take a sailing trip down the west coast and admire the eye-popping views of the iconic Pitons as you approach Soufrière Harbor. Tour the sulfurous La Soufrière "drive-in volcano," the spectacular Diamond Botanical Garden with its mineral-encrusted waterfall, and the historic Morne Coubaril agricultural estate (which also has a zip-line ride). Enjoy a Creole lunch at Fond Doux Estate, where you can also walk along the garden pathways and learn how to turn cacao beans into delicious St. Lucian chocolate.

A Day in St. Lucia's Rain Forest. One of the island's most amazing natural attractions is its vast rain forest. There are two ways to enjoy it—from above or below. Kids may prefer a thrilling zip-line trip through the forest canopy, while others may prefer the more sedate aerial tram that takes a slow, two-hour tour through the forest; both of these attractions

are in the Castries Waterworks Rain Forest east of Rodney Bay. Those looking for a more down-to-earth experience may want to take a guided hike in the Edmund Forest Reserve in the central part of the island, but you're expected to hire a guide from the Forest and Lands Department.

A Day of Shopping in Castries. St. Lucia's capital has one of the most extensive market complexes in the Caribbean. You'll find row upon row of tropical fruits and vegetables in the orange-roofed produce market, where vendors also sell spices, vanilla, and locally bottled sauces at bargain prices. Next door and across the street, you'll find huge indoor markets with souvenirs ranging from really cheesy to handcrafted beauties. For duty-free shopping, try Place Carenage or Point Seraphine.

A Day at St. Lucia's Pigeon Island. Take a taxi, minibus, or rental car to Pigeon Island National Park—a historic site and natural playground at the island's northwestern tip. You'll find ruins of 18th-century batteries and garrisons scattered around the 44-acre grounds, along with a multimedia display of the island's ecology and history in the museum and two small beaches. Bring a picnic or buy refreshments at the snack bar.

WEDDINGS AND HONEYMOONS

There's no question that Barbados and St. Lucia rank among the Caribbean's foremost honeymoon destinations. The picturesque beaches, turquoise water, swaying palm trees, balmy tropical breezes, and perpetual sunshine put people in the mood for love. St. Lucia may be the most popular wedding and honeymoon destination in the Caribbean, but at resorts on both islands you'll find wedding planners who can help you put together your perfect special day.

The Big Day

Choosing the Perfect Place. When choosing a location, remember that you really have two choices to make: the ceremony location and where to have the reception, if you're having one. For the former, there are beaches, bluffs overlooking beaches, gardens, private residences, resort lawns, and, of course, places of worship. As for the reception, there are these same choices, as well as restaurants. If you decide to go outdoors, remember the seasons—yes, the Caribbean has seasons. If you're planning a wedding outdoors, be sure you have a backup plan in case it rains. Also, if you're planning an outdoor wedding at sunset—which is very popular—be sure you match the time of your ceremony to the time the sun sets—which is at about 6 pm year-round.

Finding a Wedding Planner. If you and your loved one plan to invite more than a minister to your wedding ceremony, seriously consider an on-island wedding planner who can help select a location, coordinate the event, recommend a florist and a photographer, help plan the menu, and suggest any local traditions to incorporate into your ceremony. Alternatively, many resorts have their own on-site wedding planners and some, such as the three Sandals resorts on St. Lucia and the one on Barbados, offer free weddings with a honeymoon package.

Legal Requirements. There are no minimal residency requirements on either Barbados or St. Lucia, and no blood tests are required on either island. In Barbados you must appear in person to obtain a wedding license, but the formalities can often be completed in less than a half hour at the Ministry of Home Affairs in Bridgetown; the cost is $100 plus $13 for a stamp. For a civil marriage, a separate fee of $125 is payable to the Court; for an alternative venue, $175. And all fees must be paid in cash. In St. Lucia you can either get married after being on the island for three days (for $125), or you can obtain a "special" license anytime after arrival—even the same day you land—for $200. Plan on $60 in additional fees on top of the license cost. On both islands you must provide valid passports for identification and a certified spousal death certificate or divorce decree if you were previously married. On Barbados an official marriage officer (or magistrate or minister) must perform the actual ceremony.

Wedding Attire. In the Caribbean basically anything goes, from long, formal dresses with trains to white bikinis. Floral sundresses are fine, too. Men can wear tuxedos or a simple pair of solid-color slacks with a nice white linen shirt. If you want formal dress and tuxedo, it's usually better to bring your formal attire with you.

Photographs. Deciding whether to use the photographer supplied by your resort or an independent photographer is an important choice. Resorts that host a lot of weddings usually have their own photographers, but you can also find independent, professional island-based photographers; an independent wedding planner will know the best in the area. Look at the portfolio (many photographers will have websites), and decide whether that person can provide the kind of memories that you desire. If you're satisfied with the photographer that your resort uses, then make sure you see proofs and order prints before leaving the island.

The Honeymoon

Do you want Champagne and strawberries delivered to your room each morning? A maze of a swimming pool in which to float? A five-star restaurant in which to dine? Then a resort is the way to go, and both Barbados and St. Lucia have options in various price ranges. Whether you want a luxurious experience or a more modest one, you'll certainly find a perfect romantic escape.

On Barbados, **Cobbler's Cove Hotel** is sophisticated and classy, particularly its splurge-worthy penthouse suites. The **Atlantis Hotel** blends historic atmosphere with modern amenities in a cliffside location on the rugged east coast. Although **The Crane** is huge and the resort remote, it is located high above the ocean and next to one of the island's loveliest beaches.

On St. Lucia, **Jade Mountain Club** is the crème de la crème; every "sanctuary" has its own extravagant infinity pool with a Piton view. **Sugar Beach, A Viceroy Resort,** is a full-service, upscale resort snuggled right between the Pitons. Elegantly rustic **Ladera** is a sophisticated small inn perched 1,100 feet above the sea between the Pitons.

FAMILY TRAVEL TO BARBADOS AND ST. LUCIA

Both islands have plenty to keep children of all ages (and their parents) entertained. Some resorts and hotels welcome children, others don't, and still others restrict kids to off-season visits. All but the very fancy (and most expensive) restaurants are kid-friendly.

Barbados

Sandy Lane welcomes children at any time with programs for kids of all ages. Somewhat less pricey, **Crystal Cove Hotel** and **Tamarind** have children's programs, a great beach, and lots of water sports. On the south coast, **Turtle Beach Resort**, **Divi Southwinds Beach Resort**, **Sugar Bay Barbados**, and **Bougainvillea Beach Resort** are large resorts with great beaches and kids' activities.

Barbados has more restaurants than you can count serving any type of cuisine you have in mind, but the Friday-night **Oistins Fish Fry** is definitely family-friendly.

The the tram ride through **Harrison's Cave** and a visit to the **Barbados Wildlife Reserve** is sure to entertain the whole family. **George Washington House** has a network of secret tunnels that fascinate kids, while the **Arlington House Museum** in Speightstown has interactive exhibits, a room-sized 1747 map of Barbados, and a re-created wharf. **Folkestone Marine Park & Museum** has a playground, beach with lifeguards, and an underwater snorkeling trail.

St. Lucia

While St. Lucia has earned its "most romantic" reputation, children are welcome at most St. Lucia resorts, hotels, and villa communities. **Windjammer Landing** is a good choice, and **St. James's Club Morgan Bay** is an all-inclusive resort with kid-friendly sports and activities. **Bay Gardens Beach Resort**, though, may be the best bet; it's right on Reduit Beach, with Splash Water Park just offshore, and reasonably priced. In the south, **Sugar Beach. A Viceroy Resort** in Soufrière has children's programs; **Coconut Bay Beach Resort**, near the airport in Vieux Fort, devotes half the property to vacationing families and incorporates a water park.

Take a **catamaran cruise** to Soufrière from Rodney Bay, or visit **Pigeon Island National Landmark**, which has a beach, restaurant, museum, 18th-century garrison, and lots of space to run around. Teens will be thrilled by a **zip-line** ride through the rain forest or **horseback riding** on the beach.

BARBADOS

Updated
by Jane E.
Zarem

BARBADOS STANDS APART FROM ITS neighbors in the Lesser Antilles archipelago, the chain of islands that stretches in a graceful arc from the Virgin Islands to Trinidad. Physically, Barbados is isolated in the Atlantic Ocean—100 miles (160 km) due east of its nearest neighbor St. Lucia. And geologically, most of the Lesser Antilles are the peaks of a volcanic mountain range, whereas Barbados is the top of a single, relatively flat protuberance of coral and limestone—the source of building blocks for many a plantation manor. Several of those historic "great houses," in fact, have been carefully restored. Some are open to visitors.

Bridgetown, both capital city and commercial center, is on the southwest coast of pear-shaped Barbados. Most of the 300,000 Bajans (*Bay*-juns, derived from the phonetic British pronunciation of Barbadian) live and work in and around Bridgetown, elsewhere in St. Michael Parish, or along the idyllic west coast or busy south coast. Others reside in tiny villages that dot the interior landscape. Broad sandy beaches, craggy cliffs, and numerous coves make up the coastline; the interior is consumed by forested hills and gullies and acre upon acre of sugarcane.

Without question, Barbados is the "most British" island in the Caribbean. In contrast to the turbulent colonial past experienced by neighboring islands, which included repeated conflicts between France and Britain for dominance and control, British rule in Barbados carried on uninterrupted for 340 years—from the first established British settlement in 1627 until independence was granted in 1966. That's not to say, of course, that there weren't significant struggles in Barbados, as elsewhere in the Caribbean, between the British landowners and their African-born slaves and other indentured servants.

With that unfortunate period of slavery relegated to the history books, the British influence on Barbados remains strong today in local manners, attitudes, customs, and politics—tempered, of course, by the characteristically warm nature of the Bajan people. In keeping with British-born traditions, many Bajans worship at the Anglican church, afternoon tea is a ritual, cricket is the national pastime (a passion, most admit), dressing for dinner is a firmly entrenched tradition, and patrons at some bars are as likely to order a Pimm's Cup or a shandy as a rum and

LOGISTICS

Getting to Barbados: Several airlines fly nonstop to Barbados, or you may have to connect in Miami. Grantley Adams International Airport (BGI) is in Christ Church Parish on the south coast; the airport is about 15 minutes from hotels situated along the south coast, 45 minutes from the west coast, and 30 minutes from Bridgetown.

Hassle Factor: Low.

On the Ground: Ground transportation is available immediately outside the customs area. Airport taxis aren't metered, but fares are regulated ($38–$40 to Speightstown, $30–$35 to west-coast hotels, $16–$22 to south-coast hotels). Be sure, however, to establish the fare before getting into the taxi and confirm whether the price quoted is in U.S. or Barbadian dollars.

Getting Around the Island: You may want to rent a car if you are staying in an isolated area, although bus service is good—especially between Bridgetown and stops along the west and south coasts. Taxis, of course, are always an option.

Coke. And yet, Barbados is hardly stuffy—this is still the Caribbean, after all.

Tourist facilities are concentrated on the west coast in St. James and St. Peter parishes (appropriately dubbed the Platinum Coast) and on the south coast in Christ Church Parish. Traveling along the west coast to historic Holetown, the site of the first British settlement, and continuing north to the city of Speightstown, you can find posh beachfront resorts, luxurious private villas, and fine restaurants—all enveloped by lush gardens and tropical foliage. The trendier, more commercial south coast offers competitively priced hotels and beach resorts, and its St. Lawrence Gap area is jam-packed with restaurants and nightlife. The relatively wide-open spaces along the southeast coast are proving ripe for development, and some wonderful inns and hotels already take advantage of the intoxicating beautiful ocean vistas. For their own vacations, though, Bajans escape to the rugged east coast, where the Atlantic surf pounds the dramatic shoreline with unrelenting force.

All in all, Barbados is a sophisticated tropical island with a rich history, lodgings to suit every taste and pocketbook, and plenty to pique your interest both day and night—whether you're British or not!

TOP REASONS TO GO

Great Resorts: They run the gamut—from unpretentious to over-the-top—in terms of size, intimacy, amenities, and price. Choose one on the lively south coast or on the ritzy west coast.

Great Golf: Golfers can choose from some of the best championship courses in the Caribbean—including a public course on the south coast with very reasonable greens fees.

Restaurants Galore: Great food includes everything from street-party barbecue to the finest dining.

Wide Range of Activities: With a broad assortment of land and water sports, sightseeing options, historic sites, cultural festivals, and nightlife, there's always plenty to do in Barbados.

Welcoming Locals: Bajans are friendly, welcoming, helpful, and hospitable. You'll like them; they'll like you.

PLANNING

WHEN TO GO

Barbados is busiest in the high season, which extends from December 15 through April 15. Off-season hotel rates can be half of those required during the busy period. During the high season, too, a few hotels may require you to buy a meal plan, which is usually not required in the low season. As noted in the listings, some hotels close in September and October, the slowest months of the off-season, for annual renovations. Some restaurants may close for brief periods within that time frame as well.

DO I NEED A CAR?

You may want to rent a car if you are staying in an isolated area, although bus service is good—especially between Bridgetown and stops along the west and south coasts. Taxis are on call 24 hours a day and may suffice for visitors staying in busy resort areas. ⇨ *For more information on car travel in Barbados and car rentals, see Car Travel in Travel Smart.*

ACCOMMODATIONS

Most people stay either in luxurious enclaves on the fashionable west coast—north of Bridgetown—or on the action-packed south coast with easy access to small, independent restaurants, bars, and nightclubs. A few inns on the remote southeast and east coasts offer ocean views and tranquillity, but those on the east coast don't have good swimming

Steelpan bands perform during the Crop Over Festival, an annual six-week summer event.

beaches nearby. Prices in Barbados may be twice as high in season compared to the quieter months. Most hotels include no meals in their rates; some include breakfast, many offer a meal plan, some require you to purchase the meal plan in the high season, and a few offer all-inclusive packages.

Resorts: Great resorts run the gamut—from unpretentious to knock-your-socks-off—in terms of size, intimacy, amenities, and price. Many are well suited to families.

Small Inns: Some wonderful, cozy inns are located in the east and southeast regions of the island.

Villas and Condos: Families and long-term visitors may choose from a wide variety of condos (everything from busy time-share resorts to more sedate vacation complexes). Villas and villa complexes can be luxurious, simple, or something in between.

WHAT IT COSTS IN U.S. DOLLARS				
	$	$$	$$$	$$$$
Restaurants	under $13	$13–$20	$21–$30	over $30
Hotels	under $275	$275–$375	$376–$475	over $475

Restaurant prices are the average cost of a main course at dinner or, if dinner is not served, at lunch. Hotel prices are the lowest cost of a standard double room in high season.

SAFETY

Crime isn't a major problem in Barbados, but take normal precautions. Lock your room, and don't leave valuables—particularly passports, tickets, and wallets—in plain sight or unattended on the beach. Use your hotel safe. For personal safety, avoid walking on the beach or on unlighted streets at night. Lock your rental car, and don't pick up hitchhikers. Using or trafficking in illegal drugs is strictly prohibited in Barbados. Any offense is punishable by a hefty fine, imprisonment, or both.

WEDDINGS

There are no minimum residency requirements to get married; however, you both need to obtain a marriage license, in person, from the Ministry of Home Affairs (☎ 246/621–0227). All fees must be paid in cash. The license fee is $100 plus $13 for a stamp. For a civil marriage, a separate fee of $125 is payable to the Court; for an alternative venue, $175. If either party is divorced or widowed, appropriate paperwork must be presented to obtain the license.

Bridgetown is the capital and commercial center of Barbados.

EXPLORING BARBADOS

The terrain changes dramatically from each of the island's 11 parishes to the next, and so does the pace. Bridgetown, the capital, is a somewhat sophisticated city. West-coast resorts and private estates ooze luxury, whereas the small villages and vast sugar plantations found throughout central Barbados reflect the island's history. The relentless Atlantic surf shaped the cliffs of the dramatic east coast, and the northeast is called Scotland because of its hilly landscape and broad vistas. Along the lively south coast, the daytime hustle and bustle produce a palpable energy that continues well into the night at countless restaurants, dance clubs, and nightspots.

BRIDGETOWN

This bustling capital city is a duty-free port with a compact shopping area. The principal thoroughfare is Broad Street, which leads west from National Heroes Square.

TOP ATTRACTIONS

The Careenage. In the early days, Bridgetown's natural harbor was where schooners were turned on their sides (careened) to be scraped of barnacles and repainted. Today, The Careenage serves as a marina for pleasure yachts and excursion boats, as well as a gathering place for locals and tourists alike. A boardwalk skirts the north side of

The Careenage; on the south side, a lovely esplanade has pathways and benches for pedestrians and a statue of Errol Barrow, the first prime minister of Barbados. The Chamberlain Bridge and the Charles Duncan O'Neal Bridge span The Careenage. ⊠ *Bridgetown.*

Nidhe Israel Synagogue. Providing for the spiritual needs of one of the oldest Jewish congregations in the western hemisphere, this synagogue was formed by Sephardic Jews who arrived in 1628 from Brazil and introduced sugarcane to Barbados. The adjoining cemetery has tombstones dating from the 1630s. The original house of worship, built in 1654, was destroyed in an 1831 hurricane, rebuilt in 1833, and restored in 1987 with the assistance of the Barbados National Trust. The museum, housed in a restored coral-stone building from 1750, documents the story of the Barbados Jewish community. Friday-night services are held during the winter months, but the building is open to the public year-round. Shorts are not acceptable during services but may be worn at other times. ⊠ *Synagogue La., Bridgetown* ☎ *246/436–6869* ⊕ *www.nidheisrael.com* ⊠ *Synagogue free; museum $12.50.*

Queen's Park. Northeast of Bridgetown, this national park is the site of one of the island's two immense baobab trees. Brought to Barbados from Guinea, West Africa, around 1738, this tree has a girth of more than 60 feet. Queen's Park House, built in 1783 and the historic home of the British troop commander, has been converted into a theater (fully restored in 2017), with an exhibition room on the lower floor. Originally called King's House, the name was changed upon Queen Victoria's succession to the throne. ⊠ *Constitution Rd., Bridgetown* ☎ *246/427–2345 gallery* ⊠ *Free.*

WORTH NOTING

National Heroes Square. Across Broad Street from Parliament, this triangular plaza marks the center of town. Its monument to Lord Horatio Nelson, who visited Barbados only briefly in 1777 as a 19-year-old navy lieutenant, predates Nelson's Column in London's Trafalgar Square by 30 years (1813 vs. 1843). There's also a war memorial and a fountain commemorating the advent of running water on Barbados in 1865. ⊠ *Broad St., Bridgetown* ⊹ *Across from Parliament.*

FAMILY **Parliament Buildings.** Overlooking National Heroes Square in the center of town, these Victorian buildings were constructed around 1870 to house the British Commonwealth's third-oldest parliament (after Britain itself and Bermuda). A series of stained-glass windows in the East Wing depicts British monarchs from James I to Victoria. The National Heroes Gallery & Museum is in the West Wing. ⊠ *National Heroes Sq., Trafalgar St., Bridgetown* ☎ *246/310–5400* ⊕ *www.barbadosparliament.com* ⊠ *Museum $5* ⊙ *Closed Tues. and Sun.*

St. Michael's Cathedral. Although no one has proven it, George Washington is said to have worshiped here in 1751 during his only trip outside the United States. By then, the original structure was already nearly a century old. Destroyed twice by hurricanes, the cathedral was rebuilt in 1789 and again in 1831. Officially called "Cathedral Church of Saint Michael and All Angels," it currently seats 1,600 people and boasts the largest pipe organ in the Caribbean. ⊠ *St. Michael's Row, Bridgetown* ⊹ *East of National Heroes Sq.* ☎ *246/427–0790.*

RENTING A CAR. If you're staying on the remote southeast or east coasts, you may want to rent a car for your entire stay. In more populated areas, where taxis and public transportation are readily available, you might rent a car for a day or two of exploring on your own. Rates start at about $75 per day during the high season.

SOUTH COAST

Christ Church Parish, which is far busier and more developed than the west coast, is chockablock with condos, high- and low-rise hotels, and beach parks. It is also the location of St. Lawrence Gap, with its many places to eat, drink, shop, and party. As you move southeast, the broad, flat terrain comprises acre upon acre of cane fields, interrupted only by an occasional oil rig and a few tiny villages. Along the byways are colorful chattel houses, which were the traditional homes of tenant farmers. Historically, these typically Barbadian, ever-expandable small buildings were built so they could be dismantled and moved, as required.

TOP ATTRACTIONS

FAMILY **Barbados Concorde Experience.** The Concorde Experience focuses on the British Airways Concorde G-BOAE (Alpha Echo, for short) that for many years flew between London and Barbados. The retired supersonic jet has made its permanent home here. Besides boarding the sleek aircraft itself, you learn about how the technology was developed and how this plane differed from other jets. It's just a two-minute walk from the terminal and a perfect place to spend about an hour if you have a long layover between flights. ⊠ *Grantley Adams International Airport, adjacent to the terminal building* ☎ *246/420–7738* ⊕ *www.barbadosconcorde.com* ✆ *$20* ⊘ *Closed Sun. and Mon.*

★ Fodor's Choice **Barbados Museum & Historical Society.** Established FAMILY in 1933 in the former British Military Prison (1815) in the historic Garrison area, this intriguing museum has artifacts from Arawak days (around 400 BC) and galleries that depict 19th-century military history and everyday social history. You can see cane-harvesting tools, wedding dresses, ancient (and frightening) dental instruments, and slave sale accounts in spidery copperplate handwriting. The Harewood Gallery showcases the island's natural environment, the Cunard Gallery has a permanent col-

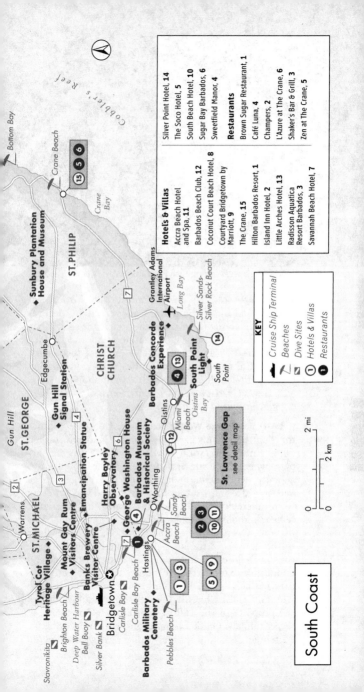

South Coast

Hotels & Villas

Accra Beach Hotel and Spa, **11**
Barbados Beach Club, **12**
Coconut Court Beach Hotel, **8**
Courtyard Bridgetown by Marriott, **9**
The Crane, **15**
Hilton Barbados Resort, **1**
Island Inn Hotel, **2**
Little Arches Hotel, **13**
Radisson Aquatica Resort Barbados, **3**
Savannah Beach Hotel, **7**
Silver Point Hotel, **14**
The Soco Hotel, **5**
South Beach Hotel, **10**
Sugar Bay Barbados, **6**
Sweetfield Manor, **4**

Restaurants

Brown Sugar Restaurant, **1**
Café Luna, **4**
Champers, **2**
L'Azure at The Crane, **6**
Shaker's Bar & Grill, **3**
Zen at The Crane, **5**

KEY

⚓ Cruise Ship Terminal
⌒ Beaches
⬛ Dive Sites
① Hotels & Villas
❶ Restaurants

The Barbados Concorde Experience focuses on the British Airways Concorde G-BOAEA.

lection of West Indian prints bequeathed by Sir Edward Cunard, and the Warmington Gallery contains decorative arts depicting the planter's lifestyle. One gallery has exhibits for children. The Shilstone Memorial Library houses rare West Indian materials—archival documents, genealogical records, photos, books, and maps—dating to the 17th century. There is also a gift shop and café. ⊠ *St. Ann's Garrison, Hwy. 7, Garrison* ☎ *246/538–0201* ⊕ *www.barbmuse.org.bb* ☞ *$10.*

★ Fodor'sChoice **George Washington House.** George Washing-
FAMILY ton slept here! This carefully restored and refurbished 18th-century plantation house in Bush Hill was the only place where the future first president of the United States actually slept outside North America. Teenage George and his older half-brother Lawrence, who was suffering from tuberculosis and seeking treatment on the island, rented this house overlooking Carlisle Bay for two months in 1751. Opened to the public in 2007, the lower floor of the house and the kitchen have period furnishings; the upper floor is a museum with both permanent and temporary exhibits that display artifacts of 18th-century Barbadian life. The site includes an original 1719 windmill and bathhouse, along with a stable added to the property in the 1800s. Kids enjoy the network of secret tunnels. Guided tours begin with an informative 15-minute film, appropriately called *George Washington*

CLOSE UP

Errol Barrow, National Hero

Errol Barrow (1920–87), trained in Britain as a lawyer and economist, led his native Barbados to independence in 1966 and became the island nation's first prime minister. During his initial tenure, which lasted through 1976, Barrow expanded the tourist industry, reduced the island's dependence on sugar, introduced national health insurance and social security, and extended free education to the community college level.

Barrow was reelected prime minister in 1986 but collapsed and died at his home a year later. He is honored as a national hero and the "Father of Independence," and his birthday—January 21—is celebrated as a national holiday. On that day in 2007, a 9-foot-tall statue of Errol Barrow was erected on the esplanade along The Careenage, picturesquely sited between the city's two bridges and facing Parliament.

in Barbados. ⊠ *Bush Hill, Garrison* ☎ *246/228–5461* ⊕ *barbadosgarrison.net/george-washington-house* 🖙 *$10* ⊘ *Closed weekends.*

★ **Fodor's Choice Sunbury Plantation House and Museum.** Lovingly rebuilt after a 1995 fire destroyed everything but the thick flint-and-stone walls of this 300-year-old great house, Sunbury offers an elegant glimpse of the 18th and 19th centuries on a Barbadian sugar estate. Period furniture, old prints, and a collection of horse-drawn carriages lend an air of authenticity. A buffet luncheon ($24 per person, $35 on Sunday) and high tea ($17.50) are served daily in the Courtyard Restaurant; you can also order à la carte. A five-course candlelight dinner ($125 per person, including drinks, minimum 12 people, reservations required) is served at the 200-year-old mahogany table in the dining room. ⊠ *Six Cross Rd.* ⊹ *Off Hwy. 5; look for the sign at the roundabout* ☎ *246/423–6270* 🖙 *$10.*

WORTH NOTING

Barbados Military Cemetery. The cemetery, also referred to as Gravesend or Garrison Military Cemetery, is near the shore behind historic St. Ann's Fort. First used in 1780, when the area was pretty much marshland, the dead were placed in shallow graves or simply left on top of the ground where, within a few short days, many were absorbed into the swamp. In the early 20th century, a number of the remaining graves were dug up to provide room for oil storage tanks; salvaged headstones were placed on a cenotaph, erected in 1920–24.

A "Cross of Sacrifice" was erected in 1982 to honor all the military dead; a second cenotaph, erected in 2003, honors the Barbadian merchant seamen who died in World War II. ⊠ *Gravesend, Needham's Point, Garrison* ✛ *Behind the Hilton Barbados Resort* ☎ *246/536-2021* ☎ *Free.*

Emancipation Statue. This powerful statue of a slave—whose raised hands, broken chains hanging from each wrist, evoke both contempt and victory—is commonly referred to as the Bussa Statue. Bussa was the man who, in 1816, led the first slave rebellion on Barbados. The work of Barbadian sculptor Karl Brodhagen, the statue was erected in 1985 to commemorate the emancipation of the slaves in 1834. ⊠ *St. Barnabas Roundabout, Haggatt Hall* ✛ *At intersection of ABC Hwy. and Hwy. 5* ☎ *Free.*

FAMILY **Harry Bayley Observatory.** Reopened in January 2014 with a fresh interior, high-tech fittings, and a new dome—and re-equipped with a 16-inch Meade telescope with the latest robotic controls and digital cameras and a new Lunt 80mm solar telescope—the observatory lets you view the moon, stars, planets, and other astronomical objects that may not be visible from mainland North America or Europe. The Friday-evening programs, which start with an informative presentation, are run by volunteers; call ahead to make sure it's open. The observatory has been the headquarters of the Barbados Astronomical Society since 1963. ⊠ *Observatory Rd., Clapham* ✛ *Off Hwy. 6* ☎ *246/622-2000, 246/622-2000* ⊕ *www.hbo.bb* ☎ *$10* ☺ *Closed Sat.–Thurs.*

South Point Light. This is the oldest of four lighthouses on Barbados. Assembled on the island in 1852, after being displayed at London's Great Exhibition the previous year, the landmark lighthouse is just east of Miami (Enterprise) Beach near the southernmost point of land on Barbados. The 89-foot tower, with its distinguishing red and white horizontal stripes, is closed to the public; but visitors may freely walk about the site, take photos, and enjoy the view. ⊠ *South Point, Lighthouse Dr., Atlantic Shores.*

EAST COAST

On the east coast, the crashing Atlantic surf has eroded the shoreline, forming steep cliffs and exposing prehistoric rocks that look like giant mushrooms. Bathsheba and Cattlewash are favorite seacoast destinations for local folks on weekends and holidays. In the central interior, narrow roads weave through tiny villages and along and between the ridges. The landscape is covered with tropical vegetation and is rife with fascinating caves and gullies. Between the sweeping views out over the Atlantic and the tiny fishing towns along the northwestern coast are forest and farm, moor and mountain. Most guides include a loop through the far north on a daylong tour of the east coast—it's a beautiful drive.

TOP ATTRACTIONS

★ Fodor'sChoice **Andromeda Botanic Gardens.** More than 600 beautiful and unusual plant specimens from around the world are cultivated in 6 acres of gardens nestled among streams, ponds, and rocky outcroppings overlooking the sea above the Bathsheba coastline near Tent Bay. The gardens were created in 1954 with flowering plants collected by the late horticulturist Iris Bannochie (1914–1988). They're now administered by the Barbados National Trust. The Gallery Shop features local art, photography, and crafts. The Garden Café serves sandwiches, salads from the gardens, desserts, and drinks. ⊠ *Bathsheba* ☎ *246/433–9384* ⊕ *www. andromedabarbados.com* ⊜ *$15.*

FAMILY **Barbados Wildlife Reserve.** This reserve at the top of Farley Hill is the habitat of herons, innumerable land turtles, screeching peacocks, shy deer, elusive green monkeys, brilliantly colored parrots (in a large walk-in aviary), snakes, and a caiman. Except for the snakes and the caiman, the animals run or fly freely—so step carefully and keep your hands to yourself. Late afternoon is your best chance to catch a glimpse of a green monkey. ⊠ *Hwy. 2* ✛ *Across from Farley Hill National Park* ☎ *246/422–8826* ⊕ *www. barbadoswildlifereserve.com* ⊜ *$15.*

WORTH NOTING

FAMILY **Animal Flower Cave.** Small sea anemones, or sea worms, resemble flowers when they open their tiny tentacles. They live in small pools in this sea cave at the island's very northern tip. The cave itself, discovered in 1750, has a coral floor that ranges from 126,000 to 500,000 years old, according to geological estimates. Coral steps lead through an opening in the "roof" into the cave. Bring your bathing suit. Depending on that day's sea swells, you can swim in the naturally formed pool—and the view of breaking waves from inside the cave is magnificent. Steep stairs, uneven surfaces, and rocks make this an unwise choice for anyone with walking difficulties. The Restaurant opens daily for lunch. ⊠ *North Point* ☎ *246/439–8797* ⊕ *www.animalflow-ercave.com* ☞ *$10.*

FAMILY **Barclays Park.** Straddling the Ermy Bourne Highway on the east coast, just north of Bathsheba, this public park was donated by Barclays Bank (now First Caribbean International Bank). Pack a picnic lunch, run around, and enjoy the gorgeous ocean view. ⊠ *Ermy Bourne Hwy., Cattlewash.*

Chalky Mount. This tiny east-coast village is perched high in the clay-yielding hills that have supplied local potters for about 300 years. A few working potteries are open daily to visitors, who can watch as artisans create bowls, vases, candleholders, and decorative objects—which are, of course, for sale. ⊠ *Coggins Hill, Chalky Mount* ☞ *Free.*

Codrington Theological College. An impressive stand of cabbage-palm trees lines the road leading to the coral-stone buildings and serene grounds of Codrington College, the oldest Anglican theological seminary in the western hemisphere, opened in 1745 on a cliff overlooking Conset Bay. The college's benefactor was Christopher Codrington III (1668–1710), a former governor-general of the Leeward Islands, whose antislavery views were unpopular in the plantocracy of the times. In an effort to "Christianize" the slaves and provide them with a general education, Codrington specified in his will that "300 Negroes at least" would always be allowed to study at the institution; the planters who acted as trustees, however, were loath to teach slaves to read and write. You may visit the chapel, stroll the grounds, enjoy the view, even have a picnic—but remember that beachwear is not appropriate here. ⊠ *Sargeant St., Codrington College* ☎ *246/416–8051* ⊕ *www.codrington. org* ☞ *Donations welcome.*

Farley Hill National Park. At this national park in northern St. Peter, across from the Barbados Wildlife Reserve, gardens and lawns—along with an avenue of towering palms and gigantic mahogany, whitewood, and casuarina trees—surround the imposing ruins of a plantation great house built by Sir Graham Briggs in 1861 to entertain royal visitors from England. Partially rebuilt for the filming of *Island in the Sun*, the classic 1957 film starring Harry Belafonte and Dorothy Dandridge, the structure was destroyed by fire in 1965. Behind the estate is a sweeping view of the region called Scotland for its rugged landscape. The park is also the site of festivals and musical events. ⊠ *Hwy. 2* ☎ *246/422–3555* ☞ *$3 per car, pedestrians free.*

St. Nicholas Abbey is the island's oldest surviving plantation home.

FAMILY **Morgan Lewis Sugar Mill.** Built in 1727, the mill was operational until 1945. Today it's the only remaining windmill in Barbados with its wheelhouse and sails intact. No longer used to grind sugarcane, the mill was donated to the Barbados National Trust in 1962 and eventually restored to original working specifications in 1998 by millwrights from the United Kingdom. A lightning strike in 2007 caused damage, and the mill remains under repair; but visitors can climb inside and see the machinery. Surrounding acres are used for dairy farming. ✛ *Southeast of Cherry Tree Hill* ☎ *246/426–2421* ⊕ *www.barbadosnationaltrust.org.*

Ragged Point. This is the location of East Coast Light, one of four strategically placed lighthouses on the island. Although civilization in the form of new homes is encroaching on this once-remote spot, the view of the entire Atlantic coastline is still spectacular—and the cool ocean breeze is refreshing on a hot day. ✉ *Marley Vale* 🎫 *Free.*

★ **Fodor'sChoice** **St. Nicholas Abbey.** The island's oldest great house (circa 1650) was named after the original British owner's hometown, St. Nicholas Parish near Bristol, and Bath Abbey nearby. Its stone-and-wood architecture makes it one of only three original Jacobean-style houses still standing in the western hemisphere. It has Dutch gables, finials of coral stone, and beautiful grounds that include an "avenue" of mahogany trees, a "gully" filled with tropical trees and plantings, formal gardens, and an old sugar mill. The first

Holetown Landing

On May 14, 1625, British Captain John Powell anchored his ship off the west coast of Barbados and claimed the island on behalf of King James I. He named his landfall Jamestown. Nearly two years later, on February 17, 1627, Captain Henry Powell landed in Jamestown with a party of 80 settlers and 10 slaves. They used a small channel, or "hole," near the settlement to offload and clean ships, so Jamestown soon became known as Holetown. Today Holetown is a vibrant town with shopping centers, restaurants, nightspots, and, of course, hotels and resorts. It is also the site of the annual Holetown Festival—a week of parades, crafts, music, and partying—held in mid-February each year to commemorate the first settlement. The celebration begins at the Holetown Monument in the center of town.

floor, fully furnished with period furniture and portraits of family members, is open to the public. A fascinating home movie, shot by a previous owner's father, records Bajan life in the 1930s. Behind the great house is a rum distillery with a 19th-century steam press; cane grinding occurs Wednesdays and Thursdays, January through May. Visitors can purchase artisanal plantation rum, browse the gift shop's traditional Barbadian products, and enjoy light refreshments at the Terrace Café. ⊠ *Cherry Tree Hill Rd., Moore Hill* ☎ *246/422–5357* ⊕ *www.stnicholasabbey.com* ⊠ *$23* ⊘ *Closed Sat.*

CHERRY TREE HILL. The cherry trees for which this spot was named have long since disappeared, but the view from Cherry Tree Hill, just east of St. Nicholas Abbey, is still one of the most spectacular in Barbados. Although only about 850 feet above sea level, it is one of the highest points on the island and affords a broad view of the rugged east coast and the entire Scotland District—so named because its rolling hills resemble the moors of Scotland. Today, when approaching from the west, you drive through a majestic stand of mature, leafy mahogany trees.

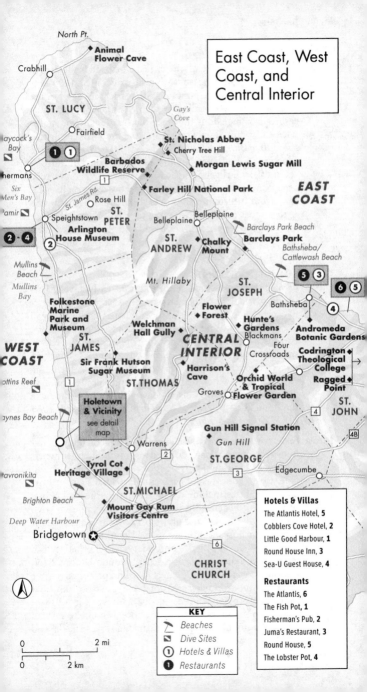

North Pt.

Animal Flower Cave

Crabhill

ST. LUCY

Fairfield

Gay's Cove

aycock's Bay

① ①

hermans

Six Men's Bay

Pamir

St. James Rd.

Rose Hill

ST. PETER

Speightstown

② - ④

Arlington House Museum

Mullins Beach

Mullins Bay

WEST COAST

Folkestone Marine Park and Museum

ST. JAMES

ottins Reef

aynes Bay Beach

Holetown & Vicinity
see detail map

St. Nicholas Abbey

Cherry Tree Hill

Barbados Wildlife Reserve

Morgan Lewis Sugar Mill

Farley Hill National Park

EAST COAST

Belleplaine

Belleplaine

Barclays Park Beach

ST. ANDREW

Chalky Mount

Barclays Park

Bathsheba/ Cattlewash Beach

⑤ ③

⑥ ⑤

ST. JOSEPH

④

Bathsheba

Flower Forest

Hunte's Gardens

Blackmans

Welchman Hall Gully

CENTRAL INTERIOR

Four Crossroads

Andromeda Botanic Gardens

Codrington Theological College

Sir Frank Hutson Sugar Museum

ST.THOMAS

Harrison's Cave

Groves

Orchid World & Tropical Flower Garden

Ragged Point

ST. JOHN

④

Gun Hill Signal Station

Gun Hill

ST. GEORGE

Warrens

②

③

4B

Edgecumbe

Tyrol Cot Heritage Village

ST.MICHAEL

Brighton Beach

avronikita

Mount Gay Rum Visitors Centre

Deep Water Harbour

Bridgetown ✪

⑥

CHRIST CHURCH

East Coast, West Coast, and Central Interior

Hotels & Villas
The Atlantis Hotel, **5**
Cobblers Cove Hotel, **2**
Little Good Harbour, **1**
Round House Inn, **3**
Sea-U Guest House, **4**

Restaurants
The Atlantis, **6**
The Fish Pot, **1**
Fisherman's Pub, **2**
Juma's Restaurant, **3**
Round House, **5**
The Lobster Pot, **4**

KEY
⚲ Beaches
◩ Dive Sites
① Hotels & Villas
❶ Restaurants

0 — 2 mi

0 — 2 km

WEST COAST

The west coast extends from just north of Bridgetown, through St. James Parish, to Speightstown in St. Peter Parish. Holetown, in St. James Parish, marks the center of the Platinum Coast—so called for the vast number of luxurious resorts and mansions that face the sea. Holetown is also where Captain John Powell and the crew of the British ship *Olive Blossom* landed on May 14, 1625, to claim the island for King James I (who had actually died of a stroke seven weeks earlier). Speightstown, the north's commercial center and once a thriving port city, now relies on its local shops and informal restaurants. Many of Speightstown's 19th-century buildings, with traditional overhanging balconies, have been restored. The island's northernmost reaches, St. Peter and St. Lucy parishes, have a varied topography and are lovely to explore.

TOP ATTRACTIONS

FAMILY **Arlington House Museum.** Learn about the early days of Barbados, particularly Speightstown, at this fascinating interactive museum in the center of town. Virtual exhibits let you "talk" with local personalities, businesspeople, vendors, and historical figures. Other focal points are the room-sized map of Barbados from 1747, the story of sugar and slavery, and a re-created wharf on the top floor—including virtual turtles swimming underneath and a pirate's running dialogue. Adults and kids alike will learn a lot—and have fun doing it. ⊠ *Queen St., Speightstown* ☎ *246/422–4064* 🖻 *$12.50* ⊘ *Closed Sun.*

FAMILY **Folkestone Marine Park and Museum.** The mission of this family-oriented marine park, located just north of Holetown, is to provide high-quality recreational activities in a sustainable way to educate and entertain Barbadians and visitors alike. Facilities include a playground, basketball court, picnic area, beach with lifeguards, and a museum (two rooms with artifacts and photos of how the sea is used for various purposes) that illuminates island marine life. For firsthand viewing, there's an underwater snorkeling trail (equipment rental, $10 for the day) around Dottins Reef, just off the beach in the 2.2-mile (3.5-km) protected marine reserve; nonswimmers can opt for a glass-bottom boat tour. The ship *Stavronikita*, deliberately sunk in 120 feet of water about a half mile from shore, is home to myriad fish and a popular dive site. A canteen serves snacks and

Cuban Monument

On October 6, 1976, Cubana Airlines Flight 455, a DC-8 aircraft en route to Cuba from Barbados, was brought down by a terrorist bombing attack, killing all 73 people on board. The aircraft crashed into the sea off Paynes Bay on the west coast of Barbados. Four anti-Castro Cuban exiles were arrested for the crime. Two were sentenced to 20-year prison terms; one was acquitted; the fourth was held for 8 years awaiting sentencing and later fled. A pyramid-shaped granite monument dedicated to the victims was installed along Highway 1 in Paynes Bay at the approximate location where the wreckage was brought ashore; the monument was unveiled during a 1998 visit by Cuban president Fidel Castro.

drinks. ⊠ *Hwy. 1, Church Point, Holetown* ☎ *246/422–2314* 🖭 *Free, exhibits $1.*

Mount Gay Rum Visitors Centre. On this popular tour, you learn the colorful story behind the world's oldest rum, made in Barbados since 1703. Although the modern distillery is in the far north in St. Lucy Parish, tour guides here explain the rum-making process. Equipment, both historic and modern, is on display, and rows and rows of barrels are stored in this location. Tours conclude with a tasting and an opportunity to buy duty-free rum and gifts—and even have lunch or cocktails (no children on cocktail tour), depending on the time of day. ⊠ *Exmouth Gap, Brandons, Spring Garden Hwy., Bridgetown* ☎ *246/227–8864* ⊕ *www.mountgayrum.com* 🖭 *$20, $70 with cocktails or lunch, $5 for transportation* ⊗ *Closed Sun.*

Sir Frank Hutson Sugar Museum. This museum is in an old boiling house in the yard of the Portvale Sugar Factory, one of two sugar refineries still in operation in Barbados. The museum has a collection of original machinery, old photographs, and other implements used to refine sugar and make molasses. A video presentation explains the production process from cutting the cane to sweetening your coffee to making rum. During the reaping season (February through May), you can also tour the modern factory to see how sugar is produced today. Call first, though, to make sure the guide (a retired worker) is on hand. ⊠ *Portvale Factory Rd.* ✛ *Off Hwy. 2A* ☎ *246/432–0100* 🖭 *$5, $8.50 with factory tour.*

Tyrol Cot Heritage Village. This coral-stone cottage just south of Bridgetown, constructed in 1854, is preserved as an example of period architecture. In 1929, it became the home of Sir Grantley Adams, the first premier of Barbados and the namesake of the island's international airport. Part of the Barbados National Trust, the cottage is filled with antiques and memorabilia that belonged to the late Sir Grantley and Lady Adams. Refreshments are available at the "rum shop." ⊠ *Codrington Hill, Bridgetown* ☎ *246/424–2074* ⊕ *www.barbadosnationaltrust.org* 🖃 *$5* ⊘ *Closed weekends.*

CENTRAL INTERIOR

The central interior of Barbados is dotted with small villages and covered with miles and miles of sugarcane. It's also marked by the island's unique cave system, a forested gully, magnificent gardens, and an amazing view of the entire south coast. Whether traveling around the south, east, or west coast, be sure to incorporate this area into your tour.

TOP ATTRACTIONS

★ **Fodor's**Choice **Flower Forest.** It's a treat to meander among fragrant flowering bushes, canna and ginger lilies, puffball trees, and more than 100 other species of tropical flora in a cool, tranquil forest of flowers and other plants. A ½-mile (1-km) path winds through the 53.6-acre grounds, a former sugar plantation; it takes about 30 to 45 minutes to follow the path, or you can wander freely for as long as you wish. Benches throughout provide places to pause and reflect. There's also a snack bar, a gift shop, and a beautiful view of Mt. Hillaby, at 1,100 feet the island's highest point. ⊠ *Hwy. 2, Richmond* ☎ *246/433–8152* ⊕ *www.flowerforestbarbados.com* 🖃 *$15.*

★ **Fodor's**Choice **Gun Hill Signal Station.** The 360-degree view from
FAMILY Gun Hill, at 700 feet, was of strategic importance to the 18th-century British army. Using lanterns and semaphore, soldiers here could communicate with their counterparts at the south coast's Garrison and the north's Grenade Hill about approaching ships, civil disorders, storms, or other emergencies. Time moved slowly in those days, and Captain Henry Wilkinson whiled away his off-duty hours by carving a huge lion from a single rock—on the hillside below the tower. Come for a short history lesson but mainly for the view; it's so gorgeous that military invalids were sent here to convalesce. There's a small café for refreshments.

The Gun Hill Signal Station lion was carved from a single rock in 1868.

✉ *Fusilier Rd., Gun Hill* ☎ *246/429–1358* ⊕ *www.barba-dosnationaltrust.org* 💲 *$6* ⊘ *Closed Sun.*

★ **Fodor's**Choice **Harrison's Cave.** This limestone cavern, com-

FAMILY plete with stalactites, stalagmites, subterranean streams, and a 40-foot underground waterfall, is a rare find in the Caribbean—and one of Barbados's most popular attractions. Tours include a nine-minute video and an hour-long underground journey via electric tram. The visitor center has interactive displays, life-size models and sculptures, a souvenir shop, restaurant, and elevator access to the tram for people with disabilities. Tram tours fill up fast, so book ahead. More-intrepid visitors may like the 1½-hour walk-in tour or 4-hour eco-adventure tour, exploring nature trails and some of the cave's natural passages. ✉ *Allen View, Welchman Hall* ✦ *Off Hwy. 2* ☎ *246/417–3700* ⊕ *www.harrisonscave.com* 💲 *Tram tour $30, walk-in $20, eco-adventure $100.*

★ **Fodor's**Choice **Hunte's Gardens.** Horticulturist Anthony Hunte spent two years converting an overgrown sinkhole (caused by the collapse of a limestone cave) into an extraordinary garden environment. Trails lead up, down, and around 10 acres of dense foliage—everything from pots of flowering plants and great swaths of thick ground cover to robust vines, exotic tropical flowers, and majestic 100-year-old cabbage palms that reach for the sun. Benches and chairs, strategically placed among the greenery, afford perfect (and fairly private) vantage points, while classical music plays overhead. Hunte lives on the property and welcomes visitors to his veranda for a glass or juice or rum punch. Just ask, and he'll be happy to tell you the fascinating story of how the gardens evolved. ✉ *Hwy. 3A, Castle Grant* ☎ *246/433–3333* ⊕ *www.huntesgardensbarbados.com* 🖃 *$15.*

WORTH NOTING

Orchid World & Tropical Flower Garden. Meandering pathways thread through gardens filled with more than 30,000 colorful orchids and other tropical plants. You'll see Vandaceous orchids attached to fences or wire frames, Schomburgkia and Oncidiums stuck on mahogany trees, Aranda and Spathoglottis orchids growing in a grotto, and Ascocendas suspended from netting in shady enclosures as well as seasonal orchids, scented orchids, and multicolor Vanda orchids. Benches are well placed to rest, admire the flowers, or take in the expansive view of the surrounding cane fields and distant hills of Sweet Vale. Snacks, cold beverages, and other refreshments are served in the café. ✉ *Hwy. 3B, Groves, Sweet Vale* ☎ *246/433–0306* ⊕ *www.orchidworldbarbados.com* 🖃 *$12.50* ⊗ *May 15–Oct. 15 closed Mon.*

Welchman Hall Gully. This 1½-mile-long (2-km-long) natural gully is really a collapsed limestone cavern, once part of the same underground network as Harrison's Cave. The Barbados National Trust protects the peace and quiet here, making it a beautiful place to hike past acres of labeled flowers and stands of trees. You can see and hear some interesting birds—and, with luck, a native green monkey. There are limited scheduled free guided tours, and a guide can be arranged with 24 hours' notice. Otherwise, the 30- to 45-minute walk is self-guided. ✉ *Welchman Hall* ☎ *246/438–6671* ⊕ *www.welchmanhallgullybarbados.com* 🖃 *$12.*

BEACHES

Geologically, Barbados is a coral-and-limestone island (not volcanic) with few rivers and, as a result, beautiful beaches—particularly along the island's southern and southeastern coastlines.

The west coast has some lovely beaches as well, but they're more susceptible to erosion after autumn storms. When the surf is too high and swimming becomes dangerous, a

CLOSE UP

Sugar: How Sweet It Is ...

Sugarcane was introduced to Barbados in the 1630s. Considered "white gold" by the original plantation owners, sugar production relied on forced labor (African slaves) and indentured servants (white civilians who wanted to emigrate overseas, kidnapped individuals, and convicted criminals dubbed "Red Legs," presumably because of the chafing marks that the chains made on their white legs). Slavery was abolished in 1834, yet records show that Barbados still had 491 active sugar plantations in 1846, along with 506 operating windmills. And until 1969, when the mechanical harvester was introduced in Barbados,

cane was cut by manual labor. Nowadays few people want the backbreaking job of cutting cane, so nearly all cane grown anywhere is cut mechanically. Today in Barbados some 1,500 small farms (about 200 acres each) produce about 60,000 tons of sugar annually, but only one operating windmill remains and just two companies refine sugar. Unfortunately, small farms and hilly terrain make mechanization inefficient. So while sugar remains an important agricultural product in Barbados, its value to the local economy has declined relative to tourism and other business interests.

red flag will be hoisted on the beach. A yellow flag—or a red flag at half-staff—means swim with caution. Topless sunbathing is not allowed anywhere in Barbados.

Beach massage, lady? Some beach vendors offer massage services—sometimes including what they call reflexology—to sunbathers. Although a beach massage sounds refreshing and may even feel good, these people are certainly not trained therapists. At best, you'll get a soothing back or foot rub. Be advised, though, that they use raw aloe vera as their massage oil, which can permanently stain clothing, towels, and chair cushions.

ST. LAWRENCE GAP

Dover Beach. All along the St. Lawrence Gap waterfront, Dover Beach is one of the most popular beaches on the south coast. The sea is fairly calm, with small to medium waves, and the white-sand beach is broad and brilliant. The resorts of Divi Southwinds and Ocean Two, as well as several restaurants, are nearby. There's a small boardwalk, a promenade with a food court, water sports and beach chair rentals, and a playground. **Amenities:** food and drink; parking (no fee); toilets; water sports. **Best for:** snorkeling; swimming. ⊠ *Hwy. 7, Dover.*

Turtle Beach. Stretching from Turtle Beach Resort and Sandals Barbados at the eastern end of St. Lawrence Gap to Bougainvillea Beach Resort on Maxwell Coast Road, this broad strand of powdery white sand is great for sunbathing, strolling, and—with low to medium surf—swimming and bodyboarding. This beach is a favorite nesting place for turtles, hence it's name; if you're lucky, you may see hundreds of tiny hatchlings emerge from the sand and make their way to the sea. ■TIP→ There's public access and parking on Maxwell Coast Road, near the Bougainvillea Beach Resort. **Amenities:** food and drink; parking (no fee). **Best for:** swimming; walking. ⊠ *St. Lawrence Gap, Maxwell.*

SOUTH COAST

A young, energetic crowd favors the south-coast beaches, which are broad and breezy, blessed with powdery white sand, and dotted with tall palms. The reef-protected areas with crystal-clear water are safe for swimming and snorkeling. The surf is medium to high, and the waves get bigger and the winds stronger (windsurfers take note) the farther southeast you go.

FAMILY   **Accra Beach** (*Rockley Beach*). This popular beach, adjacent to the Accra Beach Hotel, has a broad swath of white sand with gentle surf and a lifeguard, plenty of nearby restaurants for refreshments, a playground, and beach stalls for renting chairs and equipment for snorkeling and other water sports. The South Coast Boardwalk, great for walking or running, begins here and follows the waterfront west—past private homes, restaurants, and bars—for about a mile (1.6 km) to Needham's Point. **Amenities:** food and drink; lifeguards; parking (no fee); water sports. **Best for:** snorkeling; swimming; walking. ⊠ *Hwy. 7, Rockley.*

★   **Fodor's Choice Bottom Bay Beach.** Popular for fashion and travel-industry photo shoots, Bottom Bay is the quintessential Caribbean beach. Secluded, surrounded by a coral cliff, studded with a stand of palms, and blessed with an endless ocean view, this dreamy enclave is near the southeasternmost point of the island. The Atlantic Ocean waves can be too strong for swimming, but it's the picture-perfect

CLOSE UP

Where de Rum Come From

For more than 300 years (from 1655 through Black Tot Day, July 31, 1970), a daily "tot" of rum (2 ounces) was duly administered to each sailor in the British Navy—as a health ration. At times rum has also played a less appetizing—but equally important—role. When Admiral Horatio Nelson died in 1805 aboard ship during the Battle of Trafalgar, his body was preserved in a cask of his favorite rum until he could be properly buried.

Hardly a Caribbean island doesn't have its own locally made rum, but Barbados is truly "where de rum come from." Mount Gay, the world's oldest rum distillery, has continuously operated on Barbados since 1703, according to the original deed for the Mount Gay Estate, which itemized two stone windmills, a boiling house, seven copper pots, and a still house. The presence of rum-making equipment on the plantation at the time suggests that the previous owners were actually producing rum in Barbados long before 1703.

Today much of the island's interior is still planted with sugarcane—where the rum really does come from—and several great houses, on historic sugar plantations, have been restored with period furniture and are open to the public.

To really fathom rum, however, you need to delve a little deeper than the bottom of a glass of rum punch. Mount Gay offers an interesting 45-minute tour of its main plant, followed by a tasting. You can learn about the rum-making process from cane to cocktail, hear more rum-inspired anecdotes, and have an opportunity to buy bottles of its famous Eclipse or Extra Old rum at duty-free prices. Bottoms up!

place for a day at the beach and a picnic lunch. Park at the top of the cliff and follow the steps down to the beach. **Amenities:** none. **Best for:** solitude; swimming; walking. ⊠ *Hwy. 5, Apple Hall.*

★ **Fodor'sChoice Crane Beach.** This exquisite crescent of pink sand on the southeast coast was named not for the elegant, long-legged wading bird but for the crane used to haul and load cargo when this area served as a busy port. Crane Beach usually has a steady breeze and lightly rolling surf that varies in color from aqua to turquoise to lapis and is great for bodysurfing. Access to the beach is either down 98 steps or via a cliffside, glass-walled elevator on The Crane resort property. **Amenities:** food and drink;

lifeguards; parking (no fee); toilets. **Best for:** swimming; walking. ⊠ *Crane.*

★ Fodor'sChoice **Miami Beach** (*Enterprise Beach*). This lovely spot on the coast road, just east of Oistins, is a slice of pure white sand with shallow and calm water on one side, deeper water with small waves on the other, and cliffs on either side. Located in a mainly upscale residential area, the beach is mostly deserted except for weekends when folks who live nearby come for a swim. You'll find a palm-shaded parking area, snack carts, and chair rentals. It's also a hop, skip, and jump from Little Arches Hotel. **Amenities:** food and drink; parking (no fee). **Best for:** solitude; swimming. ⊠ *Enterprise Beach Rd., Enterprise.*

★ Fodor'sChoice **Pebbles Beach.** On the southern side of Carlisle
FAMILY Bay, just south of Bridgetown, this broad half circle of white sand is one of the island's best beaches—and it can become crowded on weekends and holidays. The southern end of the beach wraps around the Hilton Barbados; the northern end is adjacent to the Radisson Aquatica Resort Barbados and a block away from Island Inn. Park at Harbour Lights or at the Boatyard Bar and Bayshore Complex, both on Bay Street, where you can also rent umbrellas and beach chairs and buy refreshments. **Amenities:** food and drink. **Best for:** snorkeling; swimming; walking. ⊠ *Off Bay St., Garrison* ✥ *South of Bridgetown.*

FAMILY **Sandy Beach** (*Worthing Beach*). This beach has calm waters and a picturesque lagoon, making it an ideal location for families with small kids. It also has several artificial bays separated by rocks, with a shallow reef close to shore. Park right on the main road. You can rent beach chairs and umbrellas, and plenty of places nearby sell food and drinks. **Amenities:** food and drink. **Best for:** swimming; walking. ⊠ *Hwy. 7, Worthing.*

FAMILY **Silver Sands–Silver Rock Beach.** Nestled between South Point, the southernmost tip of the island, and Inch Marlow Point, Silver Point Hotel overlooks this long, broad strand of beautiful white sand that always has a strong breeze. That makes this beach the best in Barbados for intermediate and advanced windsurfers and, more recently, kiteboarders. There's a small playground and shaded picnic tables. **Amenities:** parking (no fee); water sports. **Best for:** solitude; swimming; walking; windsurfing. ⊠ *Off Hwy. 7, Silver Sands.*

EAST COAST

Be cautioned: swimming at east-coast beaches is treacherous, even for strong swimmers, and is *not* recommended. Waves are high, the bottom tends to be rocky, the currents are unpredictable, and the undertow is dangerously strong.

Bathsheba Beach. Although unsafe for swimming, the miles of untouched sand along the East Coast Road in St. Joseph Parish are great for beachcombing and wading. As you approach Bathsheba Soup Bowl, the southernmost stretch just north of Tent Bay, you'll see enormous mushroom-shaped boulders and impressive rolling surf. Expert surfers from around the world converge on the Soup Bowl each November for the Barbados Independence Pro competition. **Amenities:** none. **Best for:** solitude; sunrise; surfing; walking. ⊠ *East Coast Rd., Bathsheba.*

Cattlewash Beach. Swimming is unwise at this windswept beach with pounding surf, which follows the Atlantic Ocean coastline in St. Andrew, but you can take a dip, wade, and play in the tidal pools. Barclays Park, a 50-acre public park across the road, has a shaded picnic area. **Amenities:** none. **Best for:** solitude; sunrise; walking. ⊠ *Ermy Bourne Hwy., Cattlewash.*

WEST COAST

Gentle Caribbean waves lap the west coast, and leafy mahogany trees shade its stunning coves and sandy beaches. The water is perfect for swimming and water sports. An almost unbroken chain of beaches runs between Bridgetown and Speightstown. Elegant homes and luxury hotels face much of the beachfront property in this area, dubbed Barbados's "Platinum Coast."

West-coast beaches are considerably smaller and narrower than those on the south coast. Also, prolonged stormy weather in September and October may cause sand erosion, temporarily making the beach even narrower. Even so, west-coast beaches are seldom crowded. Vendors stroll by with handmade baskets, hats, dolls, jewelry, even original watercolors; owners of private boats offer waterskiing, parasailing, and snorkeling excursions. Hotels and beachside restaurants welcome nonguests for terrace lunches (wear a cover-up), and you can buy picnic items at supermarkets in Holetown.

CLOSE UP

Beware the Dreaded Manchineel Tree

Large, leafy manchineel trees grow along many of the west-coast beaches. Although they look like perfect shade trees, just touching a leaf or the bark can cause nasty blisters. And don't seek refuge under the tree during a rain shower, as even drips from its leaves can affect sensitive skin. The fruit of the tree, which looks like a tiny green apple, is toxic. Most of the manchineels are marked with signs or with red bands painted on the trunk. Why not just cut them all down? Their root systems are extremely important for preventing beach erosion.

2

FAMILY Brighton Beach. Calm as a lake, just north of Bridgetown, this is where you can find locals taking a quick dip on hot days—particularly weekends. **Amenities:** parking (no fee). **Best for:** swimming; walking. ⊠ *Spring Garden Hwy., Bridgetown.*

★ **Fodor's Choice Mullins Beach.** At this popular beach just south
FAMILY of Speightstown, the water is safe for swimming and snorkeling. There's easy parking on the main road, and Mullins Restaurant serves snacks, meals, and drinks—and rents chairs and umbrellas. **Amenities:** food and drink; toilets. **Best for:** sunset; swimming; walking. ⊠ *Hwy. 1B, Mullins.*

Paynes Bay Beach. The stretch of beach just south of Sandy Lane is lined with luxury hotels—Tamarind, The House, and Treasure Beach among them. It's a very pretty area, with plenty of beach to go around, calm water, and good snorkeling. Public access is available at several locations along Highway 1, though parking is limited. **Amenities:** food and drink. **Best for:** snorkeling; sunset; swimming; walking. ⊠ *Hwy. 1, Sunset Crest.*

WHERE TO EAT

First-class restaurants and hotel dining rooms serve quite sophisticated cuisine—often prepared by chefs with international experience and rivaling the dishes served in the world's best restaurants. Most menus include seafood: dolphin—the fish, not the mammal, and also called dorado or mahimahi—kingfish, snapper, and flying fish prepared every way imaginable. Flying fish is so popular that it has officially become a national symbol. Shell-fish also abounds, as do steak, pork, chicken, and local black-belly lamb.

Local specialty dishes include *buljol* (a cold salad of pickled codfish, tomatoes, onions, sweet peppers, and celery) and *conkies* (cornmeal, coconut, pumpkin, raisins, sweet potatoes, and spices, mixed together, wrapped in a banana leaf, and steamed). *Cou cou,* often served with steamed flying fish, is a mixture of cornmeal and okra, usually topped with a spicy Creole sauce made from tomatoes, onions, and sweet peppers. Bajan-style pepperpot is a hearty stew of oxtail, beef, and other meats in a rich, spicy gravy and simmered overnight.

For lunch, restaurants often offer a traditional Bajan buffet of fried fish, baked chicken, salads, macaroni pie (macaroni and cheese), and a selection of steamed or stewed provisions (local root vegetables). Be cautious with the West Indian condiments—like the sun, they're hotter than you think. Typical Bajan drinks—in addition to Banks Beer and Mount Gay, Cockspur, or Malibu rum—are *falernum* (a liqueur concocted of rum, sugar, lime juice, and almond essence) and *mauby* (a nonalcoholic drink made by boiling bitter bark and spices, straining the mixture, and sweetening it). You're sure to enjoy the fresh fruit or rum punch, as well.

What to Wear: The dress code for dinner in Barbados is conservative, casually elegant, and, occasionally, formal—a jacket and tie for gentlemen and a cocktail dress for ladies only in the fanciest restaurants and hotel dining rooms, particularly during the winter holiday season. Jeans, shorts, and T-shirts (either sleeveless or with slogans) are always frowned upon at dinner. Beach attire is appropriate only at the beach.

BRIDGETOWN

$$$ ✕**Waterfront Café.** *Caribbean.* This busy bistro on the
FAMILY walkway facing the south side of The Careenage is the perfect place to enjoy a drink, snack, or meal—and to people-watch. Locals and tourists alike gather for alfresco, all-day dining on sandwiches, salads, fish, pasta, pepperpot stew, and tasty Bajan snacks such as buljol, fish cakes, or plantation pork (plantains stuffed with spicy minced pork). **Known for:** casual waterfront dining; flying fish and cou cou; live jazz at dinnertime. Ⓢ *Average main: $28* ✉ *The*

BEST BETS FOR DINING

With so many restaurants to choose from, how will you decide where to eat? Fodor's writers and editors have selected their favorite restaurants in the Best Bets lists. The Fodor's Choice properties represent the "best of the best." Find the specific details about each restaurant in the reviews that follow.

FODOR'S CHOICE
The Atlantis, Brown Sugar Restaurant, Champers, The Cliff, The Cliff Beach Club, Daphne's, The Fish Pot, L'Azure at The Crane, Lone Star, The Mews, The Tides

BEST VIEW
The Atlantis, Champers, L'Azure at the Crane, The Lobster Pot, Lone Star, Primo, Round House, The Tides

BEST FOR FAMILIES
The Atlantis, Brown Sugar, The Cliff Beach Club, Round House

MOST ROMANTIC
The Cliff, Daphne's, Lone Star, The Mews, The Tides

BEST FOR LOCAL BAJAN CUISINE
Brown Sugar, Fisherman's Pub, Juma's, Shaker's Bar & Grill, Waterfront Café

Careenage, Bridgetown ☎ *246/427–0093* ⊕ *www.waterfrontcafe.com.bb* ☉ *Closed Sun. No dinner Mon.–Wed.*

ST. LAWRENCE GAP

$$ ✕ **Café Sol.** *Mexican.* Have a hankerin' for good Tex-Mex
FAMILY food? Enjoy nachos, tacos, burritos, empanadas, fajitas, and tostadas in this Mexican bar and grill at the western entrance to busy St. Lawrence Gap. **Known for:** busy, boisterous, and fun; good service despite the crowded space; good, filling Mexican specialties—plus "gringo" favorites. Ⓢ *Average main: $20* ⊠ *St. Lawrence Gap, Dover* ☎ *246/420–7655* ⊕ *www.cafesolbarbados.com* ☉ *Closed Mon.*

$$$$ ✕ **Primo Bar & Bistro.** *Mediterranean.* Seafood lovers will remember this as the location of Pisces, a popular "Gap" restaurant for many years. Owner and executive chef Larry Rogers tore down the earlier iteration and opened Primo, a sleek open-plan bistro that has become equally popular for waterfront dining at its best. **Known for:** fresh seafood; open-air dining; waterside location—sunset a bonus at cocktail hour. Ⓢ *Average main: $35* ⊠ *St. Lawrence Gap, Dover* ☎ *246/573–7777* ⊕ *www.primobarandbistro.com.*

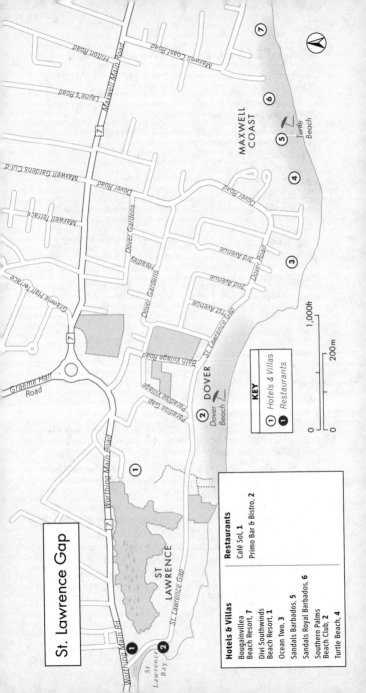

St. Lawrence Gap

KEY

① *Hotels & Villas*
❶ *Restaurants*

0 — 1,000ft
0 — 200m

MAXWELL COAST

DOVER

ST LAWRENCE

St Lawrence Bay

Turtle Beach

Dover Beach

Hotels & Villas

Bougainvillea
Beach Resort, **7**
Divi Southwinds
Beach Resort, **1**
Ocean Two, **3**
Sandals Barbados, **5**
Sandals Royal Barbados, **6**
Southern Palms
Beach Club, **2**
Turtle Beach, **4**

Restaurants

Café Sol, **1**
Primo Bar & Bistro, **2**

Worthing Main Rd.
Worthing Main Road
Graeme Hall Terrace
Graeme Hall Road
Maxwell Main Road
Hilton Road
Layne's Road
Maxwell Coast Road
Maxwell Gardens Cul-d
Maxwell Terrace
Dover Road
Dover Gardens
Headley
3rd Avenue
2nd Avenue
1st Avenue
St Lawrence Gap
Bath Village Road
Paradise Village
Paradise Gap
Dover Road

SOUTH COAST

★ Fodor's Choice 🍴 **Brown Sugar Restaurant.** *Caribbean.* Set back from the road in a traditional Bajan home, the lattice-trimmed dining patios here are filled with ferns, flowers, and water features. Brown Sugar is a popular lunch spot for local businesspeople, who come for the nearly 30 delicious local and Creole dishes spread out at the all-you-can-eat, four-course Planter's Buffet lunch. **Known for:** Bajan buffet luncheon; kids under 5 eat free (under 10 are half price); steel pan entertainment at Sunday buffet. [$] *Average main: $29* ✉ *Aquatic Gap, Garrison* ✣ *Off Bay St.* ☎ *246/426–7684* 🌐 *www.brownsugarbarbados.net* ⊗ *No lunch Sat.*
$$$
FAMILY

$$$$ 🍴 **Café Luna.** *Eclectic.* With a sweeping view of pretty Miami (Enterprise) Beach, the alfresco dining deck on top of the Mediterranean-style Little Arches Hotel is spectacular at lunchtime and magical in the moonlight. Breakfast and lunch are available only for hotel guests. **Known for:** romantic dining under the stars; mouthwatering dishes at dinner; focus on sustainable, locally produced ingredients. [$] *Average main: $32* ✉ *Little Arches Hotel, Enterprise Beach Rd., Oistins* ☎ *246/428–6172* 🌐 *www.cafelunabarbados.com.*

★ Fodor's Choice 🍴 **Champers.** *Caribbean.* Chiryl Newman's snazzy seaside restaurant is in an old Bajan home just off the main road in Rockley. The cliff-top setting overlooking the eastern end of Accra Beach offers daytime diners a panoramic view of the sea and a relaxing Caribbean atmosphere in the evening. **Known for:** upscale, consistently good Caribbean food; waterfront terrace or air-conditioned dining; on-site art gallery. [$] *Average main: $35* ✉ *Skeetes Hill, Rockley* ✣ *Off Hwy. 7* ☎ *246/434–3463* 🌐 *www.champersbarbados.com* ⊗ *No lunch Sat.*
$$$$
FAMILY

★ Fodor's Choice 🍴 **L'Azure at The Crane.** *Seafood.* Perched on an oceanfront cliff overlooking Crane Beach, L'Azure is an informal breakfast and luncheon spot by day that becomes elegant after dark. Enjoy seafood chowder or a light salad or sandwich while absorbing the breathtaking panoramic view of the beach and sea beyond. **Known for:** lovely setting whether day or evening; classy cuisine and service; Sunday gospel brunch. [$] *Average main: $35* ✉ *The Crane Resort, Crane* ☎ *246/423–6220* 🌐 *www.thecrane.com* ⊗ *No dinner Mon. and Wed.*
$$$$

$$ 🍴 **Shaker's Bar & Grill.** *Caribbean.* Locals and visitors alike gather at this no-frills hangout for drinks—perhaps a Banks beer or two, a margarita, a pitcher of sangria, or whatever

BARBADOS'S FAST-FOOD CHAIN

Chefette, Barbados's answer to the "golden arches," has 15 outlets in population centers throughout the island, primarily in Bridgetown, along the west and south coasts, and at the airport. You can get a quarter-pounder, but much more popular here are chicken breast sandwiches (barbecued, "broasted," or "krunched") and rotis (turnovers filled with meat and/or vegetables). All outlets have salads and veggie choices, nearly all sell pizza, and a couple have "BBQ Barns." Most have playgrounds and drive-through service. **■ TIP→ New Yorkers should skip the breakfast bagels. They're nothing like the hometown favorites.**

wets their whistle—and the delicious local food. Simple dishes like beer-battered flying fish, grilled catch of the day, barbecued chicken, grilled steak, or a solid cheeseburger deliver the goods, but the barbecued ribs are the main event. **Known for:** finger-lickin' barbecued ribs; small, busy, convivial "rum shop" on a quiet side street; cash only. [$] *Average main: $17* ✉ *Browne's Gap, Rockley* ☎ *246/228–8855* 🌐 *www.shakersbarbados.com/visit.html* 💳 *No credit cards* 🕒 *Closed Sun. and Mon. and mid-Aug.–mid-Sept. No lunch.*

$$$$ ✕ **Zen at The Crane.** *Asian.* Thai and Japanese specialties reign supreme in a magnificent setting overlooking Crane Beach. The centerpiece of the sophisticated, Asian-inspired decor is a 12-seat sushi bar, where chefs prepare exotic fare before your eyes. **Known for:** Thai or Japanese prix-fixe menu—or à la carte dining; traditional Japanese-style tatami room; modern, Asian-inspired decor. [$] *Average main: $32* ✉ *The Crane Resort, Crane* ☎ *246/423–6220* 🌐 *www.thecrane.com* 🕒 *Closed Tues. No lunch.*

EAST COAST

★ **$$$** **FAMILY** Fodor's Choice ✕ **The Atlantis.** *Caribbean.* For decades, an alfresco lunch on the Atlantis deck overlooking the ocean has been a favorite of both visitors and Bajans. Pleasant atmosphere and good food have always been the draw, with a casually elegant dining room and a top-notch menu that focuses on local produce, seafood, and meats. **Known for:** best place for lunch when touring the east coast; stunning ocean views from your table; Bajan buffet luncheon on

Wednesday and Sunday and kids menu every day. [$] *Average main: $29* ✉ *The Atlantis Hotel, Tent Bay* ☎ *246/433–9445* 🌐 *www.atlantishotelbarbados.com* ⏲ *Closed Sept.; Apr.–mid-Nov. no dinner Sun.*

$$$ FAMILY ✕ **Round House.** *Caribbean.* Owners Robert and Gail Manley oversee the menu for guests staying in their historic (1832) manse-turned-inn, as well as tourists enjoying the east coast and Bajans dining out. The lunch menu—served on a deck overlooking the Atlantic Ocean—includes homemade soups and quiches, sandwiches, salads, and pasta. **Known for:** casual alfresco dining overlooking smashing ocean surf; good spot for lunch when touring the east coast; even when dinner is served, the restaurant closes at 8 pm. [$] *Average main: $26* ✉ *Bathsheba* ☎ *246/433–9678* 🌐 *www.roundhousebarbados.com* ⏲ *Closed Sept.; May–Oct. no dinner; Nov.–Apr. no dinner Fri.*

HOLETOWN AND VICINITY

★ $$$$ Fodor's Choice ✕ **The Cliff.** *Eclectic.* Chef Paul Owens's mastery creates one of the finest dining experiences in the Caribbean, with prices to match. Steep steps hug the cliff on which the restaurant sits to accommodate those arriving by yacht, and every candlelit table has a sea view. **Known for:** sophisticated seaside dining experience; world-class cuisine and wine list; extraordinarily pricey. [$] *Average main: $133* ✉ *Hwy. 1, Derricks* ☎ *246/432–1922* 🌐 *www.thecliffbarbados.com* ⏲ *No lunch; Apr. 15–Dec. 15 closed Sun.*

★ $$$$ FAMILY Fodor's Choice ✕ **The Cliff Beach Club.** *International.* Just steps from The Cliff—the beach club's formal, high-end sister restaurant—the seaside views here are similarly dramatic but the atmosphere is informal, fun, and—perhaps more importantly—closer to affordable. Sandwiches (cutters), burgers, fish-and-chips, soups, and salads will fill the bill at lunchtime, but you can also choose from a variety of starters and small plates, meat and fish plates, pasta, and risotto dishes that blend right into the full dinner menu. **Known for:** sister property to ultrafancy The Cliff restaurant; excellent bistro-style cuisine; beautiful Caribbean Sea vista. [$] *Average main: $40* ✉ *Hwy. 1, Durants* ☎ *246/432–0797* 🌐 *thecliffbeachclub.com* ⏲ *Closed Mon. No dinner Sun.*

★ $$$$ Fodor's Choice ✕ **Daphne's.** *Modern Italian.* The chef and his brigade whip up contemporary Italian cuisine at The House's beachfront restaurant, a chic outpost of the London eatery of the same name. Grilled yellowfin tuna, for example, becomes "modern Italian" when combined with

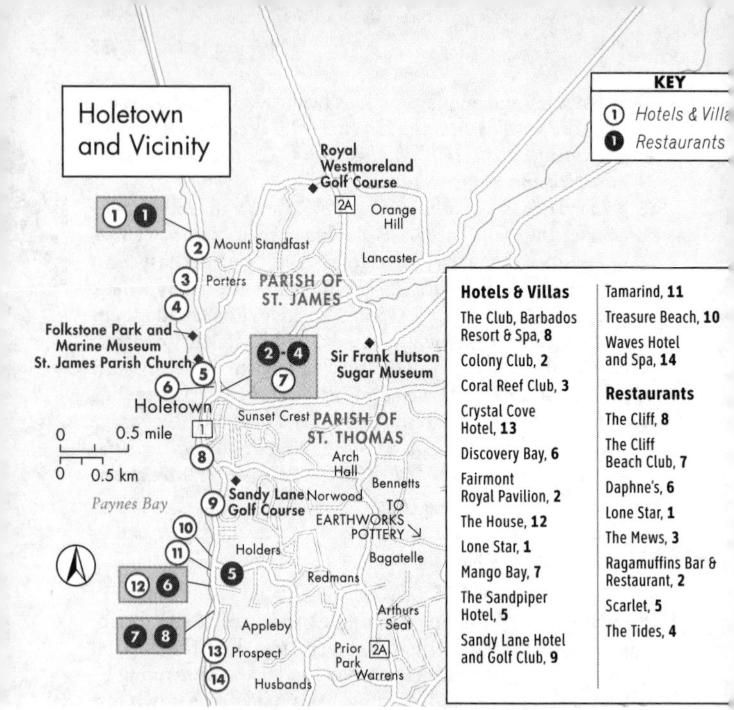
Holetown and Vicinity
KEY
Hotels & Villas
Restaurants
Royal Westmoreland Golf Course
2A
Orange Hill
Mount Standfast
Lancaster
Porters
PARISH OF ST. JAMES
Folkstone Park and Marine Museum
St. James Parish Church
Sir Frank Hutson Sugar Museum
Holetown
Sunset Crest
PARISH OF ST. THOMAS
0 0.5 mile
0 0.5 km
1
Arch Hall
Bennetts
Paynes Bay
Sandy Lane Golf Course
Norwood
TO EARTHWORKS POTTERY
Holders
Bagatelle
Redmans
Arthurs Seat
Appleby
Prospect
Prior Park
2A
Warrens
Husbands
Hotels & Villas
The Club, Barbados Resort & Spa, 8
Colony Club, 2
Coral Reef Club, 3
Crystal Cove Hotel, 13
Discovery Bay, 6
Fairmont Royal Pavilion, 2
The House, 12
Lone Star, 1
Mango Bay, 7
The Sandpiper Hotel, 5
Sandy Lane Hotel and Golf Club, 9
Tamarind, 11
Treasure Beach, 10
Waves Hotel and Spa, 14
Restaurants
The Cliff, 8
The Cliff Beach Club, 7
Daphne's, 6
Lone Star, 1
The Mews, 3
Ragamuffins Bar & Restaurant, 2
Scarlet, 5
The Tides, 4

spicy chickpeas and *peperonata* (stewed peppers, tomatoes, onions, and garlic). **Known for:** classy cuisine presented in a classy environment; delightful beachfront atmosphere; although not a "family" environment, there is a kids menu. *$ Average main: $44 ✉ The House, Hwy. 1, Paynes Bay ☎ 246/432–2731 🌐 www.daphnesbarbados.com ⏲ June–Oct. no lunch and closed Mon.*

★ **$$$$** FodorśChoice ✕ **Lone Star.** *Modern European.* At the tiny but chic Lone Star Hotel, top chefs turn the finest local ingredients into gastronomic delights. At lunch, tasty salads, sandwiches, and wood-fired pizzas are served in the oceanfront bar; after sunset, the casual daytime atmosphere turns trendy. **Known for:** lovely setting overlooking the sea; breakfast on the boardwalk; sunset cocktails in the lounge. *$ Average main: $45 ✉ Lone Star Hotel, Hwy. 1, Mount Standfast ☎ 246/629–0599 🌐 www.thelonestar.com.*

★ **$$$** FodorśChoice ✕ **The Mews.** *International.* Once the private home of actress Minnie Driver's dad, the front room is now an inviting bar; an interior courtyard is an intimate, open-air dining area; and the second floor is a maze of small dining rooms and balconies. But it's the food—classic, bistro, or tapas—that draws the visitors. **Known for:**

the atmosphere of being invited to a friend's chic home for dinner; farm-to-table dishes using fresh, locally sourced, organic ingredients; cozy downstairs cocktail bar and occasional live entertainment. $ *Average main: $28* ✉ *2nd St., Holetown* ☎ *246/432–1122* ⊕ *www.themewsbarbados.com* ⊘ *No lunch. Mid-Apr.–mid-Dec. closed Sun.*

2

$$$ ✕**Ragamuffins Bar & Restaurant.** *Caribbean.* Tiny, funky, lively, and informal, here you can dine inside in an authentic chattel house or outside on the porch. Although the restaurant focuses on fun, the chef specializes in the freshest seafood, perfectly broiled T-bone steaks, West Indian curries, and vegetarian dishes such as Bajan stir-fried vegetables with noodles. **Known for:** good food, good music, and good fun; unpretentious, friendly, welcoming atmosphere; Sunday-night Drag Show, a must. $ *Average main: $22* ✉ *1st St., Holetown* ☎ *246/432–1295* ⊕ *www.ragamuffinsbarbados.com* ⊘ *No lunch.*

$$$ ✕**Scarlet.** *Eclectic.* Movers and groovers come to this bright-red building on the side of the road to chill over a martini and share nibbles, such as a plate of Bajan fish cakes with "calypso" dip. Or they settle in after cocktails for a burger with sophisticated toppings, grilled lamb cutlets, lemongrass salmon skewers, or perhaps Baxter's Road chicken. **Known for:** red building, red walls, red cocktails …; generous portions of elegant food; close quarters and sometimes quite busy. $ *Average main: $28* ✉ *Hwy. 1, Paynes Bay* ☎ *246/432–3663* ⊕ *www.scarletbarbados.com* ⊘ *Closed Sun. and Mon. No lunch.*

★ Fodor'sChoice ✕**The Tides.** *Modern European.* Perhaps the most **$$$$** intriguing feature of this stunning setting in what was once a private mansion—besides the sound of waves crashing onto the shore just feet away—is the row of huge tree trunks growing right through the dining room. The food is equally dramatic. **Known for:** long considered one of the island's best restaurants; chic "tree house" with a sea view; the cozy lounge and on-site art gallery. $ *Average main: $45* ✉ *Balmore House, Hwy. 1, Holetown* ☎ *246/432–8356* ⊕ *www.tidesbarbados.com* ⊘ *No lunch Mon.–Sat.*

WEST COAST

★ Fodor'sChoice ✕**The Fish Pot.** *Caribbean.* Bright and cheery by **$$$$** day and relaxed and cozy by night, the Fish Pot offers a tasty dining experience in a setting that's classier than its name might suggest. Just north of the little fishing village of Six Men's Bay, on the northwestern coast of Barbados, this attractive seaside restaurant serves excellent internationally inspired, "modern" Caribbean cuisine and some of the island's freshest fish. Gaze seaward through windows framed with pale-green louvered shutters while lunching on a seafood crêpe, a grilled panini, snow-crab salad, or perhaps pasta with seafood or roasted-pepper-and-chili tomato sauce. **Known for:** casual gourmet dining; fresh seafood by the seaside; perfect spot for lunch when headed north. [$] *Average main: $35* ✉ *Little Good Harbour Hotel, Hwy. 1B* ☎ *246/439–3000* 🌐 *www.littlegoodharbourbarbados.com.*

$ 🍴 **Fisherman's Pub.** *Caribbean.* As local as local gets, this FAMILY open-air, waterfront beach bar (a former rum shop) is built on stilts a stone's throw from the Speightstown fish market. For years, fishermen and other locals have come here for the inexpensive, authentic Bajan lunch buffet. **Known for:** truly local food in a truly local environment; fill up for a few bucks; right on the waterfront. [$] *Average main: $12* ✉ *Queen St., Speightstown* ☎ *246/422–2703* 🌐 *fishermanpub.restaurantsnapshot.com.*

$$$ 🍴 **Juma's Restaurant.** *Caribbean.* Once you've stepped FAMILY through the somewhat innocuous roadside building, you're transported to an open beachfront environment decorated with African-inspired artwork, thatched ceilings, and an endless view of the ocean. But wait … there's more; the cuisine here features French and Thai dishes (seafood thermidor, beef fillet with peppercorn sauce, red or green curry with jasmine rice), along with local Bajan specialties (saltfish cakes, flying fish cutters). **Known for:** eclectic menu; Sunday-afternoon beach barbecue; complimentary transportation from west-coast locations with minimum spend. [$] *Average main: $29* ✉ *Queen St., Speightstown* ☎ *246/432–0232* 🌐 *www.jumasrestaurant.com.*

$$$ 🍴 **The Lobster Pot.** *Seafood.* Overlooking the beach in the FAMILY middle of Speightstown, this is the place to come for lobster: lobster bisque, lobster salad, grilled lobster, lobster thermidor, lobster potpie, lobster burger … you name it. Landlubbers, on the other hand, might enjoy plantain-stuffed chicken breast, pork spareribs, curried goat, or a steak. **Known for:** lobster, of course; start with breakfast, then enjoy the complimentary beach sun loungers; Sunday-afternoon beach barbecue with live music. [$] *Average main: $30* ✉ *Queen St., Speightstown* ☎ *246/432–0287* 🌐 *www.thelobsterpotbarbados.com* ⏲ *Closed Mon.*

WHERE TO STAY

Most visitors stay on either the fashionable west coast, north of Bridgetown, or on the action-packed south coast. On the west coast, the beachfront resorts in St. Peter and St. James parishes are mostly luxurious, self-contained enclaves. Highway 1, a two-lane road with considerable traffic, runs past these resorts, which can make strolling to a nearby bar or restaurant a bit difficult. Along the south coast in Christ Church Parish, many hotels are clustered near the busy strip known as St. Lawrence Gap, convenient to small restaurants, bars, and nightclubs. On the much more remote east coast, a couple of small inns offer ocean-front views and get-away-from-it-all tranquillity.

In keeping with the smoke-free policy enforced throughout Barbados, smoking is restricted to open outdoor areas such as the beach. It is not permitted in hotels (neither rooms nor public areas such as the pool) or in restaurants.

Prices in Barbados may be considerably higher in season (December 15–April 15) than in the quieter months. Most hotels include no meals in their rates, but some include breakfast; most offer optional meal plans. A few may require you to purchase a meal plan in the high season. Several offer all-inclusive packages.

Resorts run the gamut—from unpretentious to exceedingly formal—in terms of size, intimacy, amenities, and price. Families and long-term visitors may choose from a wide variety of villas and condos. A few small, cozy inns are found along the east and southeast coasts, as well as the northwest. They can be ultraluxurious, fairly simple, or something in between.

Villa and condo complexes, which are continually cropping up along the south and west coasts of Barbados, may be the most economical option for families, other groups, or couples vacationing together. Nonowner vacationers rent individual units directly from the property managers, the same as reserving hotel accommodations. Units with fully equipped kitchens, two to six bedrooms, and as many baths run $200 to $2,500 per night in the off-season—double that in winter.

Hotel reviews have been shortened. For full information, visit Fodors.com.

BEST BETS FOR LODGING

Fodor's offers a selective listing of quality lodging experiences, from the island's best boutique hotel to its most luxurious beach resort. Here we've compiled our top recommendations based on the different types of lodging found on the island. Properties that provide a particularly remarkable experience are designated in the listings with the Fodor's Choice logo.

FODOR'S CHOICE
Atlantis Hotel, Cobblers Cove Hotel, Colony Club, Coral Reef Club, Fairmont Royal Pavilion, The House, Ocean Two, Sandals Barbados, The Sandpiper, Sandy Lane, Sweetfield Manor

BEST FOR HONEYMOONERS
Cobblers Cove Hotel, Colony Club, Coral Reef Club, Fairmont Royal Pavilion, The House, Sandals Barbados, The Sandpiper, Sweetfield Manor

BEST FOR FAMILIES
Bougainvillea, Crystal Cove, Divi Southwinds Beach Resort, Hilton Barbados Resort, Southern Palms Beach Club, Tamarind, Turtle Beach

PRIVATE VILLAS AND CONDOS

Local real-estate agencies will arrange vacation rentals of privately owned villas and condos along the west coast in St. James and St. Peter. All villas and condos are fully furnished and equipped, including appropriate staff depending on the size of the villa or unit—which can range from one to eight bedrooms; the staff usually works six days a week. Most villas have TVs and other entertainment devices; all properties have telephones, and some have Internet access. International telephone calls are usually blocked; plan on using your own mobile phone or a phone card. Vehicles generally are not included in the rates, but rental cars can be arranged for and delivered to the villa upon request. Linens and basic supplies (such as bath soap, toilet tissue, and dishwashing detergent) are normally included.

Units with one to six bedrooms and as many baths run $200 to $2,500 per night in summer and double that in winter. Rates include utilities and government taxes. The only additional cost is for groceries, staff gratuities, and extraordinary or optional requests. A security deposit is required upon booking and refunded seven days after departure less any damages or unpaid miscellaneous charges.

Apartments are available for vacation rentals in buildings or complexes that can have as few as 3 or 4 units or as many as 30 to 40 units—or even more. Prices range from $30 to $300 per night.

VILLA RENTAL CONTACTS

Altman Real Estate. ✉ *Hwy. 1, Derricks, Durants* ☎ *246/432–0840, 866/360–5292 in U.S.* 🌐 *www.altmanbarbados.com.*

Blue Sky Luxury. ✉ *Newton House, Hwy. 1B, Little Bataleys* ☎ *246/622–4466, 866/404–9600 in U.S.* 🌐 *www.blueskyluxury.com.*

Island Villas. ✉ *Trents Bldg., Holetown* ☎ *246/422–3333, 866/978–8499 in U.S.* 🌐 *www.island-villas.com.*

APARTMENT RENTAL CONTACTS

Barbados Tourism Marketing, Inc. This office has a list of apartments in prime resort areas on the south and west coasts, complete with facilities offered and current rates. ✉ *Warrens Office Complex, 1st fl., West Wing, Warrens* ☎ *246/427–2623, 800/221–9831 in U.S.* 🌐 *www.visitbarbados.org.*

ST. LAWRENCE GAP

$$ 🏨 **Bougainvillea Beach Resort.** *Resort.* Attractive seaside town houses, each with a separate entrance, wrap around the pool or face the beachfront; the suites are huge compared with hotel suites elsewhere in this price range, are decorated in appealing Caribbean pastels, and have full kitchens. **Pros:** great for families but also appeals to couples and honeymooners; tennis court and air-conditioned fitness center; three pools, one with a swim-up bar, and lots of water sports. **Cons:** rooms are on four levels with no elevator; sea can be a little rough for swimming; service/attitude could use a little boost. [$] *Rooms from: $304* ✉ *Maxwell Coast Rd., Maxwell* ☎ *246/628–0990, 800/495–1858 in U.S.* 🌐 *www.bougainvillearesort.com* 🛏 *138 suites* 🍴 *No meals.*
FAMILY

$ 🏨 **Divi Southwinds Beach Resort.** *Resort.* This all-suites resort is situated on 20 acres of lawn and gardens bisected by action-packed St. Lawrence Gap. The property south of "The Gap" wraps around a stunning half mile of Dover Beach, where 16 beach villas provide an intimate setting steps from the sand. **Pros:** beautiful beach plus three pools; close to shopping, restaurants, and nightspots; kids club. **Cons:** water sports cost extra; some rooms aching for renovations. [$] *Rooms from: $264* ✉ *St. Lawrence Main Rd.,*
FAMILY

Turtle Time

Along Turtle Beach, which stretches in front of both Sandals Barbados and the aptly named Turtle Beach Resort, mother hawksbill turtles dig a pit in the sand, lay 100 or more eggs, cover the nest with sand, and then return to the sea. The eggs, which look just like Ping-Pong balls, are usually deposited between May and November and take about 60 days to hatch. If you happen to be strolling along the beach at the time they emerge, you'll see a mass of newborn turtles scrambling out of the sand

and making a dash (at turtle speed, of course) for the sea. Although the journey takes only a few minutes, this can be a very dangerous time for the tiny turtles. They are easy prey for gulls and large crabs. The folks involved in the Barbados Sea Turtle Project (☎ 246/230–0142) at the University of the West Indies are working hard to protect and conserve the marine turtle populations in Barbados through educational workshops, tagging programs, and other research efforts.

Hwy. 7, Dover ☎ *246/428–7181, 800/367–3484* ⊕ *www.divisouthwinds.com* ⋧ *133 rooms* ⦿ *No meals.*

★ **Fodor's**Choice ⊡ **Ocean Two.** *Resort.* Couples and families
$$$ are drawn to this sophisticated, high-rise resort on Dover
FAMILY Beach at the eastern end of lively St. Lawrence Gap. Most accommodations are residential-style suites, with sitting rooms and full kitchens—even a dishwasher and washer/dryer! A few are standard hotel rooms, and all but a handful of "bay view" two-bedroom suites have a full ocean view. **Pros:** large, luxurious accommodations; beautiful beach and inviting pool; in-room spa services. **Cons:** showers only, no tubs; Taste restaurant could be more tasty—and it's expensive—but plenty of dining options nearby; a little more service and less attitude would be good. Ⓢ *Rooms from: $379* ⊠ *St. Lawrence Gap, Dover* ☎ *246/418–1800* ⊕ *www.oceantwobarbados.com* ⋧ *86 rooms* ⦿ *No meals.*

★ **Fodor's**Choice ⊡ **Sandals Barbados.** *Resort.* Romance is defi-
$$$$ nitely in the air at this truly magnificent (couples-only) Sandals property, which surrounds an 8-acre garden and lagoon—the longest and largest in Barbados. **Pros:** great beach and beautiful garden; myriad activities, including unlimited scuba diving, windsurfing, and sailing; a great place for weddings, honeymoons, and vow renewals; ocean-front and swim-up lagoon rooms are top choices. **Cons:** fabulously expensive, so look for frequent promotional offers;

with so much to do, it's easy to forget there's a whole island to explore; too few pool chaises to meet demand. $ *Rooms from: $1,004* ⊠ *St. Lawrence Gap, Maxwell* ⊹ *At Maxwell Coast Rd.* ☎ *246/620–3600, 888/726–3257* ⊕ *www.sandals. com/barbados* ⮑ *280 rooms* ◯ *All-inclusive.*

$$$$ ⛫ **Sandals Royal Barbados.** *All-Inclusive.* Sandal's second resort on the island, opened in December 2017 adjacent to sister resort Sandals Barbados, features all concierge- and butler-level suites with all the implied pampering. **Pros:** suites are ultraluxurious, ultraromantic … ultra-ultra; with 17 possible dining options, you'll never go hungry; complimentary airport shuttle service. **Cons:** with so much to do on-site, you may not experience the island itself; spa services cost extra; getting a taxi is always an issue at Sandals, as you're urged to use their own tour service. $ *Rooms from: $857* ⊠ *Maxwell Coast Rd., Maxwell* ☎ *246/620–3600, 800/726–3257 in U.S.* ⊕ *www.sandals.com/royalbarbados* ⮑ *222 suites* ◯ *All-inclusive.*

$$ ⛫ **Southern Palms Beach Club.** *Resort.* This resort is pretty in
FAMILY pink, you might say, with its (pink) plantation-style main building opening onto an inviting pool area and 1,000 feet of white sandy beach. **Pros:** friendly and accommodating staff; hotel food and entertainment are very good, and other options are nearby; nice beach. **Cons:** rooms are large and clean but bathrooms are dated; beach vendors can be a nuisance (not the hotel's fault); uncomfortable pool loungers should be replaced. $ *Rooms from: $325* ⊠ *St. Lawrence Gap, Dover* ☎ *246/428–7171* ⊕ *www.southernpalms.net* ⮑ *91 rooms* ◯ *No meals.*

$$$$ ⛫ **Turtle Beach.** *Resort.* Families flock to this resort because it
FAMILY offers large, bright, family-friendly suites and enough all-included activities for everyone. **Pros:** good choice for families; daily rounds of golf at Barbados Golf Club included; lots of complimentary water sports. **Cons:** refrigerators are stocked only in one-bedroom suites; pools are small relative to the number of kids in them; buffet meals are a little tired. $ *Rooms from: $945* ⊠ *St. Lawrence Gap, Dover* ⊹ *At Maxwell Coast Rd.* ☎ *246/428–7131* ⊕ *www.turtle-beachresortbarbados.com* ⮑ *161 suites* ◯ *All-inclusive.*

SOUTH COAST

$ ⛫ **Accra Beach Hotel and Spa.** *Resort.* A full-service resort in the middle of the busy south coast, Accra is large, modern, competitively priced, and faces a great beach. **Pros:** can't beat that beach; walk to shopping, restaurants, and nightspots; reasonable prices. **Cons:**"island view" rooms facing the street have an unattractive view and can be noisy; rooms could use some TLC; customer service is lax. $ *Rooms from: $247* ✉ *Hwy. 7, Rockley* ☎ *246/435–8920* 🌐 *www.accrabeachhotel.com* 🛏 *221 rooms* 🍴 *No meals.*

$$ FAMILY **Barbados Beach Club.** *Resort.* Designed with families in mind, this four-story hotel (with elevators) sits on a beautiful stretch of south-coast beach—and offers tremendous value. **Pros:** great beach; good value; wonderful for kids. **Cons:** rooms really need refreshing; meals at set times, not all day; food varies daily but is rather uninspired. $ *Rooms from: $326* ✉ *Maxwell Coast Rd., Maxwell* ☎ *246/428–9900* 🌐 *www.barbadosbeachclub.com* 🛏 *110 rooms* 🍴 *All-inclusive.*

$ FAMILY **Coconut Court Beach Hotel.** *Hotel.* This beachfront hotel is popular among families, who love the activities room for kids, the kitchenettes, and the fact that children under 12 stay free. **Pros:** safe swimming and snorkeling at the beautiful beach; free airport shuttle and Bridgetown shopping shuttle services; easy walk to The Garrison, South Coast Boardwalk, restaurants, shops. **Cons:** close to the road, so noise can be an issue; rooms are rather basic and simply decorated; restricted views of the beach in "west wing" rooms. $ *Rooms from: $255* ✉ *Main Rd., Hastings* ☎ *246/427–1655, 888/506–0448 in U.S.* 🌐 *www.coconut-court.com* 🛏 *112 rooms* 🍴 *Breakfast.*

$ **Courtyard Bridgetown by Marriott.** *Hotel.* Comfortable, contemporary, convenient, and economical, this place is pleasant and the rooms are well appointed. **Pros:** good value; especially suited to business travelers; modern, attractive accommodations. **Cons:** long walk to beach and restaurants; comparatively little "Caribbean resort" atmosphere; limited on-site dining options. $ *Rooms from: $246* ✉ *Hwy. 7, Hastings Main Rd., Garrison* ⊕ *Set back a block from the road* ☎ *246/625–0000* 🌐 *www.marriott.com* 🛏 *118 rooms* 🍴 *No meals.*

$$$ FAMILY **The Crane.** *Resort.* Hugging a seaside bluff on the southeast coast, The Crane incorporates the island's oldest hotel in continuous operation; the original coral-stone hotel building (1887) is the centerpiece of a luxurious, 40-acre villa complex. **Pros:** enchanting view, beach, and pools; complimentary kids club; fabulous suites and five great restaurants. **Cons:** remote location; rental car recommended; villas are considerably more expensive and more modern than historic hotel rooms. $ *Rooms from: $457*

✉ *Crane* ☎ *246/423–6220, 866/978–5942 in U.S.* 🌐 *www.thecrane.com* 🛏 *252 rooms* 🍴 *No meals.*

$$ 🏨 **Hilton Barbados Resort.** *Hotel.* Beautifully situated on the
FAMILY sandy Needham's Point peninsula, all 350 units in this high-rise resort hotel have private balconies overlooking either the ocean or Carlisle Bay; 77 rooms on executive floors offer a private lounge and concierge services. **Pros:** great location near town and on a beautiful beach; lots of services and amenities; accessible rooms available. **Cons:** service/communication should be better; huge group/convention hotel; lacks island ambience. [$] *Rooms from: $360* ✉ *Aquatic Gap, Needham's Point, Garrison* ☎ *246/426–0200* 🌐 *www.hiltonbarbadosresort.com* 🛏 *350 rooms* 🍴 *No meals.*

$$$ 🏨 **Island Inn Hotel.** *Hotel.* Constructed in 1804 as a rum storage facility for the British Regiment, this quaint, all-inclusive boutique hotel—less than a mile from Bridgetown and steps away from beautiful Pebbles Beach on Carlisle Bay—appeals to singles, couples, and families. **Pros:** friendly, accommodating, attractive atmosphere; smartly decorated rooms; excellent all-inclusive value. **Cons:** small pool; rooms near the front may be noisier and don't have a patio; near but not directly on the beach. [$] *Rooms from: $425* ✉ *Aquatic Gap, Garrison* ☎ *246/436–6393* 🌐 *www.islandinnbarbados.com* 🛏 *24 rooms* 🍴 *All-inclusive.*

$$ 🏨 **Little Arches Hotel.** *Hotel.* Just east of the fishing village of Oistins, this classy boutique hotel has a distinctly Mediterranean atmoshere and a perfect vantage point overlooking the sea. **Pros:** stylish accommodations; complimentary full breakfasts with weeklong stay; across from Miami Beach. **Cons:** fairly remote residential area; road traffic is sometimes distracting; small pool. [$] *Rooms from: $340* ✉ *Enterprise Beach Rd., Oistins* ☎ *246/420–4689* 🌐 *www.littlearches.com* 🛏 *10 rooms* 🍴 *No meals.*

$$ 🏨 **Radisson Aquatica Resort Barbados.** *Hotel.* Rooms in this high-rise hotel overlooking pretty Carlisle Bay, just south of Bridgetown, are modern and sleek with espresso-color furniture, sparkling white linens, desk with ergonomic chair, comfortable sitting chair and ottoman, 42-inch flat-screen TV, and the latest in-room technology. **Pros:** excellent beach; beautiful sunsets from ocean-facing rooms; convenient location. **Cons:** pool area could use more umbrellas; noisy air-conditioning, no room refrigerator; skip the restaurant and opt for neighboring Brown Sugar or the Hilton. [$] *Rooms from: $358* ✉ *Aquatic Gap, Gar-*

rison ☎ 246/426–6000 ⊕ www.radisson.com/barbados ⤳ 124 rooms ꧁Breakfast.

$ ▨ **Savannah Beach Hotel.** *Hotel.* Appealing to those who don't require organized entertainment, the Savannah is convenient for walks to the Garrison Historic Area, the Barbados Museum, and the racetrack—and minutes from Bridgetown by car or taxi. **Pros:** inviting pool; convenient to Bridgetown and sites; friendly, accommodating staff. **Cons:** beach is somewhat rocky; few activities for kids other than the beach; some rooms need a little TLC. Ⓢ *Rooms from: $273* ✉ *Hastings Main Rd., Hastings* ☎ 246/434–3800 ⊕ www.savannahbarbados.com ⤳ 93 rooms ꧁Breakfast.

$$ ▨ **Silver Point Hotel.** *Hotel.* This remote, gated community of modern condos at Silver Sands–Silver Rock Beach is operated as a trendy boutique hotel that appeals to singles, couples, and families—but especially to windsurfers and kitesurfers. **Pros:** stylish suites; perfect location for windsurfers and kitesurfers; gated community. **Cons:** far from anything but the beach, so a rental car is recommended; sea can be rough for swimming; no entertainment other than the beach. Ⓢ *Rooms from: $280* ✉ *Silver Rock Beach, Silver Sands, Silver Sands* ☎ 246/420–4416 ⊕ www.silverpointhotel.com ⤳ 58 suites ꧁No meals.

$$$$ ▨ **The SoCo Hotel.** *Hotel.* Sophisticated travelers, particularly couples, love this ultramodern, adults-only boutique hotel strategically poised on the beachfront in Hastings. **Pros:** stylish rooms; lovely beach with long boardwalk; excellent restaurant. **Cons:** showers only, no tubs; mixed reviews on the food; morning road noise can be an issue. Ⓢ *Rooms from: $591* ✉ *Hastings Main Rd., Hastings* ☎ 246/537–7626 ⊕ www.thesocohotel.com ⤳ 24 rooms ꧁All-inclusive.

$ ▨ **South Beach Hotel.** *Rental.* You enter the sleek lobby of
FAMILY this cool condo-style hotel, across the street from spectacular Accra Beach, via a footbridge across a double-wide lap pool that runs the length of the property. **Pros:** near shopping, restaurants, and nightlife; Accra Beach is great for families; washer/dryer on every floor. **Cons:** beach is across the street; only pool, while beautiful looking, is a shallow lap pool; more "Miami Beach" than "Caribbean" style. Ⓢ *Rooms from: $225* ✉ *Main Rd., Rockley* ✚ *At Accra Beach* ☎ 246/435–8561 ⊕ www.southbeachbarbados.com ⤳ 49 rooms ꧁Breakfast.

$$$$ ▨ **Sugar Bay Barbados.** *All-Inclusive.* Tropical gardens and
FAMILY a dramatic water feature mask the proximity of the main road to this large, all-inclusive beachfront resort near the Garrison Historic Area. **Pros:** great beach for swimming and

snorkeling; walking distance to Garrison sights; friendly, accommodating staff. **Cons:** one pool is small and larger pool is often full of kids; limited access to specialty restaurants without a surcharge; dining and entertainment area gets congested. [$] *Rooms from: $500* ✉ *Hastings Main Rd., Hastings* ☎ *246/622–1101* 🌐 *www.sugarbaybarbados.com* 🛏 *138 rooms* 🍴 *All-inclusive.*

★ Fodor's Choice 🏨 **Sweetfield Manor.** *B&B/Inn.* Perched on a
$$ ridge about a mile from Bridgetown, this romantic, restored plantation house (circa 1900) was once the residence of the Dutch ambassador and is now the island's most delightful bed-and-breakfast. **Pros:** peaceful enclave, primarily for adults; inviting pool and gardens; delicious gourmet breakfast; perfect wedding venue. **Cons:** long walk (or short car ride) to beach; rental car advised; not appropriate for kids or those with physical disabilities. [$] *Rooms from: $338* ✉ *Brittons New Rd., Brittons Hill* ☎ *246/269–7294* 🌐 *www.sweetfieldmanor.com* 🛏 *10 rooms* 🍴 *Breakfast.*

DID YOU KNOW? **Portuguese explorer Pedro a Campos is credited with naming Barbados. In 1536, when he stopped by the island en route to Brazil, he and his crew were intrigued by the bearded appearance of the indigenous fig trees. "Os Barbados," or "the bearded ones," he proclaimed—and the name stuck.**

EAST COAST

★ Fodor's Choice 🏨 **The Atlantis Hotel.** *B&B/Inn.* Renowned for
$$ its spectacular oceanfront location, this hotel has been a fixture on the rugged east coast for more than a century. **Pros:** historical and modern blend beautifully; spectacular oceanfront location; popular restaurant. **Cons:** for oceanfront rooms, smashing waves can be noisy at night; no beach for swimming but there is a pool; remote location, so rental car is advised. [$] *Rooms from: $281* ✉ *Tent Bay* ☎ *246/433–9445* 🌐 *www.atlantishotelbarbados.com* 🕒 *Closed Sept.* 🛏 *9 rooms* 🍴 *Breakfast.*

$ 🏨 **Round House Inn.** *B&B/Inn.* It's hard to tell which is more appealing: the view of the rugged coastline or the magnificent historic (1832) manse strategically perched on the cliff to take advantage of the view. **Pros:** fabulous ocean views; small and intimate; quiet and peaceful—bring a good book. **Cons:** really remote location; no TV (if you care); no beach for swimming. [$] *Rooms from: $175* ✉ *Bathsheba* ☎ *246/433–9079* 🌐 *www.roundhousebarbados.com* 🛏 *4 rooms* 🍴 *Breakfast.*

$ **Sea-U Guest House.** *B&B/Inn.* Uschi Wetzels, a German travel writer in an earlier life, became smitten with the wild and woolly east coast of Barbados while on assignment and returned in 1999 to build this delightful guesthouse. **Pros:** peaceful and relaxing; couldn't be friendlier; dinner available most nights. **Cons:** remote location; few on-site activities; no TV or in-room telephone; some rooms have no air-conditioning. [$] *Rooms from: $219* ✉ *Tent Bay* ☎ *246/433–9450* 🌐 *www.seaubarbados.com* 🛏 *10 rooms* 🍴 *Breakfast.*

HOLETOWN AND VICINITY

$$$$ **The Club, Barbados Resort & Spa.** *Resort.* This is one of the island's few adults-only (age 16 and up) all-inclusive resorts and the only one on the west coast; only spa and salon services and room service cost extra. **Pros:** intimate atmosphere; walk to Holetown and Sandy Lane Beach; waterskiing included. **Cons:** beach erodes to almost nothing sometimes—usually after fall storms—but the sandy beach deck is a good substitute; not fully accessible to people with disabilities; three-night stay required in high season. [$] *Rooms from: $840* ✉ *Hwy. 1, Vauxhall, Holetown* ☎ *246/432–7840, 866/317–8009* 🌐 *www.theclubbarbados.com* 🛏 *158 rooms* 🍴 *All-inclusive.*

★ Fodor's Choice **Colony Club.** *Resort.* The signature hotel of
$$$$ seven Elegant Hotel properties on Barbados is certainly elegant, but with a quiet, friendly, understated style primarily targeted to adults. **Pros:** swim-up rooms and bar; Bait-to-Plate fishing trip with the chef; complimentary motorized and nonmotorized water sports. **Cons:** pricey; kid-friendly activities only summer and holidays; beach comes and goes, depending on storms. [$] *Rooms from: $1,040* ✉ *Hwy. 1, Porters* ☎ *246/422–2335, 855/805–6646* 🌐 *eleganthotels.com/colony-club* ⊗ *Closed Sept.* 🛏 *96 rooms* 🍴 *Breakfast.*

★ Fodor's Choice **Coral Reef Club.** *Resort.* This upscale resort,
$$$$ with pristine coral-stone cottages scattered over 12 acres of flower-filled gardens, offers elegance in a welcoming, informal atmosphere. **Pros:** delightful appearance and atmosphere; beautiful suites with huge verandas; delicious dining. **Cons:** few room TVs; narrow beach sometimes disappears, depending on weather; no kids mid-January through February; seven-night minimum stay during winter and spring holidays. [$] *Rooms from: $1,147* ✉ *Hwy. 1, Porters* ☎ *246/422–2372*

🌐 *www.coralreefbarbados.com* ⏲ *Closed mid-May–mid-July and Sept.* 🛏 *88 rooms* 🍴 *Breakfast.*

$$$$ **FAMILY** 🏨 **Crystal Cove Hotel.** *Resort.* This seaside colony of attached duplex cottages, whitewashed and trimmed in perky pastels, appeals to both couples and families. **Pros:** kids club with activities all day and nanny service at night; exchange dining program with sister resorts on the west coast; all water sports, including waterskiing and banana boat or tube rides, are complimentary. **Cons:** few activities immediately outside the resort, although it's not far from Bridgetown; lots of stairs make it difficult for physically challenged visitors; quality and variety of culinary offerings could use improvement. [$] *Rooms from: $975* ✉ *Hwy. 1, Appleby* ☎ *246/432–2683, 855/258–0902 in U.S.* 🌐 *eleganthotels.com/crystal-cove* 🛏 *88 rooms* 🍴 *All-inclusive.*

$$ 🏨 **Discovery Bay.** *Hotel.* Considering the beachfront location and convenience to shopping, restaurants, and nightlife opportunities (all a five-minute walk from your room), the price at this resort in Holetown is fairly reasonable. **Pros:** convenient Holetown location; family-friendly; ground-floor rooms suitable for guests with restricted physical abilities. **Cons:** rooms and service still relatively "rustic"; extra cost for à la carte meals and snacks; only buffet and table d'hôte meals included; extra cost for some water sports and activities. [$] *Rooms from: $373* ✉ *Hwy. 1, Holetown* ☎ *246/432–1301* 🌐 *www.rexresorts.com/discovery-bay* 🛏 *86 rooms* 🍴 *All-inclusive.*

★ **$$$$** Fodor'sChoice 🏨 **Fairmont Royal Pavilion.** *Resort.* Every unit in this luxurious, adults-oriented resort (kids welcome mid-March through October) has immediate access to 11 acres of tropical gardens and an uninterrupted sea view from a broad balcony or patio. **Pros:** top-notch service—everyone remembers your name; excellent dining; swimming with turtles included. **Cons:** dining—and everything else—is expensive; rooms need refurbishing (currently under way); breakfast buffet needs inspiration. [$] *Rooms from: $1,087* ✉ *Hwy. 1, Porters* ☎ *246/422–5555, 866/540–4485* 🌐 *www.fairmont.com/barbados* ⏲ *Closed Oct.–mid-Nov.* 🛏 *73 rooms* 🍴 *No meals.*

★ **$$$$** Fodor'sChoice 🏨 **The House.** *Hotel.* Privacy, luxury, and service are hallmarks of this intimate adults-only sanctuary adjacent to sister resort Tamarind. **Pros:** pure relaxation in stylish surroundings; privacy assured; complimentary half-hour massage. **Cons:** small pool and narrow beach; no kids under 18 (settle kids and nanny next door at Tamarind); not enough sunbeds in pool area. [$] *Rooms* *from: $1,195* ✉ *Hwy. 1, Paynes Bay* ☎ *246/432–5525, 855/220–8459 in U.S.* 🌐 *www.thehousebarbados.com* ⇨ *34 rooms* 🍴 *Breakfast.*

$$$$ 🏨 **Lone Star Hotel.** *Hotel.* This 1940s-era service station was transformed into a sleek beachfront boutique hotel that—fortunately or unfortunately—has since been discovered by celebrities. **Pros:** rub shoulders and chill with celebs (perhaps); great cuisine; complimentary airport transfers; you'll love the decor. **Cons:** no activities except for the beach; no pool; close to road, so early morning traffic can be noisy. $ *Rooms from: $695* ✉ *Hwy. 1, Mount Standfast* ☎ *246/629–0599* 🌐 *www.thelonestar.com* ⇨ *6 rooms* 🍴 *Breakfast.*

$$$$ FAMILY 🏨 **Mango Bay.** *Resort.* This beachfront resort in the heart of Holetown is within walking distance of shops, restaurants, nightspots, historic sites, and the public bus to Bridgetown and Speightstown. **Pros:** the location in Holetown; food is good, but there's only one restaurant; accommodating staff. **Cons:** small pool; vendors on the beach can be annoying; noise can be an issue for rooms facing the bar area. $ *Rooms from: $755* ✉ *2nd St., Holetown* ☎ *246/432–1384* 🌐 *www.mangobaybarbados.com* ⇨ *76 rooms* 🍴 *All-inclusive.*

★ Fodor's Choice $$$$ FAMILY 🏨 **The Sandpiper Hotel.** *Resort.* An intimate vibe and (practically) private beach keep guests coming back to this family-oriented hideaway, with accommodations spread throughout 7 acres of gardens. **Pros:** private and sophisticated; dining, spa, and tennis privileges at nearby Coral Reef Club; Tree Top suites are fabulous—but pricey. **Cons:** beach is small, typical of west-coast beaches; book far in advance, as hotel is small and popular (75% repeat guests); no room TVs. $ *Rooms from: $895* ✉ *Hwy. 1, Folkestone, Holetown* ☎ *246/422–2251* 🌐 *www.sandpiperbarbados.com* ⊗ *Closed Sept.* ⇨ *50 rooms* 🍴 *Breakfast.*

★ Fodor's Choice $$$$ FAMILY 🏨 **Sandy Lane Hotel and Golf Club.** *Resort.* Few places in the Caribbean can compare to Sandy Lane's luxurious facilities and ultrapampering service—or to its astronomical prices. **Pros:** cream of the crop; excellent dining; lovely beach; amazing spa; great golf. **Cons:** over the top for most mortals; although you don't need to dress up to walk through the lobby, you'll feel that you should; beach loungers packed too closely together. $ *Rooms from: $1,750* ✉ *Hwy. 1, Paynes Bay, Holetown* ✥ *1.5 miles (2 km) south of town* ☎ *246/444–2000, 866/444–4080 in U.S.* 🌐 *www.sandylane.com* ⛳ *Two 18-hole championship courses, one 9-hole course* ⇨ *113 rooms* 🍴 *Breakfast.*

$$$$ FAMILY 🏨 **Tamarind.** *Resort.* This sleek Mediterranean-style resort, which sprawls along 750 feet of prime west-coast beachfront, is large enough to cater to active families and sophisticated couples, including honeymooners. **Pros:** very big resort, yet layout affords privacy; right on superb Paynes Bay beach; lots of complimentary water sports, including waterskiing and banana boat rides. **Cons:** some rooms could use a little TLC; uninspired buffet breakfast; rooms on the road side of the property suffer from traffic noise. [$] *Rooms from: $855* ✉ *Hwy. 1, Paynes Bay* ☎ *246/432–1332, 855/326–5189 in U.S.* 🌐 *eleganthotels.com/tamarind* 🛏 *104 rooms* 🍴 *Breakfast.*

$$$$ 🏨 **Treasure Beach.** *Hotel.* Quiet, upscale, and intimate, this adults-only boutique hotel was gutted and completely refurbished in late 2017. **Pros:** cozy retreat; complimentary art gallery tour; chef-taught food-styling and pastry-making classes; complimentary dinner with a five-night stay. **Cons:** narrow beach; offshore turtle swimming attracts boatloads of tourists; no kids allowed. [$] *Rooms from: $699* ✉ *Hwy. 1, Paynes Bay* ☎ *246/428–7131, 888/996–9948 in U.S.* 🌐 *eleganthotels.com/treasure-beach* 🛏 *35 rooms* 🍴 *Breakfast.*

$$$$ 🏨 **Waves Hotel and Spa.** *All-Inclusive.* The main part of this hotel—lobby, most guest rooms, restaurant, snack bar, bar and lounge, and a pool—is perched on a cliff overlooking a sandy beach, while adults-only guest rooms are across the road, along with the spa, a specialty restaurant, and a second pool. **Pros:** relaxed atmosphere for both couples and families; friendly, accommodating staff; motorized water sports (and instruction) are included. **Cons:** adults-only rooms are across the street from the beach; no connecting rooms for families with kids; pools are small. [$] *Rooms from: $650* ✉ *Hwy. 1, Prospect Bay* ☎ *246/424–7571, 855/465–8886 in U.S.* 🌐 *eleganthotels.com/waves* 🛏 *70 rooms* 🍴 *All-inclusive.*

WEST COAST

★ $$$$ Fodor's Choice 🏨 **Cobblers Cove Hotel.** *Resort.* Flanked by tropical gardens on one side and the sea on the other, this English country–style resort has elegant suites, each with a comfy sitting room with sofa bed, a small library, and a wall of louvered shutters that open wide to a patio. **Pros:** peaceful and quiet; lovely grounds; amazing penthouse suites. **Cons:** small beach; no room TVs; only bedrooms have air-conditioning. [$] *Rooms from: $821* ✉ *Road View, Hwy. 1B,*

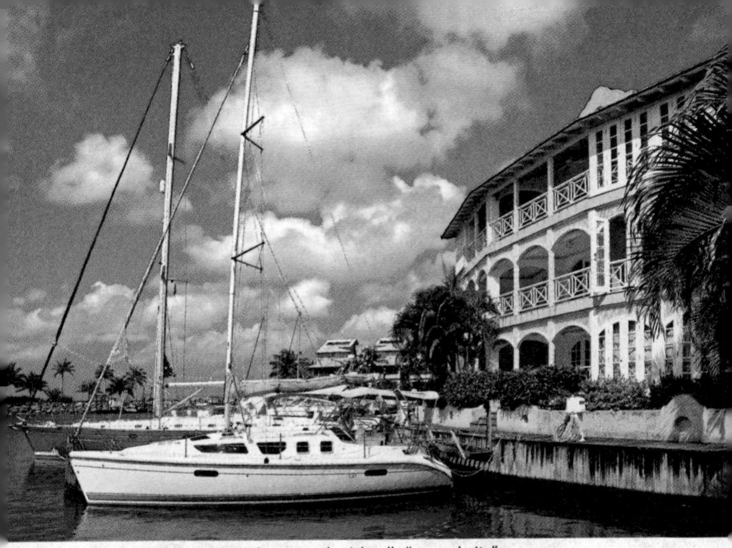
Port St. Charles Marina in Speightstown, the island's "second city"

Speightstown ☎ *246/422–2291* 🌐 *www.cobblerscove.com* ⏲ *Closed Aug.–mid-Oct.* 🛏 *42 suites* 🍴 *Breakfast.*

$$$$ FAMILY 🏨 **Little Good Harbour.** *Rental.* A cluster of spacious self-catering cottages, built in updated chattel-house style with gingerbread balconies, overlooks a narrow strip of beach in far north Barbados—just beyond the fishing community of Six Men's Bay. This little enclave, with one-, two-, and three-bedroom (mostly) duplex suites, is a perfect choice for self-sufficient travelers who don't need the hand-holding that resorts provide and relish the chance to experience a delightful slice of Bajan village life. **Pros:** spacious units with fully equipped kitchens; laid-back atmosphere; good choice for families. **Cons:** busy road; air-conditioning in bedrooms only; remote location; tiny beach. [$] *Rooms from: $525* ✉ *Hwy. 1B* ☎ *246/439–3000* 🌐 *www.littlegoodharbourbarbados.com* ⏲ *Closed Sept.* 🛏 *20 suites* 🍴 *No meals.*

NIGHTLIFE

When the sun goes down, the people come out to "lime" (which can mean anything from a casual chat to a full-blown "jump-up" or street party). Performances by world-renowned stars and regional groups are major events, and tickets can be hard to come by—but give it a try. Most resorts have nightly entertainment in season, and nightclubs often have live bands for listening and

DID YOU KNOW?

Although the surf is too rough for swimming, Bathsheba Soup Bowl hosts the Independence Classic Surfing Championship every November.

CLOSE UP

Nightspots Aplenty

St. Lawrence Gap, the narrow waterfront byway with restaurants, bars, and hotels one right after another, is where the action is on the south coast. In Holetown, on the west coast, the restaurants and clubs on 1st and 2nd streets are giving "The Gap" a run for its money. Along with a half dozen or so restaurants that offer fare ranging from ribs or pizza to elegant cuisine, a handful of nightspots and night "experiences" have cropped up recently. After-dinner drinks at the Mews or Red Door Lounge are popular any evening, but on Sunday evenings locals and tourists alike descend on One Love Bar for the karaoke and to Ragamuffin's restaurant, next door, for the after-dinner drag show.

dancing. The busiest bars and dance clubs rage until 3 am. On Saturday nights some clubs—especially those with live music—charge a cover of $15 or more.

Barbados supports the rum industry with more than 1,600 "rum shops," simple bars where (mostly) men congregate to discuss the world or life in general, drink rum, and eat a cutter (sandwich). In more sophisticated establishments you can find upscale rum cocktails made with the island's renowned Mount Gay and Cockspur brands—and no shortage of Barbados's own Banks Beer.

BRIDGETOWN AREA

Harbour Lights. This open-air, beachfront club claims to be the "home of the party animal." Wednesday and Friday nights are the hottest, with dancing under the stars to reggae and soca music. But on Monday and Wednesday evenings, there's a family-friendly "cultural" dinner show on the beach, along with three live bands and a Bajan barbecue dinner, and drinks. ■TIP→ $44 includes the Monday or Wednesday evening dinner show, drinks, and transportation. ⊠ *Marine Villa, Bay St., Bridgetown* ✚ *South of town, Carlisle Bay* ☎ *246/436–7225* ⊕ *www.harbour-lightsbarbados.com.*

DID YOU KNOW? **Did You Know? Baxter's Road is sometimes called "The Street That Never Sleeps." Night owls head for Baxter's Road, in Bridgetown, any night of the week for after-hours fun and food. The strip of rum shops begins to hit its stride at 11**

The Oistins Fish Fry is held every Friday night in the south-coast fishing village.

pm, but locals usually show up around 3 am. Street vendors sell freshly made "Baxter's Road" fried chicken and other snacks all night long, but Enid's is the place to see and be seen.

Waterfront Café. From November through April, there's live jazz Thursday, Friday, and Saturday evenings. The location alongside the wharf and small dance floor are also draws. ⊠ *The Careenage, Bridgetown* ☎ *246/427–0093* ⊕ *www. waterfrontcafe.com.bb* ☙ *Closed Sun.–Wed.*

ST. LAWRENCE GAP

The Old Jamm Inn. "Booze, beats, and burgers" are the attractions at this music venue in St. Lawrence Gap. Listen, dance, and enjoy live performances by local performers and/or DJs who spin tunes in all styles. Add a juicy burger, Bajan fish cakes, or jerk pork—and rum drinks are always two-for-one. It's a party every night! ⊠ *St. Lawrence Gap, Dover* ☎ *246/428–3919* ⊕ *www.theoldjamminn.com.*

Scoopie's Jazz. It's small, it's local, it's in The Gap—and the live jazz will soothe you whether you grab a bite to eat or just sit with a drink. You might even take a spin around the small dance floor. ⊠ *St. Lawrence Gap, Dover* ✛ *At 3rd Ave.* ☎ *246/537–0347.*

SOUTH COAST

FAMILY **Bubba's Sports Bar.** Merrymakers and sports lovers find live action on three 10-foot video screens and a dozen TVs, along with bar food and drinks. ☒ *Rockley Main Rd., Worthing* ☎ *246/435–8731* ⊕ *www.bubbassportsbar.net.*

★ **Fodor'sChoice Oistins Fish Fry.** This is the place to be on Friday
FAMILY evening, when this south-coast fishing village becomes a lively and convivial outdoor street party suitable for the whole family. Barbecued chicken and a variety of fish, along with all the traditional sides, are served fresh from the grill and consumed at roadside picnic tables. Servings are huge, and prices are inexpensive—about $10–$15 per plate. Drinks, music, and dancing add to the fun. ☒ *Oistins Main Rd., Oistins.*

HOLETOWN

Drift Ocean Terrace Lounge. Sophisticated in style and seductive in setting, this is a lovely spot to celebrate a romantic evening with Champagne, a tropical cocktail, or a glass of blush wine and delicious small plates from the "night bites" menu. Drift opens at 5 pm. ☒ *Hwy. 1, Holetown* ☎ *246/432–2808* ⊕ *www.driftinbarbados.com.*

Duke's Night Lounge. Good place to chill, good vibes, good party atmosphere on Friday, Saturday, and Sunday nights starting at 10 pm. Drink, dance, or head outside to the hookah lounge. ☒ *1st St., Holetown* ☎ *246/836–2023* ⊕ *www. dukesbarbados.com.*

Red Door Lounge. Cocktails, DJs, live music, and conversation—this local hot spot is the place to be on Friday and Saturday nights from 9 pm until 4 am. ☒ *2nd St., Holetown* ☎ *246/620–3761* ⊕ *reddoorbarbados.com.*

SHOPPING

WHAT TO BUY

One of the most long-lasting souvenirs to bring home from Barbados is a piece of authentic Caribbean art. The colorful flowers, quaint villages, mesmerizing seascapes, and fascinating cultural experiences and activities that are endemic to the region and familiar to visitors have been translated by local artists onto canvas and into photographs, sculpture, and other mediums. Gift shops and even some restaurants display local artwork for sale, but the broadest array of artwork will be found in a gallery.

Typical crafts include pottery, shell and glass art, wood carvings, handmade dolls, watercolors, and other artwork (both originals and prints).

Although many of the private homes, great houses, and museums in Barbados are filled with priceless antiques, you'll find few for sale—mainly British antiques and some local pieces, particularly mahogany furniture. Look especially for planters' chairs and the classic Barbadian rocking chair, as well as old prints and paintings.

DUTY-FREE SHOPPING

Duty-free luxury goods—china, crystal, cameras, porcelain, leather items, electronics, jewelry, perfume, and clothing—are found in Bridgetown's Broad Street department stores and their branches, at the high-end Limegrove Lifestyle Centre in Holetown, at the Bridgetown Cruise Terminal (for passengers only), and in the departure lounge at Grantley Adams International Airport. Prices are often 30% to 40% less than full retail. To buy goods at duty-free prices, you must produce your passport, immigration form, or driver's license, along with departure information (such as flight number and date) at the time of purchase—or you can have your purchases delivered free to the airport or harbor for pickup. Duty-free alcohol, tobacco products, and some electronic equipment *must* be delivered to you at the airport or harbor.

GROCERIES

If you've chosen self-catering lodgings, are looking for snacks, or just want to explore a local grocery store, you'll find large, modern supermarkets at Sunset Crest in Holetown on the west coast; in Oistins, at Sargeant's Village (Sheraton Mall), and in Worthing on the south coast; and at Warrens (Highway 2, north of Bridgetown) in St. Michael.

BRIDGETOWN

Bridgetown's **Broad Street** is the primary downtown shopping area. **The Colonnade Mall**, in the historic Colonnade Building on Broad Street, has about 40 shops that sell everything from Piaget watches to postcards; across the street, **Mall 34** has more than 20 shops where you can buy duty-free goods, souvenirs, and snacks. At the **cruise-ship terminal** shopping arcade, passengers can buy both duty-free goods and Barbadian-made crafts at more than 30 boutiques and a dozen vendor carts and stalls. And allow time before boarding your plane to shop in the **airport departure**

lounge, which has a dozen or more shops that sell duty-free alcohol, souvenirs, clothing, and more.

A free Bridgetown shopping shuttle serves hotels on the south and west coasts, so guests can visit downtown shops, see the sights, and perhaps have lunch. The shuttle operates Monday through Saturday, departing from the hotels at 9:30 and 11 am and returning from Bridgetown at 1:30 and 3 pm. Reserve your seat with your hotel concierge a day ahead.

DEPARTMENT STORES

Cave Shepherd. The main store on Broad Street sells an array of clothing and luxury goods. Branches are at Holetown's Sunset Crest mall on the west coast and the Vista shopping complex in Worthing and Sheraton Mall in Sargeants on the south coast; the airport departure lounge and cruise-ship terminal each have a boutique. ⊠ *10-14 Broad St., Bridgetown* ☎ *246/629–4400* ⊕ *www.mycaveshepherd.com.*

DUTY-FREE GOODS

Little Switzerland. This mini-chain's shop is at The Colonnade Mall in Bridgetown, where you can find perfume, jewelry, cameras, audio equipment, Swarovski and Waterford crystal, and Wedgwood china. ⊠ *The Colonnade Mall, Broad St., Bridgetown* ☎ *246/431–0030* ⊕ *www.littleswitzerland.com.*

The Royal Shop. The Royal Shop carries fine watches and jewelry fashioned in Italian gold, Caribbean silver, diamonds, and other gems in its main shop on Broad Street and branch shop at the cruise-ship terminal. ⊠ *Royal Towers, 32 Broad St., Bridgetown* ☎ *246/429–7072* ⊕ *royalportfolio.com/store/the-royal-shop-barbados.*

SOUTH COAST

At **Chattel House Village,** a cluster of boutiques in St. Lawrence Gap, you can buy locally made crafts and other souvenirs. In Rockley, Christ Church, **Quayside Shopping Center** houses a small group of boutiques, restaurants, and services.

Best of Barbados. Architect Jimmy Walker founded these shops to showcase the works of his artist wife. Products range from her framable prints, housewares, and textiles to arts and crafts in both native style and modern designs. Everything is made or designed on Barbados. Branch shops are at Chattel House Village in Holetown, at Southern Palms Resort in St. Lawrence Gap, at the cruise-ship terminal, and in the airport departure lounge.

✉ *Quayside Centre, Main Rd., Rockley* ☎ *246/622–1761* ⊕ *www.best-of-barbados.com.*

WEST COAST

Holetown has the upscale **Limegrove Lifestyle Centre**, a stylish shopping mall with high-end designer boutiques, as well as **Chattel House Village**, a cluster of small shops selling local products, fashions, beachwear, and souvenirs. Also in Holetown, **Sunset Crest** has a huge Massy supermarket, a branch of the Cave Shepherd department store, a bank, a pharmacy, and several small shops.

★ Fodor'sChoice **Earthworks Pottery.** At this family-owned and -operated pottery workshop, items range from dishes and knickknacks to complete dinner services and one-of-a-kind art pieces. The characteristically blue or green—and, more recently, peach and brown—pottery decorates hotel rooms and is sold in gift shops throughout the island, but the biggest selection (including "seconds") is here, where you also can watch the potters at work. And they'll carefully pack your purchase for traveling or ship it home for you! ✉ *2 Edgehill Heights, Edgehill* ☎ *246/425–0223* ⊕ *www. earthworks-pottery.com* ⊘ *Closed Sun.*

Gallery of Caribbean Art. This gallery is committed to promoting Caribbean art from Haiti and Cuba in the north to Curaçao and Guyana in the south—and, particularly, the works of Barbadian artists. ✉ *Northern Business Centre, Queen St., Speightstown* ☎ *246/419–0858* ⊕ *www.artgallerycaribbean.com* ⊘ *Closed Sun.*

On the Wall Art Gallery. Artist and gallery owner Vanita Comissiong offers an array of original paintings by Barbadian artists, along with handmade arts and crafts and jewelry products. An additional gallery is located in a dedicated space at Champers restaurant in Rockley on the south coast. ✉ *Earthworks Pottery, 2 Edgehill Heights* ☎ *246/438–9246* ⊕ *www.onthewallartgallery.com* ⊘ *Closed Sun.*

Red Clay Pottery and Fairfield Gallery. This workshop and gallery has been operated by potter Denis Bell all his life, "save a little time spent doing some engineering and raising a family." Visitors are welcome to watch the potters at work in the studio, which is in an old sugar-boiling house, and, in the adjacent shop, purchase plates, platters, bowls, place settings, and fine decorative items designed by Bell's daughter, Maggie. Call ahead if you'd like a

Cricket is the national pastime (and passion) of many Bajans.

tour. ✉ *Fairfield House, Fairfield Cross Rd., Bridgetown* ☎ *246/424–3800* ⊘ *Closed Sun.*

SPORTS AND ACTIVITIES

Cricket, football (soccer), polo, and rugby are extremely popular sports in Barbados for participants and spectators alike, with local, regional, and international matches held throughout the year. Check local newspapers for information about schedules and tickets.

DIVING AND SNORKELING

More than two dozen dive sites lie along the west coast between Maycocks Bay and Bridgetown and off the south coast as far as the St. Lawrence Gap. Certified divers can explore flat coral reefs and see dramatic sea fans, huge barrel sponges, and more than 50 varieties of fish. Nine sunken wrecks are dived regularly, and at least 10 more are accessible to experts. Underwater visibility is generally 80 to 90 feet. The calm waters along the west coast are also ideal for snorkeling. The marine reserve, a stretch of protected reef between Sandy Lane and the Colony Club, contains beautiful coral formations accessible from the beach.

Barbados Blue offers snorkeling and diving in Carlisle Bay.

DIVE SITES

On the west coast, **Bell Buoy** is a large, dome-shaped reef where huge brown coral tree forests and schools of fish delight all categories of divers at depths ranging from 20 to 60 feet. At **Dottins Reef**, off Holetown, you can see schooling fish, barracudas, and turtles at depths of 40 to 60 feet. **Maycocks Bay**, on the northwest coast, is a particularly enticing site; large coral reefs are separated by corridors of white sand, and visibility is often 100 feet or more. The 165-foot freighter *Pamir* lies in 60 feet of water off Six Men's Bay; it's still intact, and you can peer through its portholes and view dozens of varieties of tropical fish. **Silver Bank** is a healthy coral reef with beautiful fish and sea fans; you may get a glimpse of the *Atlantis* submarine at 60 to 80 feet. Not to be missed is the *Stavronikita*, a scuttled Greek freighter at about 135 feet; hundreds of butterfly fish hang out around its mast, and the thin rays of sunlight filtering down through the water make fully exploring the huge ship a wonderfully eerie experience.

Farther south, **Carlisle Bay** is a natural harbor and marine park just below Bridgetown. Here you can retrieve empty bottles thrown overboard by generations of sailors and see cannons and cannonballs, anchors, and six unique shipwrecks (*Berwyn, Fox, CTrek, Eilon*, the barge *Cornwallis*, and *Bajan Queen*) lying in 25 to 60 feet of water, all close enough to visit on the same dive. The *Bajan Queen,* a cruise vessel that sank in 2002, is the island's newest wreck.

Dive shops provide a two-hour beginner's "resort" course ($100–$110) followed by a shallow dive, or a weeklong certification course (about $450). Once you're certified, a one-tank dive runs about $70; a two-tank dive is $120. All equipment is supplied, and you can purchase multidive packages. Gear for snorkeling is available (free or for a small rental fee) from most hotels. Snorkelers can usually accompany dive trips for $30 for a one- or two-hour trip. Most dive shops have relationships with several hotels and offer special dive packages, with transportation, to hotel guests.

DIVE OPERATORS

Barbados Blue. Located within the Hilton Barbados hotel complex at Needham's Point, Barbados Blue offers daily scuba and snorkeling trips to Carlisle Bay Marine Park—think shipwrecks and hawksbill turtles—as well as private boat charters and PADI classes. Scuba and snorkeling gear are available to rent, along with underwater digital cameras, and hotel pickup can be arranged. Added bonuses: The facility is 100% eco-ware, it's the only dive operator with two marine biologists on staff, and your money directly benefits the marine park. ⊠ *Hilton Barbados, Aquatic Gap, Garrison* ☎ *246/434–5764, 800/929–7154 in U.S.* ⊕ *www. divebarbadosblue.com.*

Dive Hightide Watersports. On the west coast, Dive Hightide Watersports offers three dive trips daily—one- and two-tank dives and night reef–wreck–drift dives—for up to eight divers, along with PADI instruction, equipment rental, and free transportation. ⊠ *Coral Reef Club, Hwy. 1, Holetown* ☎ *246/432–0931, 800/970–0016, 800/513–5763* ⊕ *www. divehightide.com.*

Dive Shop, Ltd. Next to the marine park on Carlisle Bay, just south of Bridgetown, the island's oldest dive shop offers daily reef and wreck dives, plus beginner classes, certification courses, and underwater photography instruction. Underwater cameras are available for rent. Free transfers are provided between your hotel and the dive shop. ⊠ *Amey's Alley, Upper Bay St., Garrison* ✢ *Next to Nautilus Beach Apts.* ☎ *246/426–9947* ⊕ *www.thediveshop-barbados.com.*

Reefers & Wreckers Scuba Diving. The island's most northerly dive shop provides easy access to the north's unspoiled reefs, runs daily trips to dive sites and wrecks all along the west coast and in Carlisle Bay, and offers PADI courses ranging from "discover" to "divemaster"—including nitrox, advanced open water, night diver, deep diver, drift diver, and rescue diver. ✉ *Queen St., Speightstown* ✛ *Next to Orange St. Grocer* ☎ *246/422–5450* ⊕ *www.reeferswreckersbarbados.com.*

FISHING

Fishing is a year-round activity in Barbados, but prime time is January through April, when game fish are in season. Whether you're a serious deep-sea fisher looking for marlin, sailfish, tuna, and other billfish or you prefer angling in calm coastal waters where wahoo, barracuda, and other smaller fish reside, you can choose from a variety of half- or full-day charter trips departing from The Careenage in Bridgetown. Expect to pay $175 per person for a shared half-day charter; for a private charter, expect to pay $500 to $600 per boat for a four-hour half-day or $950 to $1,000 for an eight-hour full-day charter. Spectators who don't fish are welcome for $50 per person.

Billfisher Deepsea Fishing. *Billfisher III*, a 40-foot Viking Sport Fisherman, accommodates up to six passengers with three fishing chairs and five rods. Captain Ralphie White's full-day charters include a full lunch; all trips include drinks and transportation to and from the boat. ✉ *Bridge House Wharf, The Careenage, Bridgetown* ☎ *246/431–0741* ⊕ *www.greatadventuresbarbados.com.*

Cannon Charters. *Cannon II*, a 42-foot Hatteras Sport Fisherman, has three chairs and five rods and accommodates six passengers. Drinks and snacks are complimentary, and lunch is served on full-day charters. ✉ *The Careenage, Bridgetown* ☎ *246/424–6107* ⊕ *www.fishingbarbados.com.*

High Seas Charters. *Ocean Hunter*, a 42-foot custom-built sportfishing boat, has an extended cockpit that easily accommodates six people. Choose a four-, six-, or eight-hour charter. All tackle and bait are supplied, as well as drinks and snacks. Charter rates include hotel transfers. ✉ *The Careenage* ☎ *246/233–2598* ⊕ *www.sportfishingbarbados.com.*

Sports Legend: Sir Garfield Sobers

Cricket is more than a national pastime in Barbados. It's a passion. And no one is more revered than Sir Garfield Sobers, the greatest sportsman ever to hail from Barbados and globally acknowledged as the greatest all-round cricketer the game has ever seen. Sobers played his first test match in 1953 at the age of 17 and continually set and broke records until his last test match in 1973. He was an equally accomplished batsman and bowler. Knighted by Queen Elizabeth II in 1974 for his contributions to the sport, he was honored as a national hero of Barbados in 1999. A bronze statue honoring His Excellency, the Right Honorable Sir Garfield Sobers (or Sir Gary, as he's known locally) dominates the entry to Kensington Oval, the stadium in Bridgetown used mainly for cricket.

GOLF

Barbadians love golf, and golfers love Barbados. Courses open to visitors are listed below.

Barbados Golf Club. The first public golf course on Barbados, an 18-hole championship course (two returning 9s), was redesigned in 2000 by golf course architect Ron Kirby. The course has hosted numerous competitions, including the European Senior tour in 2003. Several hotels offer preferential tee-time reservations and reduced rates. Cart, trolley, club, and shoe rentals are all available. ⊠ *Hwy. 7, Durants* ☎ *246/428–8463* ⊕ *www.barbadosgolfclub.com* ⌧ *$105 for 18 holes; $65 for 9 holes; 3-, 5-, and 7-day passes $255, $400, $525, respectively* ⚑ *18 holes (2 returning 9s), 6805 yards, par 72.*

★ **Fodor'sChoice Country Club at Sandy Lane.** At this prestigious club, golfers can play the Old Nine or either of two 18-hole championship courses: the Tom Fazio–designed Country Club Course and the spectacular Green Monkey Course, which is reserved for hotel guests and club members. The layouts offer a limestone-quarry setting (Green Monkey), a modern style with lakes (Country Club), and traditional small greens and narrow fairways (Old Nine). Golfers can use the driving range for free. The Country Club Restaurant and Bar, overlooking the 18th hole, is open to the public. Caddies, trolleys, clubs, and shoes are available for rent, as are GPS-equipped carts that alert you to upcoming hazards, give tips on how to play holes, and let you order refreshments. ⊠ *Sandy La., Hwy. 1* ☎ *246/444–2000* ⊕ *www.san-dylane.com/golf* ⊡ *Country Club: $240 for 18 holes ($200 hotel guests); $150 for 9 holes ($130 guests); 7-day pass $1,350 ($1,250 guests). Green Monkey: $390 for 18 holes (guests only). The Old Nine: $90 for 9 holes ($75 guests); 7-day pass $560 ($450 guests)* ⅄ *Green Monkey: 18 holes, 7343 yards, par 72; Country Club: 18 holes, 7060 yards, par 72; Old Nine: 9 holes, 3345 yards, par 36.*

Royal Westmoreland Golf Club. This well-regarded Robert Trent Jones Jr.–designed, 18-hole championship course meanders through 500 tropically landscaped acres. Highlights include challenging greens, a great set of par-3, and ocean views from every hole. The course is for members and villa renters, with tee times for visitors subject to availability. Greens fees include an electric cart (required); club and shoe rentals are available. ⊠ *Royal Westmoreland Resort, Westmoreland* ☎ *246/419–7242* ⊕ *www.royal-westmore-land.com* ⊡ *$250 for 18 holes (day rate for nonresidents)* ⅄ *18 holes, 7045 yards, par 72.*

GUIDED TOURS

Taxi drivers will give you a personalized tour of Barbados for about $35 to $40 per hour for up to three people. Or you can choose an overland mountain-bike journey, a 4x4 safari expedition, or a full-day bus excursion. The prices vary according to the mode of travel and the number and kind of attractions included. Ask guest services at your hotel to help you make arrangements.

Island Safari. Discover all the popular attractions and scenic locations via a 4x4 jeep—including some gullies, forests, and remote areas that are inaccessible by conventional cars and buses. A full-day tour (5½ hours) includes snacks or lunch. You can also arrange your own private safari (three to six hours). ⊠ *CWTS Complex, Salters Rd., Lower Estate* ☎ *246/429–5337* ⊕ *www.islandsafari.bb* ⊡ *From $98.*

HIKING

Hilly but not mountainous, the island's northern interior and east coast are ideal for hiking.

Arbib Heritage and Nature Trail. Maintained by the Barbados National Trust, these are actually two trails. The Whim Adventure trail offers a rigorous hike (3½ hours) through gullies and plantations to old ruins and remote north-coun-

The Sandy Lane Gold Cup is held annually at the Barbados Turf Club.

try areas; the shorter, easier Round-de-Town Stroll (2 hours) goes through Speightstown's side streets and past an ancient church and chattel houses. Guided hikes run from 9 to 2 on Wednesday, Thursday, and Saturday (with a minimum of four people); group rates are available. Book ahead, preferably four days in advance. Not recommended for children under five. ⊠ *Barbados National Trust, Wildey House, Errol Barrow Hwy., Wildey* ☎ *246/426–2421* ⊕ *www.barbadosnationaltrust.org* 🎟 *$25.*

Hike Barbados. Free walks sponsored by the Barbados National Trust are led year-round on Sunday from 6 to 9 am and from 3:30 to 6:30 pm; once a month, a moonlight hike at 5:30 pm substitutes for the afternoon hike (bring a flashlight). Experienced guides group you with others of similar ability on "Stop and Stare" walks, 5 to 6 miles (8 to 10 km); medium hikes, 8 to 10 miles (13 to 16 km); medium-fast hikes, 10 to 12 miles (16 to 19 km); or really fast hikes, 12 to 14 miles (19 to 23 km). Wear loose clothes, sensible shoes, sunscreen, and a hat, and bring a camera and water. Routes and locations change, but each hike is a loop, finishing where it began. Check newspapers or call the Trust for schedules and meeting places. ⊠ *Barbados National Trust, Wildey House, Errol Barrow Hwy., Wildey* ☎ *246/436–9033, 246/426–2421.*

HORSE RACING

Barbados Turf Club. Horse racing is administered by the Barbados Turf Club. Races take place on alternate Saturdays throughout the year at the Garrison Savannah, a 6-furlong grass oval in Christ Church, about 3 miles (5 km) south of Bridgetown. The important races are the Sandy Lane Barbados Gold Cup, held in late February or early March, and the Massy United Insurance Barbados Derby Day, in early August. Post time is 1:30 pm. Prices are higher on Gold Cup day. ⊠ *Garrison Savannah, Garrison* ☎ *246/626–3980* ⊕ *www.barbadosturfclub.org* ⊡ *From $5.*

SEA EXCURSIONS

Minisubmarine voyages are enormously popular with families and those who enjoy watching fish but don't wish to get wet. Party boats depart from Bridgetown's Deep Water Harbour for sightseeing and snorkeling or romantic sunset cruises. Prices are $70 to $125 per person for four- or five-hour daytime cruises and $60 to $85 for three- or four-hour sunset cruises, depending on the type of refreshments and entertainment included; transportation to and from the dock is provided. For an excursion that may be less splashy in terms of a party atmosphere—but is definitely splashier in terms of the actual experience—turtle tours allow participants to swim with and feed a resident group of hawksbill and leatherback sea turtles.

FAMILY *Atlantis* **Submarine.** This 50-foot, 48-passenger submarine turns the Caribbean into a giant aquarium. The 90-minute voyage (including 45 minutes underwater) takes in wrecks and reefs as deep as 150 feet. Children love the adventure, but they must be at least 3 feet tall. ⊠ *Shallow Draught, Bridgetown* ☎ *246/436–8929* ⊕ *www.barbados.atlantis-submarines.com* ⊡ *From $104.*

FAMILY *Cool Runnings* **Catamaran Cruises.** Captain Robert Povey, owner of *Cool Runnings* catamaran, skippers a five-hour lunch cruise with stops to swim with the fishes, snorkel with sea turtles, and explore a shallow shipwreck. A four-hour sunset cruise includes swimming, snorkeling, and exploring underwater as the sun sinks. Delicious meals with wine, along with an open bar, are part of all cruises. ⊠ *Carlisle House, Carlisle Wharf, Hincks St., Bridgetown* ☎ *246/436–0911* ⊕ *www.coolrunningsbarbados.com* ⊡ *Lunch cruise $90, sunset cruise $80.*

2

FAMILY **Black Pearl Party Cruises.** The whole family will get a kick out of a "pirate" ship adventure on *Jolly Roger 1*. The four-hour daytime cruises along the island's west coast include a barbecue lunch or dinner, free-flowing drinks, lively music, swimming with turtles, and pirate activities such as walking the plank and rope swinging. A three-hour sunset cruise every Thursday includes cocktails, dinner, unlimited drinks, and an elaborate show. ⊠ *Carlisle House, The Careenage, Bridgetown* ☎ *246/826–7245, 246/826–7245* ⊕ *www.barbadosblackpearl-jollyroger1. com* ⊑ *$87.50 for day cruises.*

★ Fodor'sChoice **Tiami Catamaran Cruises.** Tiami operates five cata-
FAMILY maran party boats for luncheon cruises to a secluded bay for swimming with turtles or for romantic sunset and moonlight cruises. Daytime cruises include buffet lunch, open bar, and three swim/snorkel stops. Evening cruises include a swim/snorkel stop as the sun goes down, buffet dinner, and cocktails. ■ TIP→ Round-trip hotel transfers are complimentary for all cruises. ⊠ *Shallow Draught, Bridgetown* ☎ *246/430–0900* ⊕ *www.tiamicatamarancruises.com* ⊑ *From $70.*

SEA URCHIN ALERT. **Black sea urchins lurk on the shallow sea bottom and near reefs, and their venom-filled spines can cause painful wounds. They've even been known to pierce wet suits, so divers should be careful when brushing up against submerged rock walls. Getting several stings might cause muscle spasms and breathing difficulties; victims should get help immediately.**

SURFING

The best surfing is at Bathsheba Soup Bowl on the east coast; the Barbados Independence SurfPro championship (an international competition) is held here every November. But, the water on the windward (Atlantic Ocean) side of the island is safe only for the most experienced surfers. Surfers also congregate at Surfer's Point, at the southern tip of Barbados near Inch Marlow, where the Atlantic Ocean meets the Caribbean Sea.

Dread or Dead Surf Shop. This surf shop promises to get beginners from "zero to standing up and surfing" in one afternoon. The three-hour course—"or until you stand up or give up"—includes a board, wax, rash guard (if necessary), a ride to and from the surf break, and instruction; additional two-and-one-half-hour lessons can be purchased after the three-hour course. More-experienced surfers can simply rent boards. ✉ *Hastings Main Rd., Hastings* ☎ *246/228–4785* ⊕ *www.dreadordead.com* ⊠ *From $75.*

Zed's Surfing Adventures. This outfit rents surfboards, provides lessons, and offers surf tours including equipment, guide, and transportation to surf breaks appropriate for your experience. Two-hour group lessons are held regularly; a six-hour package includes three lessons and a week's board rental. Surfboard rentals for experienced surfers and private lessons are always available. ✉ *Surfer's Point, Inch Marlowe* ☎ *246/428–7873* ⊕ *www.zedssurftravel.com* ⊠ *From $80.*

WINDSURFING AND KITEBOARDING

Barbados is one of the prime locations in the world for windsurfing—and, increasingly, for kiteboarding. Winds are strongest November through April at the island's southern tip, at Silver Sands–Silver Rock Beach, which is where the Barbados Windsurfing Championships are held in mid-January. Use of windsurfing boards and equipment as well as instruction are often among the amenities included at larger hotels, and some also rent to nonguests. Kiteboarding is a more difficult sport that requires several hours of instruction to reach proficiency; Silver Sands is about the only location where you'll find kiteboarding equipment and instruction. Stand-up paddling has also become increasingly popular, and most surf shops (and many resorts) offer paddling equipment and instruction.

deAction Surf Shop. Directly on Silver Sands–Silver Rock Beach, Brian "Irie Man" Talma's shop stocks a range of rental surfing equipment and offers beginner windsurfing, kiteboarding, surfing, and stand-up paddling lessons. Conditions are ideal, with waves off the outer reef and flat water in the inner lagoon. Kiteboarding, which isn't easy, generally involves six hours of instruction broken up into two or three sessions: from flying a small kite to getting the body dragged with a big kite to finally getting up on the board. All equipment is provided. ✉ *Silver Sands–Silver Rock Beach, Silver Sands* ☎ *246/428–2027* ⊕ *www.briantalma.com.*

FAMILY **Paddle Barbados.** Paddleboarding is the new "it" water sport, and Paddle Barbados offers instruction, rentals, and paddling tours around the harbor. You can also just paddle on your own. A quick lesson will get you up on the board and paddling away in about 10 minutes. ✉ *Barbados Cruising Club, Aquatic Gap, Garrison* ☎ *246/249–2787* ⊕ *www.paddlebarbados.com.*

ST. LUCIA

Updated
by Jane E.
Zarem

A VERDANT, MOUNTAINOUS ISLAND HALFWAY between Martinique and St. Vincent, St. Lucia has evolved into one of the Caribbean's most popular vacation destinations—particularly for honeymooners and other romantics enticed by the island's striking natural beauty, its many splendid resorts and appealing inns, and its welcoming atmosphere.

The capital city of Castries and nearby villages in the northwest are home to 40% of the 180,000 St. Lucians. This area—along with Rodney Bay Village farther north, Marigot Bay just south of the capital, and Soufrière on the southwestern coast—are the destinations of most vacationers. In the central and southwestern parts of the island dense rain forest, jungle-covered mountains, and vast banana plantations dominate the landscape. A tortuous road follows most of the coastline, bisecting small villages, cutting through mountains, and passing by fertile valleys. On the southwest coast, Petit Piton and Gros Piton, the island's unusual twin peaks that rise out of the sea to more than 2,600 feet, are familiar landmarks for sailors and aviators alike as well as a UNESCO World Heritage site. Divers are attracted to the reefs in the National Marine Reserve between the Pitons and extending north past Soufrière, the capital during French colonial times. Most of the natural tourist attractions are in this area, along with several more fine resorts and inns.

The pirate François Le Clerc, nicknamed Jambe de Bois (Wooden Leg) for obvious reasons, was the first European "settler" in St. Lucia. In the late 16th century Le Clerc holed up on Pigeon Island, just off St. Lucia's northernmost point, using it as a staging ground for attacking passing ships. Now Pigeon Island National Landmark is a public park connected by a causeway to the mainland; Sandals Grande St. Lucian Spa & Beach Resort, one of the largest resorts in St. Lucia, and The Landings, a luxury villa community, sprawl along that causeway.

Like most of its Caribbean neighbors, St. Lucia was first inhabited by Arawaks and then the Carib people. British settlers attempted to colonize the island twice in the early 1600s, but it wasn't until 1651, after the French West India Company suppressed the local Caribs, that Europeans gained a foothold. For 150 years battles over possession of the island were frequent between the French and the British, with a dizzying 14 changes in power before the British finally took possession in 1814. The Europeans established sugar plantations, using slaves from West Africa to work the fields. By 1838, when the slaves were emancipated, more than 90% of the population was of African descent—roughly the same proportion as today.

On February 22, 1979, St. Lucia became an independent state within the British Commonwealth of Nations, with a resident governor-general appointed by the Queen. Still, the island appears to have retained more relics of French influence—notably the island patois, cuisine, village names, and surnames—than of the British. Most likely, that's because the British contribution primarily involved the English language, the educational and legal systems, and the political structure, whereas the French culture historically had more influence on the arts—culinary, dance, and music.

The island becomes especially tuneful for 10 days every May, when the St. Lucia Jazz Festival welcomes renowned international musicians who perform for enthusiastic fans at Pigeon Island National Park and other island venues. St. Lucians themselves love jazz—and, interestingly, country music—while the beat of Caribbean music also resonates throughout the island.

PLANNING

WHEN TO GO

The high season runs from mid-December through mid-April and during the annual St. Lucia Jazz Festival and Carnival events; at other times of the year, hotel rates may be significantly cheaper. December and January are the coolest months, and June through August are the hottest. Substantial rain (more than just a tropical spritz) is more likely from June through November.

FESTIVALS AND EVENTS

The **St. Lucia Jazz,** in early May, kicks off Soleil, St. Lucia's Summer Festival, and is the year's big event; during that week you may have trouble finding a hotel room at any price.

St. Lucia's summer **Carnival** is held in Castries beginning in late June and continuing into July.

The **St. Lucia Billfishing Tournament,** which attracts anglers from far and wide, is held in October.

LOGISTICS

Getting to St. Lucia: St. Lucia's primary gateway is Hewanorra International Airport (UVF) in Vieux Fort, on the island's southern tip. Regional airlines fly into George F. L. Charles Airport (SLU) in Castries, commonly called Vigie Airport and more convenient to resorts in the north. The 40-mile (64-km) drive between Hewanorra and resorts in the north takes about 90 minutes; between Hewanorra and Marigot Bay, about 60 minutes; and between Hewanorra and Soufrière, about 45 minutes.

Hassle Factor: Medium to high due to the long drive from Hewanorra International Airport.

On the Ground: Taxis are available at both airports, although transfers may be included in your travel package. It's an expensive ride to the north from Hewanorra—$80–$100 for up to four passengers—and $75–$80 to Soufrière. A helicopter shuttle cuts the transfer time to about 10 minutes, but the cost doubles.

Getting Around the Island: A car is more important if you are staying at a small inn or hotel away from the beach. If you're staying at an all-inclusive beach resort and you don't plan to leave for meals, taxis may be the better bet.

October is also Creole Heritage Month, which culminates in **Jounen Kwéyòl Entenasyonnal** (International Creole Day) on the last Sunday of the month.

In early December, the finish of the **Atlantic Rally for Cruisers**, the world's largest ocean-crossing race, is marked by a week of festivities at Rodney Bay.

DO I NEED A CAR?

A car is more important if you are staying at a small inn or hotel away from the beach. Just keep in mind that driving is on the left, British-style. If you're staying at an all-inclusive beach resort and you don't plan to leave for meals, taxis may be the better bet. Privately owned and operated minivans constitute St. Lucia's bus system, an inexpensive and efficient means of transportation used primarily by locals and a good way to travel between Castries and the Rodney Bay area. Water taxis are also available in some places and can save time. ⇨ *For more information on car travel in St. Lucia and car rentals, see Car Travel in Travel Smart.*

TOP REASONS TO GO

The Beauty: Magnificent, lush scenery makes St. Lucia one of the most beautiful Caribbean islands.

The Romance: A popular honeymoon spot, St. Lucia boasts numerous romantic retreats.

The Indulgent Accommodations: Sybaritic lodging options include an all-inclusive spa resort with daily pampering, a posh sanctuary sandwiched between a mountain and the beach, and two picturesque resorts with prime locations between the Pitons.

The Music: Performers and fans from all over the world come for the annual St. Lucia Jazz event.

The Welcome: The friendly St. Lucians love sharing their island and their cultural heritage with visitors.

SAFETY

Although crime isn't a significant problem in St. Lucia, take the same precautions you would at home—lock your door, secure your valuables, and don't carry too much money or flaunt expensive jewelry on the street. It's safe (not to mention convenient) to ride local buses in the Rodney Bay area.

ACCOMMODATIONS

Nearly all of St. Lucia's resorts and small inns face unspoiled beaches or are hidden away on secluded coves or tucked into forested hillsides in three locations along the calm Caribbean (western) coast. They're in the greater Castries area between Marigot Bay, a few miles south of the city, and Labrelotte Bay in the north; in and around Rodney Bay and north to Cap Estate; and in and around Soufrière on the southwest coast near the Pitons. There's a pair of resorts in Vieux Fort, near Hewanorra. The advantage of being in the north is that you have access to a wider range of restaurants and nightlife; in the south, you may be limited to hotel offerings—albeit some of the best—and a few other dining options in and around Soufrière.

Beach Resorts: Most people choose to stay in one of St. Lucia's many beach resorts, most of which are upscale and fairly pricey. Several are all-inclusive, including three Sandals resorts, two Sunswept resorts (The BodyHoliday and Rendezvous), St. James's Club Morgan Bay Resort & Spa, East Winds Inn, Coconut Bay Beach Resort & Spa and

Serenity at Coconut Bay, and Royalton St. Lucia Resort & Spa. Others may offer an all-inclusive option.

Small Inns: If you are looking for something more intimate and perhaps less expensive, a locally owned inn or small hotel is a good option; it may or may not be directly on the beach.

Villas: Luxury villa communities that operate like hotels are a good alternative for families. Several are in the north in the Cap Estate area.

WHAT IT COSTS IN U.S. DOLLARS			
$	**$$**	**$$$**	**$$$$**
Restaurants under $13	$13–$20	$21–$30	over $30
Hotels under $275	$275–$375	$376–$475	over $475

Restaurant prices are the average cost of a main course at dinner or, if dinner is not served, at lunch. Hotel prices are the lowest cost of a standard double room in high season.

WEDDINGS

Marriage licenses cost $125 with a required three-day waiting period or $200 with no waiting period, plus $60 for the associated registrar and certificate fees. You'll need to produce valid passports and original or certified copies of birth certificates and, if applicable, divorce decrees or death certificates. Some resorts offer free weddings when combined with a honeymoon stay.

EXPLORING ST. LUCIA

Except for a small area in the extreme northeast, one main highway circles all of St. Lucia. The road snakes along the coast, cuts across mountains, makes hairpin turns and sheer drops, and reaches dizzying heights. It takes at least four hours to drive the whole loop. Even at a leisurely pace with frequent sightseeing stops, and whether you're driving or being driven, the curvy roads make it a tiring drive in a single outing.

The West Coast Road between Castries and Soufrière (a 1½-hour journey) has steep hills and sharp turns, but it's well marked and incredibly scenic. South of Castries the road tunnels through Morne Fortuné, skirts the island's largest banana plantation (more than 127 varieties of bananas, called "figs" in this part of the Caribbean, grow

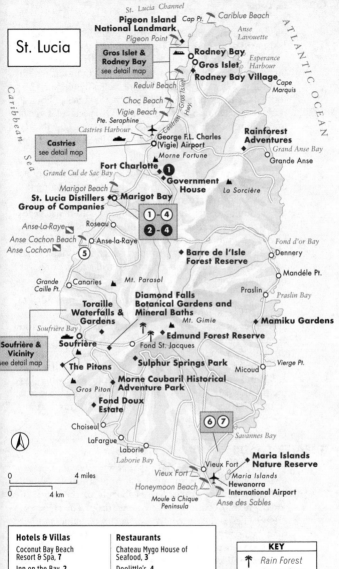

St. Lucia

St. Lucia Channel

Pigeon Island
National Landmark
Pigeon Point

Cap Pt. ⌐ *Cariblue Beach*

Anse Lavouette

**Gros Islet &
Rodney Bay**
see detail map

Rodney Bay
Gros Islet
Rodney Bay Village

Esperance Harbour

Cape Marquis

Reduit Beach

Choc Beach

Vigie Beach
Pte. Seraphine
Castries Harbour

Castries
see detail map

George F.L. Charles
(Vigie) Airport

**Rainforest
Adventures**

Grand Anse Bay

Grande Anse

Morne Fortune

Fort Charlotte

Grande Cul de Sac Bay

**Government
House**

La Sorcière

Marigot Beach

**St. Lucia Distillers
Group of Companies**

Marigot Bay

① – ④
② – ④

Roseau

Anse-La-Raye
Anse Cochon Beach
Anse Cochon

Anse-la-Raye

⑤

**Barre de l'Isle
Forest Reserve**

Fond d'or Bay

Dennery

Mandéle Pt.

*Grande
Caille Pt.*

Canaries

Mt. Parasol

Praslin

Praslin Bay

**Diamond Falls
Botanical Gardens and
Mineral Baths**

**Toraille
Waterfalls &
Gardens**

Mt. Gimie

Edmund Forest Reserve

Mamiku Gardens

Soufrière Bay

Soufrière

Fond St. Jacques

The Pitons

Sulphur Springs Park

Vierge Pt.

Micoud

Gros Piton

**Morne Coubaril Historical
Adventure Park**

**Fond Doux
Estate**

Choiseul

LaFargue

Laborie

Laborie Bay

⑥⑦

Savannes Bay

**Maria Islands
Nature Reserve**

Vieux Fort

Vieux Fort

Maria Islands

**Hewanorra
International Airport**

Honeymoon Beach

*Moule à Chique
Peninsula*

Anse des Sables

Caribbean Sea

ATLANTIC OCEAN

Ⓝ

0 |——| 4 miles
0 |——| 4 km

Hotels & Villas

Coconut Bay Beach
Resort & Spa, **7**

Inn on the Bay, **2**

Mango Beach Inn, **4**

Marigot Bay Resort & Marina
by Capella, **1**

Marigot Beach Club
& Dive Resort, **3**

Serenity at Coconut Bay, **6**

Ti Kaye Resort & Spa, **5**

Restaurants

Chateau Mygo House of
Seafood, **3**

Doolittle's, **4**

Hurricane Hole Bar &
Restaurant, **2**

The Pink Plantation House, **1**

KEY

🌴 *Rain Forest*

⚓ *Cruise Ship Terminal*

≥ *Beaches*

◩ *Dive Sites*

① *Hotels & Villas*

❶ *Restaurants*

on the island), and passes through tiny fishing villages. Just north of Soufrière the road negotiates the island's fruit basket, where most of the mangoes, breadfruit, tomatoes, limes, and oranges are grown. In the mountainous region that forms a backdrop for Soufrière, you will notice 3,118-foot Mt. Gimie (pronounced Jimmy), St. Lucia's highest peak. Approaching Soufrière, you'll have spectacular views of the Pitons; the spume of smoke wafting out of the thickly forested mountainside just east of Soufrière emanates from the so-called drive-in volcano.

The landscape changes dramatically between the Pitons and Vieux Fort on the island's southeastern tip. Along the South Coast Road traveling southeasterly from Soufrière, the terrain starts as steep mountainside with dense vegetation, progresses to undulating hills, and finally becomes rather flat and comparatively arid. Anyone arriving at Hewanorra International Airport, which is in Vieux Fort, and staying at a resort near Soufrière will travel along this route, a journey of about 45 minutes each way.

From Vieux Fort north to Castries, a 1½-hour drive, the East Coast Road twists through Micoud, Dennery, and other coastal villages. It then winds up, down, and around mountains, crosses Barre de l'Isle Ridge, and slices through the rain forest. Much of the scenery is breathtaking. The Atlantic Ocean pounds against rocky cliffs, and acres and acres of bananas and coconut palms blanket the hillsides. If you arrive at Hewanorra and stay at a resort near Castries or Rodney Bay, you'll travel along the East Coast Road.

GREATER CASTRIES AND THE NORTH

Castries, a busy commercial city that wraps around a sheltered bay, is St. Lucia's capital and home to some 70,000 residents. Morne Fortuné rises sharply to the south of town, creating a dramatic green backdrop. The charm of Castries lies almost entirely in its current liveliness rather than its history, because four fires between 1796 and 1948 destroyed most of the colonial buildings. Freighters (exporting bananas, coconut, cocoa, mace, nutmeg, and citrus fruits) and cruise ships come and go frequently, making Castries Harbour one of the Caribbean's busiest ports.

Castries and the north are the most developed parts of St. Lucia. The roads are straight, mostly flat, and easy to navigate. Rodney Bay Marina and most of the island's resorts, restaurants, and nightspots are north of Castries, and the beaches in the north are some of the island's best. Pigeon Island, one of the island's most important historical sites, is at the island's northwestern tip. Marigot Bay, about 15 minutes south of the city, is both a yacht haven and a lovely destination for landlubbers.

RODNEY BAY, THEN AND NOW. **A mosquito-infested swamp near Reduit Beach was drained and opened up to the sea in the 1970s, creating a beautiful lagoon and ensuring the value of the surrounding real estate for tourism development. Today Rodney Bay Village is a hive of tourist activity, with hotels, restaurants, much of the island's nightlife, and, of course, Rodney Bay Marina.**

TOP ATTRACTIONS

★ Fodor'sChoice **Marigot Bay.** This is one of the prettiest natural harbors in the Caribbean. In 1778, British admiral Samuel Barrington sailed into this secluded bay-within-a-bay and, the story goes, covered his ships with palm fronds to hide them from the French. Today this small community, just 4 miles (7 km) south of Castries, is a favorite anchorage for boaters and a peaceful destination for landlubbers, with a luxury resort, several small inns and restaurants, and a marina village with a snack shop, grocery store, and boutiques. A 24-hour ferry (EC$5 round-trip) connects the bay's two shores—a voyage that takes a minute or so each way. ⊠ *Marigot Bay.*

FAMILY **Pigeon Island National Landmark.** Jutting out from the northwest coast, Pigeon Island connects to the mainland via a causeway. Tales are told of the pirate Jambe de Bois (Wooden Leg), who once hid out on this 44-acre hilltop islet—a strategic point during the French and British struggles for control of St. Lucia. Now Pigeon Island is a national park and a venue for concerts, festivals, and family gatherings. There are two small beaches with calm waters for swimming and snorkeling, a restaurant, and picnic areas. Scattered around the grounds are ruins of barracks, batteries, and garrisons that date from 18th-century French and English battles. In the Museum and Interpretative Centre, housed in the restored British officers' mess, a multimedia display explains the island's ecological and historical significance. The site is administered by the St. Lucia National Trust. ⊠ *Pigeon Island* ☎ *758/452–5005* ⊕ *www.slunatrust.org* ☜ *$8.*

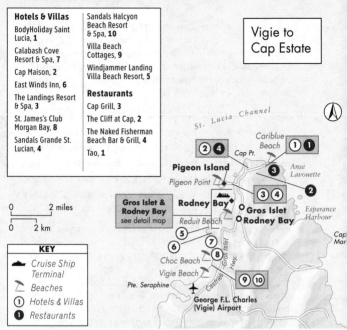

Vigie to Cap Estate

Hotels & Villas

BodyHoliday Saint Lucia, **1**

Calabash Cove Resort & Spa, **7**

Cap Maison, **2**

East Winds Inn, **6**

The Landings Resort & Spa, **3**

St. James's Club Morgan Bay, **8**

Sandals Grande St. Lucian, **4**

Sandals Halcyon Beach Resort & Spa, **10**

Villa Beach Cottages, **9**

Windjammer Landing Villa Beach Resort, **5**

Restaurants

Cap Grill, **3**

The Cliff at Cap, **2**

The Naked Fisherman Beach Bar & Grill, **4**

Tao, **1**

KEY

⚓ *Cruise Ship Terminal*

⌇ *Beaches*

① *Hotels & Villas*

❶ *Restaurants*

FAMILY Rainforest Adventures. Ever wish you could get a bird's-eye view of the rain forest? Or at least experience it without hiking up and down miles of mountain trails? Here's your chance. Depending on your athleticism and spirit of adventure, choose a two-hour aerial tram ride, a zip-line experience, or both. Either activity guarantees a magnificent view as you peacefully ride above or actively zip through the canopy of the 3,442-acre Castries Waterworks Rain Forest in Babonneau, 30 minutes east of Rodney Bay. On the tram ride, eight-passenger gondolas glide slowly among the giant trees, twisting vines, and dense thickets of vegetation accented by colorful flowers, as a tour guide explains and shares anecdotes about the various trees, plants, birds, and other wonders of nature found in the area. The zip line, on the other hand, is a thrilling experience in which you're rigged with a harness, helmet, and clamps that attach to cables strategically strung through the forest. Short trails connect 18 platforms, so riders come down to earth briefly and hike to the next station before speeding through the forest canopy to the next stop. There's even a nighttime zip-line tour. ■ TIP→ Bring binoculars and a camera. ⊠ *Chassin, Babonneau* ☎ *758/458–5151, 866/759–8726 in the U.S.* ⊕ *www.rainforestadventure.com* ☛ *Tram $80, zip line $80, combo $95.*

Rodney Bay Village. Hotels, popular restaurants, a huge mall, and the island's only casino surround a natural bay and an 80-acre man-made lagoon named for Admiral George Rodney, who sailed the British navy out of Gros Islet in 1780 to attack and ultimately destroy the French fleet. With 253 slips, Rodney Bay Marina is one of the Caribbean's premier yachting centers; each December, it's the destination of the Atlantic Rally for Cruisers, a transatlantic sailing competition for racing yachts. Yacht charters and sightseeing day trips can be arranged at the marina. Rodney Bay Village is about 15 minutes north of Castries. ⊠ *Rodney Bay.*

3

WORTH NOTING

★ Fodor'sChoice **Castries Market.** Under a brilliant orange roof,
FAMILY this bustling market is at its liveliest on Saturday morning, when farmers bring their produce and spices to town—as they have for more than a century. (It's closed Sunday.) Next door to the produce market is the **Craft Market,** where you can buy pottery, wood carvings, handwoven straw articles, and innumerable souvenirs, trinkets, and gewgaws. At the **Vendors' Arcade,** across Peynier Street from the Craft Market, you'll find still more handicrafts and souvenirs. ⊠ *Jeremie and Peynier Sts., Castries.*

Cathedral of the Immaculate Conception. Directly across Laborie Street from Derek Walcott Square stands Castries's Roman Catholic cathedral, which was built in 1897. Though it appears rather somber on the outside, the interior walls are decorated with colorful murals reworked by St. Lucian artist Dunstan St. Omer just prior to Pope John Paul II's visit in 1985. This church has an active parish and is open daily for both public viewing and religious services. ⊠ *Micoud St., Castries.*

Derek Walcott Square. The city's green oasis is bordered by Brazil, Laborie, Micoud, and Bourbon streets. Formerly Columbus Square, it was renamed to honor the late Derek Walcott, the hometown poet who won the 1992 Nobel Prize in Literature and one of two Nobel laureates from St. Lucia (the late Sir W. Arthur Lewis won the 1979 Nobel Prize in Economics). Some of the 19th-century buildings that have survived fire, wind, and rain can be seen on Brazil Street, the square's southern border. On the Laborie Street side, there's a huge, 400-year-old samaan (monkey pod) tree with leafy branches that shade a good portion of the square. ⊠ *Bordered by Brazil, Laborie, Micoud, and Bourbon Sts., Castries.*

DID YOU KNOW?

Pigeon Island, a reputed pirate hideout, is now a national park with beaches that offer good snorkeling opportunities.

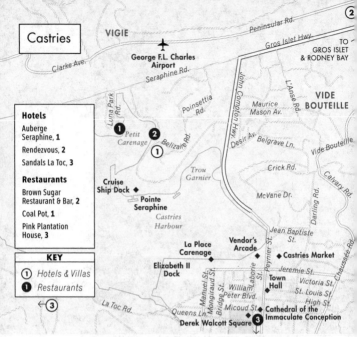

Castries

VIGIE

Peninsular Rd.
Gros Islet Hwy.

TO GROS ISLET & RODNEY BAY

Clarke Ave.

George F.L. Charles Airport

Seraphine Rd.

John Compton Hwy.

Poinsettia Rd.

Luna Park Rd.

VIDE BOUTEILLE

Maurice Mason Av.

L'Anse Rd.

Desir Av. Belgrave Ln.

Vide Bouteille

Belzaire Rd.

Crick Rd.

Calvary Rd.

Trou Garnier

McVane Dr.

Darling Rd.

Petit Carenage

Cruise Ship Dock ◆

Pointe Seraphine

Castries Harbour

Jean Baptiste St.

Vendor's Arcade ◆

La Place Carenage

Elizabeth II Dock

Peynier St.

◆ **Castries Market**

Jeremie St.

Town Hall

Victoria St.

Chaussee Rd.

Laborie St.

William Peter Blvd.

St. Louis St.

High St.

Manuel St.

Mongiraud St.

Bridge St.

Micoud St.

Queens Ln.

Cathedral of the Immaculate Conception

La Toc Rd.

Derek Walcott Square

Hotels

Auberge Seraphine, **1**

Rendezvous, **2**

Sandals La Toc, **3**

Restaurants

Brown Sugar Restaurant & Bar, **2**

Coal Pot, **1**

Pink Plantation House, **3**

KEY

① Hotels & Villas

❶ Restaurants

Fort Charlotte. Begun in 1764 by the French as the Citadelle du Morne Fortuné, Fort Charlotte was completed after 20 years of battling and changing hands. Its old barracks and batteries are now government buildings and local educational facilities, but you can drive around and look at the remains of redoubts, a guardroom, stables, and cells. You can also walk up to the Inniskilling Monument, a tribute to the 1796 battle in which the 27th Foot Royal Inniskilling Fusiliers wrested the Morne from the French. At the military cemetery, first used in 1782, faint inscriptions on the tombstones tell the tales of French and English soldiers who died in St. Lucia. Six former governors of the island are also buried here. From this point atop Morne Fortuné, you have a beautiful view of Castries Harbour, Martinique farther north, and the Pitons to the south. ⊠ *Morne Fortuné*.

Government House. The official residence of the governor-general—and one of the island's few remaining examples of Victorian architecture—is perched high above Castries, halfway up Morne Fortuné (Hill of Good Fortune), which forms a backdrop for the capital city. Morne Fortuné has also seen more than its share of *bad* luck, including devastating hurricanes and four fires that leveled Castries. Within

Government House is **Le Pavillon Royal Museum,** which houses important historical photographs and documents, artifacts, crockery, silverware, medals, and awards; original architectural drawings of the house are displayed on the walls. Note that you must make an appointment to visit. ⊠ *Morne Fortuné* ☎ *758/452–2481* ✆ *Free.*

La Place Carenage. On the south side of the harbor near the pier and markets is a duty-free shopping complex with a handful of shops and a café. It's busiest when a cruise ship is in port. ⊠ *Jeremie St., Castries* ☎ *758/453–2451* ⊕ *carenagemall.com.*

Pointe Seraphine. This duty-free shopping complex is on the north side of the harbor, about a 20-minute walk or 2-minute cab ride from the city center; a launch ferries passengers across the harbor when cruise ships are in port. Pointe Seraphine's attractive Spanish-style architecture houses more than 20 upscale duty-free shops, a tourist information kiosk, a taxi stand, and car-rental agencies. The shopping center is adjacent to a cruise-ship pier and is busiest when ships are in port. ⊠ *Castries Harbour, Castries* ☎ *758/457–3425* ⊕ *www. pointeseraphine.lc* ☉ *Closed Sun. (unless a ship is in port).*

St. Lucia Distillers Group of Companies. St. Lucia Distillers, which produces the island's own Bounty and Chairman's Reserve rums, offers 90-minute Rhythm of Rum tours that cover the history of sugar, the background of rum, a detailed description of the distillation process, colorful displays of local architecture, a glimpse at a typical rum shop, Caribbean music, and a chance to sample the company's rums and liqueurs. The distillery is at the Roseau Sugar Factory in the Roseau Valley, on the island's largest banana plantation a few miles south of Castries and not far from Marigot. Reservations for the tour are essential. ⊠ *Roseau Sugar Factory, West Coast Rd., Roseau Valley, Marigot Bay* ☎ *758/456–3148* ⊕ *www.saintluciarums.com* ✆ *$10.*

THE "SNAKE MAN." Driving along the West Coast Road just north of Canaries, don't be surprised if you see a man selling coconuts on the northbound side of the road with a boa constrictor wrapped around his neck. The "snake man" has been a fixture here for years—usually from mid morning to mid afternoon—and we're sure the startled looks on tourists' faces give him a kick. Taxi drivers will stop if you want some coconut water or just a closer look. For a small tip, the "snake man" will let you take his picture—wearing his boa, of course.

Dunstan St. Omer

The murals of Dunstan St. Omer (1927–2015), one of St. Lucia's leading artists—if not *the* leading artist—adorn many walls and churches throughout the island, and his paintings and portraits are prized both locally and internationally. St. Omer is best known locally for frescoing the walls of the **Cathedral of the Immaculate Conception** in Castries, with the images of black saints just prior to a visit by Pope John Paul II in 1985. He also designed St. Lucia's national flag. A 2004 recipient of the St. Lucia Cross, the nation's highest award, he inspired generations of youngsters for more than 30 years as an art instructor in the public schools. St. Omer was also the father of nine children, two of whom—Luigi and Julio—inherited their father's talent and have followed in his footsteps.

SOUFRIÈRE

The oldest town in St. Lucia and the island's former French colonial capital, Soufrière was founded by the French in 1746 and named for its proximity to the volcano of the same name. The wharf is the center of activity in this sleepy town (population, about 9,000), particularly when a ship anchors in pretty Soufrière Bay. French colonial influences are evident in the second-story verandas, gingerbread trim, and other appointments of the wooden buildings that surround the market square. The market building itself is decorated with colorful murals.

The site of much of St. Lucia's renowned natural beauty, Soufrière is also the destination of most sightseeing trips. This is where you can get up close to the landmark Pitons and visit the "drive-in" volcano, botanical gardens, working plantations, waterfalls, and countless other examples of the natural beauty for which St. Lucia is deservedly famous.

TOP ATTRACTIONS

★ Fodor'sChoice **Diamond Falls Botanical Gardens and Mineral Baths.** These splendid gardens are part of Soufrière Estate, a 2,000-acre land grant presented by King Louis XIV in 1713 to three Devaux brothers from Normandy in recognition of their services to France. The estate is still owned by their descendants; Joan DuBouley Devaux maintains the gardens. Bushes and shrubs bursting with brilliant flowers grow beneath towering trees and line pathways that lead to a natural gorge. Water bubbling to the surface from underground sulfur springs streams downhill in rivulets to become Diamond Waterfall, deep within the botanical gardens. Through the centuries, the rocks over which the cascade spills have become encrusted with minerals tinted yellow, green, and purple. Near the falls, mineral baths are fed by the underground springs. King Louis XVI of France provided funds in 1784 for the construction of a building with a dozen large stone baths to fortify his troops against the St. Lucian climate. It's claimed that the future Joséphine Bonaparte bathed here as a young girl while visiting her father's plantation nearby. During the Brigand's War, just after the French Revolution, the bathhouse was destroyed. In 1930 André DuBoulay had the site excavated, and two of the original stone baths were restored for his use. Outside baths were added later. For a small fee, you can slip into your swimsuit and soak for 30 minutes in one of the outside pools; a private bath costs slightly more. ⊠ *Soufrière Estate, Diamond Rd., Soufrière* ☏ *758/459–7155* ⊕ *www.diamondstlucia.com* ⌤ *$7, public bath $6, private bath $7.*

Edmund Forest Reserve. Dense tropical rain forest that stretches from one side of St. Lucia to the other, sprawling over 19,000 acres of mountains and valleys, is home to a multitude of exotic flowers, trees, plants, and rare birds—including the brightly feathered Jacquot parrot. The Edmund Forest Reserve, on the island's western side, is most easily accessible from the road to Fond St. Jacques, which is just east of Soufrière. A trek through the verdant landscape, with spectacular views of mountains, valleys, and the sea beyond, can take three or more hours. The ranger station at the reserve entrance is a 30-minute drive from Soufrière and 90 minutes or more from the northern end of St. Lucia. You'll need a four-wheel-drive vehicle to drive inland to the trailhead, which can take another hour. The trek itself is a strenuous hike, requiring stamina and sturdy hiking shoes. Your hotel can help you obtain permission from the St. Lucia Forestry Department to access reserve trails and to arrange for a naturalist or forest officer guide—necessary because the vegetation is so dense. ⊠ *Soufrière* ☏ *758/468–5649 Forestry Dept.* ⌤ *Nature trails $10, guide $25.*

★ Fodor'sChoice **Fond Doux Estate.** One of the earliest French
FAMILY estates established by land grants (1745 and 1764), this plantation still produces cocoa, citrus, bananas, coconut, and vegetables on 135 hilly acres. The restored 1864 plantation house is still in use as well. A 90-minute guided

DID YOU KNOW?

The Devaux family has owned Diamond Falls Botanical Gardens and Mineral Baths since 1713; the minerals in the sulfurous water cascading over the waterfall have stained the underlying rocks, making them sparkle—like diamonds.

walking tour begins at the cocoa fermentary, where you can see the drying process. You then follow a trail through the cultivated area, where a guide points out various fruit- or spice-bearing trees, tropical flowers, and indigenous birds (and their unique songs). Additional trails lead to old military ruins, a religious shrine, and a vantage point for viewing the spectacular Pitons. Cool drinks and a Creole buffet lunch are served at the Cocoa Pod restaurant. Souvenirs, including just-made chocolate sticks, are sold at the boutique. ⊠ *Vieux Fort Rd., Château Belair* ☎ *758/459–7545* ⊕ *www. fonddouxestate.com* ☎ *$20 with snacks, $40 with lunch.*

★ Fodor'sChoice **The Pitons.** Rising precipitously from the cobalt-blue Caribbean just south of Soufrière Bay, these two unusual mountains—named a UNESCO World Heritage site in 2004—have become the iconic symbol of St. Lucia. Covered with thick tropical vegetation, the massive outcroppings were formed by a volcanic eruption 30 to 40 million years ago. They are not identical twins, since 2,619-foot Gros Piton is taller and 2,461-foot Petit Piton is broader. It's possible to climb the Pitons, but it's a strenuous trek. Gros Piton is the easier climb and takes about four hours round-trip. Either climb requires permission and a guide; register at the base of Gros Piton. ⊠ *Soufrière.*

★ Fodor'sChoice **Sulphur Springs Park.** As you approach the crater
FAMILY of the "drive-in volcano," your nose will pick up a strong scent emanating from more than 20 belching pools of murky water, crusty sulfur deposits, and other multicolor minerals baking and steaming on the surface. You don't actually drive all the way in. Rather, you drive within a few hundred feet of the gurgling, steaming mass and then walk behind your guide—whose service is included in the admission price—around a fault in the substratum rock. Following the fascinating, educational half-hour tour, you're welcome to take a quick dip in the nearby hot, mineral-rich bathing pools—which can also be pretty stinky on a hot day, but your skin will thank you! ⊠ *Malgretoute, Soufrière* ⊹ *Off West Coast Rd., south of town* ☎ *758/459–7686* ⊕ *www.soufrierefoundation.org* ☎ *$5 tour, $5 bath, $11 combo.*

WORTH NOTING

FAMILY **Morne Coubaril Historical Adventure Park.** On the site of an 18th-century estate, a 250-acre land grant in 1713 by Louis XIV of France, the original plantation house has been rebuilt and a farm workers' village has been re-created. It

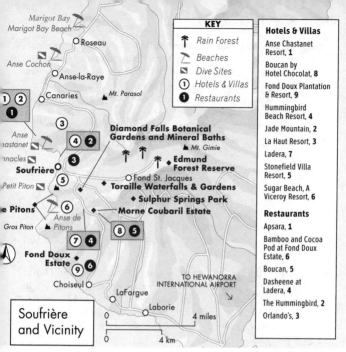

KEY

🌴 *Rain Forest*
⚓ *Beaches*
◣ *Dive Sites*
① *Hotels & Villas*
❶ *Restaurants*

Hotels & Villas

Anse Chastanet Resort, 1

Boucan by Hotel Chocolat, 8

Fond Doux Plantation & Resort, 9

Hummingbird Beach Resort, 4

Jade Mountain, 2

La Haut Resort, 3

Ladera, 7

Stonefield Villa Resort, 5

Sugar Beach, A Viceroy Resort, 6

Restaurants

Apsara, 1

Bamboo and Cocoa Pod at Fond Doux Estate, 6

Boucan, 5

Dasheene at Ladera, 4

The Hummingbird, 2

Orlando's, 3

does a good job of showing what life was like for both the owners (a single family owned the land until 1960) and those who did all the hard labor over the centuries producing cotton, coffee, sugarcane, and cocoa. Cocoa, coffee, coconuts, manioc, and tropical fruits are still grown on the estate using traditional agricultural methods. On the 45-minute Historical Estate Tour, guides show how coconuts are opened and roasted for use as oil and animal feed and how cocoa is fermented, dried, crushed by dancing on the beans, and finally formed into chocolate sticks. Manioc roots (also called cassava) are grated, squeezed of excess water, dried, and turned into flour used for baking. The grounds are lovely for walking or hiking, and the views of mountains and Soufrière Bay are spellbinding. More adventurous visitors will enjoy zip-lining past Petit Piton and through the adjacent rain forest—or horseback riding around the area. A large, open-air restaurant serves a Creole buffet luncheon by reservation only. ⊠ *West Coast Rd., Soufrière* ✛ *2 miles (3 km) south of Soufrière* ☎ *758/459–7340* ⊕ *www.mornecoubarilestate.com* 🖅 *$11 estate tour, with lunch $25; $75 zip line; $75–$120 horseback riding.*

FAMILY **Toraille Waterfalls & Gardens.** A mile or so inland from Soufrière and a stone's throw from the road through Fond St. Jacques, Toraille Waterfall cascades over a cliff and down about 50 feet to a pool. You're invited to don your bathing suit (changing rooms are available) and take a refreshing plunge or let the falling water massage your back and shoulders. A nature trail leads through the surrounding lush tropical gardens. ☏ 758/459–7527 ⊕ *soufrierefoundation.org* 🖃 *$3*.

VIEUX FORT AND THE EAST COAST

Vieux Fort, on the southeastern tip of St. Lucia, is the island's second-largest town (Castries is the only "official" city) and the location of Hewanorra International Airport, which serves all commercial jet aircraft arriving on and departing from the island.

Although less developed for tourism than the island's north and west, the area around Vieux Fort and points north along the east coast are home to some of St. Lucia's unique ecosystems and interesting natural attractions. From the Moule à Chique Peninsula, the island's southernmost tip, you can see much of St. Lucia to the north and the island of St. Vincent 21 miles (34 km) to the south. This is where the waters of the clear Caribbean Sea blend with those of the deeper blue Atlantic Ocean.

TOP ATTRACTIONS

Barre de l'Isle Forest Reserve. St. Lucia is divided into eastern and western halves by Barre de l'Isle ridge. A mile-long (1½-km-long) trail cuts through the reserve, and four lookout points provide panoramic views. Visible in the distance are Mt. Gimie, immense green valleys, both the Caribbean Sea and the Atlantic Ocean, and coastal communities. The trailhead is a half-hour drive from Castries. It takes about an hour to walk the trail—an easy hike—and another hour to climb Mt. LaCombe Ridge. Permission from the St. Lucia Forestry Department is required to access the trail in Barre de l'Isle; a naturalist or forest officer guide will accompany you. ⊠ *Micoud Hwy., Ravine Poisson* ✛ *Midway between Castries and Dennery* ☏ *758/468–5635 Forestry Dept.* 🖃 *$10 for the guide* ☞ *Call weekdays 8:30–4:30.*

Mamiku Gardens. One of St. Lucia's loveliest botanical gardens surrounds the hilltop ruins of the Micoud Estate. Baron Micoud, an 18th-century colonel in the French army and governor-general of St. Lucia, deeded the land to his

St. Lucia's Two Nobel Laureates

Sir W. Arthur Lewis won the Nobel Memorial Prize in Economic Science in 1979. Born in St. Lucia in 1915, Lewis graduated with distinction from the London School of Economics and went on to earn a PhD in industrial economics. His life interest—and his influence—was in economic development and the transformation and expansion of university education in the Caribbean. Lewis died in 1991 and was buried on the grounds of Sir Arthur Lewis Community College on Morne Fortuné in St. Lucia.

Sir Derek Walcott was born in Castries in 1930. *Omeros*—an epic poem about his journey around the Caribbean, the American West, and London—contributed to his winning the Nobel Prize in Literature in 1992. Walcott was also a writer, playwright, and watercolor painter. He taught poetry and drama in the United States, Canada, and England and gave lectures and readings throughout the world. In 2016 he was honored by Queen Elizabeth II as the Knight Commander of the Order of St. Lucia. Walcott died in 2017 and is also buried on Morne Fortuné.

wife, Madame de Micoud, to avoid confiscation by the British during one of the many times when St. Lucia changed hands. Locals abbreviated her name to "Ma Micoud," which, over time, became Mamiku. (The estate did become a British military outpost in 1796, but shortly thereafter was burned to the ground by slaves during the Brigand's War.) The estate is now primarily a banana plantation, but the gardens themselves—including several secluded or "secret" gardens—are filled with tropical flowers and plants, delicate orchids, and fragrant herbs. ⊠ *Micoud Hwy., Praslin* ✛ *Just north of Micoud* ☎ *758/455–3729* ⊕ *www.mamikugardens. com* ⊑ *$8, guided tour $10* ☞ *Guided tours must be booked at least 3 days in advance.*

WORTH NOTING

Maria Islands Nature Reserve. Two tiny islands in the Atlantic Ocean off St. Lucia's southeastern coast make up the reserve, which has its own interpretive center. The 25-acre Maria Major and the 4-acre Maria Minor are inhabited by two rare species of reptiles: the colorful Zandoli Terre ground lizard and the harmless Kouwes grass snake. They share their home with frigate birds, terns, doves, and other wildlife. There's a small beach for swimming and snorkeling, as well as an undisturbed forest, a vertical cliff covered with cacti, and a coral reef for snorkeling or diving. The St. Lucia National Trust offers tours, including a canoe trip to the islands, by appointment only; bring your own picnic lunch, as there are no facilities. ⊠ *Vieux Fort* ☎ *758/454–5014 for tour reservations* ⊕ *www.slunatrust.org* ⊠ *$35.*

BEACHES

The sand on St. Lucia's beaches ranges from golden to black, and the island has some of the best off-the-beach snorkeling in the Caribbean—especially along the western coast north of Soufrière.

St. Lucia's longest, broadest, and most popular beaches are in the north, which is also the flattest part of this mountainous island and the location of most resorts, restaurants, and nightlife. Many of the island's biggest resorts front the beaches from Choc Bay to Rodney Bay and north to Cap Estate. Elsewhere, tiny coves with inviting crescents of sand offer great swimming and snorkeling opportunities. Beaches are all public, but hotels flank many along the northwestern coast. A few secluded stretches of beach on the southwestern coast, south of Marigot Bay and accessible primarily by boat, are popular swimming and snorkeling stops on catamaran day sails or powerboat sightseeing trips. Don't swim along the windward (eastern) coast, as the Atlantic Ocean is too rough—but the views are spectacular. Coconut Bay Beach Resort and Serenity by Coconut Bay, both in Vieux Fort at the southernmost tip of the island, share a beautiful beach facing the Atlantic; the water is rough—but an artificial reef makes it safe for swimming and water sports, especially kitesurfing.

Anse Chastanet. In front of the resort of the same name and Jade Mountain, this palm-studded, dark-sand beach just north of Soufrière Bay has a backdrop of green mountains, brightly painted fishing skiffs bobbing at anchor, calm waters for swimming, and some of the island's best reefs for snorkeling and diving right from shore. Anse Chastanet Resort's gazebos are among the palms; its dive shop, restaurant, and bar are on the beach and open to the public. The mile-long dirt road from Soufrière, though, is a challenge even for taxi drivers, given its (by design) state of disrepair. **Amenities:** food and drink; parking (no fee); toilets; water sports. **Best for:** snorkeling; sunset; swimming. ⊠ *Anse Chastanet Rd., Soufrière* ✛ *1 mile (1½ km) north of Soufrière.*

Embracing Kwéyòl

English is St. Lucia's official language, but most St. Lucians speak and often use Kwéyòl—a French-based Creole language—for informal conversations among themselves. Primarily a spoken language, Kwéyòl in its written version doesn't look at all like French; pronounce the words phonetically, though—*entenasyonnal* (international), for example, or the word *Kwéyòl* (Creole) itself—and you indeed sound as if you're speaking French.

Pretty much the same version of the Creole language, or patois, is spoken on the nearby island of Dominica. Otherwise, the St. Lucian Kwéyòl is quite different from that spoken in other Caribbean islands that have a French and African heritage, such as Haiti, Guadeloupe, and Martinique—or elsewhere, such as Louisiana, Mauritius, and Madagascar. The Kwéyòl

spoken in St. Lucia and Dominica is mostly unintelligible to people from those other locations—and vice versa.

St. Lucia embraces its Creole heritage by devoting the month of October each year to celebrations that preserve and promote Creole culture, language, and traditions. In selected communities throughout the island, events and performances highlight Creole music, food, dance, theater, native costumes, church services, traditional games, folklore, native medicine—a little bit of everything, or *tout bagay*, as you say in Kwéyòl.

Creole Heritage Month culminates at the end of October with all-day events and activities on Jounen Kwéyòl Entenasyonnal, or International Creole Day, which is recognized by all countries that speak a version of the Creole language.

Anse Cochon. This dark-sand beach in front of Ti Kaye Resort & Spa is accessible by boat or by jeep via Ti Kaye's mile-long, tire-crunching access road. The calm water and adjacent reefs, part of the National Marine Reserve, are superb for swimming, diving, and snorkeling. Most catamaran cruises to Soufrière stop here on the northbound leg so that day-trippers can take a quick swim. Moorings are free, and boaters and swimmers can enjoy refreshments at Ti Kaye's beach bar. Snorkeling equipment is available ($10) at the dive shop on the beach. **Amenities:** food and drink; toilets; water sports. **Best for:** snorkeling; swimming. ⊠ *Off West Coast Rd., Anse La Raye ✛ 3 miles (5 km) south of Anse la Raye.*

Anse des Pitons (*Sugar Beach*). The white sand on this crescent beach, snuggled between the Pitons, was imported years ago and spread over the natural black sand. Accessible through the Sugar Beach, a Viceroy Resort, property or by boat, Anse des Pitons (Sugar Beach) offers crystal-clear water for swimming, excellent snorkeling and diving, and breathtaking scenery—you're swimming right between the Pitons, after all. The underwater area here is protected as part of the National Marine Reserve. Neighboring resorts Ladera and Boucan provide shuttle service to the beach. **Amenities:** food and drink; toilets; water sports. **Best for:** snorkeling; sunset; swimming. ⊠ *Val des Pitons, Soufrière* ✢ *3 miles (5 km) south of Soufrière.*

Marigot Beach (*Labas Beach*). Calm waters rippled only by passing yachts lap a sliver of sand on the north side of Marigot Bay adjacent to the Marigot Beach Club & Dive Resort, across the bay from Marigot Bay Resort & Marina by Capella, and a short walk from Mango Beach Inn. Studded with palm trees, the tiny but extremely picturesque beach is accessible by a ferry (EC$5 round-trip) that operates continually from one side of the bay to the other, with pickup at the Marina Village dock. You can find refreshments at adjacent or nearby restaurants. **Amenities:** food and drink; toilets; water sports. **Best for:** swimming, sunset. ⊠ *Marigot Bay.*

FAMILY **Pigeon Point.** This small beach within the national landmark, on the northwestern tip of St. Lucia, has golden sand, a calm sea, and a view that extends from Rodney Bay to Martinique. It's a perfect spot for picnicking, and you can take a break from the sun by visiting the nearby Pigeon Island Museum and Interpretive Centre. **Amenities:** food and drink; toilets. **Best for:** snorkeling; solitude; swimming. ⊠ *Pigeon Island National Landmark, Pigeon Island* 🖃 *$7 park admission.*

★ Fodor'sChoice **Reduit Beach.** Many feel that Reduit (pronounced
FAMILY red-wee) is the island's finest beach. The long stretch of golden sand that frames Rodney Bay is within walking distance of many hotels and restaurants in Rodney Bay Village. Bay Gardens Beach Resort and Royal St. Lucia by Rex Resorts face the beachfront; blu St. Lucia, Harmony Suites, and Ginger Lily hotels are across the road. At the Royal's water-sports center, you can rent sports equipment and beach chairs and take windsurfing or waterskiing lessons. Kids (and adults alike) love Splash Island Water Park,

an open-water inflatable playground near Bay Gardens Beach Resort with a trampoline, climbing wall, monkey bars, swing, slide, and more. **Amenities:** food and drink; toilets; water sports. **Best for:** snorkeling; sunset; swimming; walking; windsurfing. ⊠ *Rodney Bay*.

Vigie/Malabar Beach. This 2-mile (3-km) stretch of lovely white sand runs parallel to the George F. L. Charles Airport runway in Castries and continues on past the Rendezvous resort, where it becomes Malabar Beach. In the area opposite the airport departure lounge, a few vendors sell refreshments. **Amenities:** food and drink. **Best for:** swimming. ⊠ *Castries* ⊹ *Adjacent to George F.L. Charles Airport runway*.

WHERE TO EAT

Bananas, mangoes, passion fruit, plantains, breadfruit, okra, avocados, limes, pumpkins, cucumbers, papaya, yams, christophenes (also called chayote), and coconuts are among the fresh fruits and vegetables that grace St. Lucian menus. The French influence is strong, and most chefs cook with a Creole flair. Resort buffets and restaurant fare include standards like steaks, chops, pasta, and pizza—and every menu lists fresh fish along with the ever-popular lobster.

Caribbean standards include callaloo, stuffed crab back, pepperpot stew, curried chicken or goat, and *lambi* (conch). The national dish of salt fish and green fig—a stew of dried, salted codfish and boiled green banana—is, let's say, an acquired taste. A runner-up in terms of local popularity is bouyon, a cooked-all-day soup or stew that combines meat (usually pig tail), "provisions" (root vegetables), pigeon peas, dumplings, broth, and local spices. Soups and stews are traditionally prepared in a coal pot—unique to St. Lucia—a rustic clay casserole on a matching clay stand that holds the hot coals.

Chicken and pork dishes and barbecues are also popular here. Fresh lobster is available in season, which lasts from August through February. As they do throughout the Caribbean, local vendors set up barbecue grills along the roadside, at street fairs, and at Friday-night "jump-ups" and do a bang-up business selling grilled fish or chicken legs, bakes (fried biscuits), and beer—you can get a full meal for less than $10. Most other meats are imported—beef

BEST BETS FOR DINING

With so many restaurants to choose from, how will you decide where to eat? Fodor's writers and editors have selected their favorite restaurants in the Best Bets lists below. The Fodor's Choice properties represent the "best of the best." Find the specific details about each restaurant in the reviews that follow.

FODOR'S CHOICE
The Cliff at Cap, Coal Pot, Dasheene at Ladera, Jacques Waterfront Dining,Tao

BEST VIEW
Chateau Mygo, The Cliff at Cap, Coal Pot, Dasheene at Ladera

BEST FOR FAMILIES
Doolittle's

MOST ROMANTIC
Boucan, Coal Pot, Tao

BEST FOR LOCAL ST. LUCIAN CUISINE
Jardin Cacao at Fond Doux Estate, Lifeline Restaurant at the Hummingbird

from Argentina and Iowa, lamb from New Zealand. Piton is the local brew; Bounty, the local rum.

Guests at St. Lucia's many popular all-inclusive resorts take most meals at hotel restaurants—which are generally quite good and, in some cases, exceptional—but it's fun when vacationing to try some of the local restaurants, as well—for lunch when sightseeing or for a special night out.

What to Wear: Dress on St. Lucia is casual but conservative. Shorts are usually fine during the day, but bathing suits and immodest clothing are frowned upon anywhere but at the beach. Nude or topless sunbathing is prohibited. In the evening the mood is casually elegant, but even the fanciest places generally expect only a collared shirt and long pants for men and a sundress or slacks for women.

VIGIE TO CAP ESTATE

$$ 🍴 **Cap Grill.** *Steakhouse.* At the St. Lucia Golf Resort & Country Club, this restaurant serves breakfast, lunch, and early supper all day every day (7 to 7) and Sunday brunch in air-conditioned comfort or alfresco on the dining porch. In any case, your table will overlook the golf course. **Known for:** mingling with golfers; great burgers and steaks; convivial sports bar. [$] *Average main: US$20* ✉ *St. Lucia Golf Resort & Country Club, Cap Estate* ☎ *758/450–8523* 🌐 *www.stluciagolf.com* 🕒 *No dinner.*

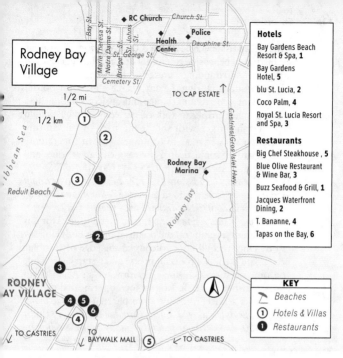

Rodney Bay Village

TO CAP ESTATE

Church St.

◆ RC Church

St. Johns St.

Bay St.

Marie Theresa St.

Notre Dame St.

Bridge St.

St. George St.

Cemetery St.

◆ Health Center

◆ Police

Dauphine St.

1/2 mi

1/2 km

Caribbean Sea

Reduit Beach

Rodney Bay Marina

Rodney Bay

Castries/Gros Islet Hwy.

RODNEY BAY VILLAGE

TO CASTRIES

TO BAYWALK MALL

TO CASTRIES

Hotels

Bay Gardens Beach Resort & Spa, **1**

Bay Gardens Hotel, **5**

blu St. Lucia, **2**

Coco Palm, **4**

Royal St. Lucia Resort and Spa, **3**

Restaurants

Big Chef Steakhouse , **5**

Blue Olive Restaurant & Wine Bar, **3**

Buzz Seafood & Grill, **1**

Jacques Waterfront Dining, **2**

T. Bananne, **4**

Tapas on the Bay, **6**

KEY
⌐ *Beaches*
① *Hotels & Villas*
❶ *Restaurants*

★ **Fodor's**Choice ✕ **The Cliff at Cap.** *Eclectic.* High on top of a cliff
$$$$ at the northern tip of St. Lucia, the open-air dining room at
Cap Maison welcomes diners to what executive chef Craig
Jones calls "nouveau" French–West Indian cuisine. True,
he incorporates local vegetables, fruits, herbs, and spices
with the best meats and fresh-caught seafood you'll find
on the island; but the technique and presentation—and
the service—lean more toward the French. **Known for:** the
superb dining; the panoramic view; the daily (but pricey)
tastings in the wine cellar. ⑤ *Average main: US$36 ⌧ Cap
Maison, Smuggler's Cove Dr., Cap Estate* ☎ *758/457–8681*
⊕ *www.thecliffatcap.com.*

★ **Fodor's**Choice ✕ **Coal Pot.** *French.* Popular since it opened in
$$$$ 1968, this tiny waterfront restaurant overlooks pretty Vigie
Cove. Come for a light lunch—perhaps a bowl of creamy
pumpkin soup, Greek salad with chicken or shrimp, or
broiled fresh fish—or enjoy an exquisite French-inspired
dinner under the stars. **Known for:** outstanding cuisine
and service; picturesque harbor views; repeat customers
who love the place. ⑤ *Average main: US$32 ⌧ Seraphine
Rd., Vigie* ☎ *758/452–5566* ⊗ *Closed Sun. No lunch Sat.*

$$$$ 🍴 **The Naked Fisherman Beach Bar & Grill.** *Seafood.* The rather sophisticated beachside restaurant at Cap Maison is tucked into a cliff surrounding a crescent of sand at the northern tip of St. Lucia. During the day, match a glass (or bottle) of excellent wine to an arugula-and-apricot salad, grilled island catch, Caribbean roti, or perfectly cooked Wagyu beef or fish burger with shoestring fries—while staring across the sea as far as Martinique. **Known for:** remote beach location; sophisticated environment; great wines and great food. [$] *Average main: US$35* ✉ *Cap Maison, Smugglers Cove Rd., Cap Estate* ✥ *On the beach, 92 steps down (and back up) from the road* ☎ *758/457–8694* 🌐 *nakedfishermanstlucia.com* 🕒 *No dinner Sun.–Tues.*

★ Fodor's Choice 🍴 **Tao.** *Asian.* For a special evening, head for this

$$$$ Cap Estate restaurant on the premises of the BodyHoliday resort. On a second-floor balcony at the edge of Cariblue Beach, you'll enjoy a pleasant breeze and a starry sky while you dine on fusion cuisine—mouthwatering Asian tastes with a Caribbean touch. **Known for:** sophisticated cuisine; top-drawer service; romantic atmosphere. [$] *Average main: US$35* ✉ *BodyHoliday St. Lucia, Cariblue Beach, Cap Estate* ☎ *758/450–8551* 🌐 *www.thebodyholiday.com* 🕒 *No lunch.*

GREATER CASTRIES

$$ 🍴 **Brown Sugar Restaurant & Bar.** *Caribbean.* Perfect for lunch while touring Castries, a romantic dinner, or before a flight from nearby George F. L. Charles Airport, this open-air dining deck in a lovely garden setting overlook Vigie Cove Marina. The menu features Caribbean cuisine—an island salad with pineapple coconut dressing, paupiettes of fish with Creole sauce, cinnamon- and cumin-infused braised lamb, or curried chicken—plus loaded cheeseburgers, pasta Alfredo, and spicy wings with a secret sauce. **Known for:** pretty views; reasonable prices; tasty, well-prepared dishes. [$] *Average main: US$20* ✉ *Vigie Cove, Vigie* ☎ *758/458–9131* 🌐 *www.brownsugarrestaurantandbar.com* 🕒 *Closed Mon. No lunch Sun.*

$$$ 🍴 **The Pink Plantation House.** *Caribbean.* A 140-year-old, pretty in pink, French Colonial plantation house is the setting for authentic French Creole cuisine—the inspiration of local artist Michelle Elliott, whose ceramics and paintings are displayed for sale in a cozy room set up as a gift shop. Diners enjoy grilled fish, steak, rack of lamb, jumbo shrimp, or chicken breast matched with interesting homemade sauces and accompanied by steamed rice, fried plantains, sautéed vegetables, breadfruit/sweet potato

balls, local peas, and christophene (chayote) gratin. **Known for:** scenic garden setting; historic environment; excellent regional cuisine. $ *Average main: US$25* ✉ *Chef Harry Dr., Morne Fortuné* ☎ *758/452–5422* ⏲ *Closed Sat.*

RODNEY BAY VILLAGE

$$$$ 🍴 **Big Chef Steakhouse.** *Steakhouse.* It's not always easy to find a good thick steak outside of a major city—or perhaps Texas!—but Big Chef owners Marc and Rosie Joinville have being delivering mouthwatering steaks (and more) for more than a decade. Chef Rosie trained at London's Cordon Bleu Cooking School, worked all over the world, and has run several restaurants in St. Lucia, so she knows what she's doing in the kitchen! **Known for:** thick, juicy steaks; Chef Rosie's rich desserts; friendly service. $ *Average main: US$36* ✉ *Reduit Beach Ave., opposite Baywalk Mall, Rodney Bay* ☎ *758/450–0210* 🌐 *bigchefsteakhouse.com* ⏲ *No lunch.*

$$$$ 🍴 **Blue Olive Restaurant & Wine Bar.** *Mediterranean.* At this cozy spot on the Rodney Bay waterfront, Chef Xavier Rabot's culinary team blends Mediterranean and Caribbean cuisine to create dishes like stuffed crab back, creamy coquille St.-Jacques, or catch of the day with Creole sauce as a main. To find the restaurant, you need to walk down a small lane off the main road—past a pizza place—but don't let that dissuade you! **Known for:** beautiful setting at the water's edge; reasonable prices for good food; attentive service but definitely not rushed. $ *Average main: US$35* ✉ *Seagrape Ave., Rodney Bay* ☎ *758/458–2433* 🌐 *blueolivestlucia.com* ⏲ *No lunch Sun.*

$$$ 🍴 **Buzz Seafood & Grill.** *Seafood.* Opposite the Royal St. Lucia by Rex Resorts hotel and Reduit Beach, this dining spot is part of Rodney Bay's "restaurant central." After cool drinks and warm appetizers at the bar, diners make their way to the dining room or garden for some serious seafood or a good steak, West Indian pepperpot stew, spicy Moroccan-style lamb shanks, or simple chicken and chips. The seared yellowfin tuna, potato-crusted red snapper, and seafood Creole are big hits, too. **Known for:** flashy tropical cocktails; meals cooked to order; vegetarian choices. $ *Average main: US$30* ✉ *Reduit Beach Ave., Rodney Bay* ☎ *758/458–0450* 🌐 *www.buzzseafoodgrill.com* ⏲ *Closed Mon. No lunch.*

★ Fodors Choice 🍴 **Jacques Waterfront Dining.** *French.* Chef-owner
$$$$ Jacky Rioux (aka Froggie Jacques) creates magical dishes

in his waterfront restaurant set within the gardens of Harmony Suites Hotel in Rodney Bay. The cooking is decidedly French, as is Rioux, but fresh produce and local spices create a memorable fusion cuisine. **Known for:** long-standing reputation for quality cuisine; waterfront location; impressive wine list. [$] *Average main: US$32* ✉ *Harmony Suites Hotel, Reduit Beach Ave., Rodney Bay* ☎ *758/458–1900* 🌐 *www.jacquesrestaurant.com.*

$$$ ✕ **Tapas On The Bay.** *Tapas.* The sister restaurant to Big Chef Steakhouse, this waterfront spot serves small plates—more than a dozen classic and inspired choices, all served with homemade bread, olives, aioli, olive oil, chutneys, and salsa—as well as full meals like the beef and chorizo burger or coconut steamed fish. Pair your meal with a glass (or pitcher) of sangria or perhaps a glass (or bottle) of robust red wine from Spain—and if your dining partners don't mind, a Cuban cigar. **Known for:** small plates, large portions; harbor view; happy hours and (Friday night) entertainment. [$] *Average main: US$24* ✉ *Waterfront, Rodney Bay* ✣ *behind Big Chef Steakhouse* ☎ *758/451–2433* 🌐 *tapasonthebay.com* ⏲ *Closed Tues.*

$$$ ✕ **Ti Bananne.** *Caribbean.* Poolside at the Coco Palm hotel,
FAMILY this alfresco bistro and bar attracts mostly hotel guests for breakfast but a wider clientele for lunch or dinner—and happy hour. A live band entertains most evenings and always at the Friday-night Caribbean buffet. **Known for:** easy, breezy dining; friendly bar; poolside live music. [$] *Average main: US$27* ✉ *Coco Palm Resort, Off Reduit Beach Ave., Rodney Bay* ☎ *758/456–2800* 🌐 *www.coco-resorts.com.*

MARIGOT BAY

$$$ ✕ **Chateau Mygo House of Seafood.** *Seafood.* Walk down a
FAMILY garden path to Chateau Mygo (a colloquial corruption of "Marigot") or sail up on your boat, pick out a table on the deck of this popular dockside restaurant, and soak up the waterfront atmosphere of what may be the Caribbean's prettiest bay. The tableau is mesmerizing—and that's at lunch, when you can order a sandwich, burger, roti, fish- or chicken-and-chips, salads, or grilled fish or savory coconut chicken with peas and rice and vegetables. **Known for:** casual waterside dining on Marigot Bay; local seafood (and other) specialties; live local music and dancing (weekly). [$] *Average main: US$22* ✉ *Marigot Bay* ☎ *758/458–3947* 🌐 *www.chateaumygo.com.*

Amazing views at Dasheene Restaurant in the Ladera Resort

$$$ 🍴 **Doolittle's.** *Seafood.* Named for the protagonist in the
FAMILY original (1967) *Dr. Doolittle* movie, part of which was filmed in Marigot Bay, this indoor-outdoor restaurant at Marigot Beach Club & Dive Resort is on the north side of the bay. **Known for:** casual atmosphere; close to the beach; evening entertainment. [$] *Average main: US$28* ✉ *Marigot Beach Club & Dive Resort, Marigot Bay* ☎ *758/451–4974* 🌐 *www.marigotbeachclub.com.*

$$ 🍴 **Hurricane Hole Bar & Restaurant.** *Café.* Join the yachties
FAMILY and nearby hotel guests for breakfast, lunch, afternoon tea, a casual evening meal, cocktails or a cold drink, or just dessert at this café in the Marina Village on Marigot Bay. Eat in (well, outside on the dock), get it to go, or select something quickly from the grab 'n' go counter. **Known for:** alfresco dining at the marina; all-day menu; quick service. [$] *Average main: US$14* ✉ *Marina Village, Marigot Bay* ☎ *758/458–5300.*

SOUFRIÈRE

$$$$ 🍴 **Apsara.** *Indian.* India has had an important influence on the Caribbean islands, from the heritage of their people to the colorful madras plaids and the curry flavors that are a staple of Caribbean cuisine. At night, Anse Chastanet's Trou au Diable restaurant transforms into Apsara, an extraordinarily romantic, candlelit, beachfront dining experience with modern Indian cuisine. **Known for:** exotic cuisine in an island setting; accessible by land or water; chef visits with diners at table to discuss cuisine. $ *Average main: US$38* ✉ *Anse Chastanet, 1 Anse Chastanet Rd., Soufrière* ☎ *758/459–7000* 🌐 *www.ansechastanet.com* ⏲ *Closed Tues. No lunch.*

$$$ FAMILY 🍴 **Bamboo and Cocoa Pod at Fond Doux Estate.** *Caribbean.* The small, rustic restaurant on this working plantation is one of the most popular spots to enjoy a Creole lunch when touring the natural sights in and around Soufrière. Help yourself to the buffet, containing stewed chicken, grilled fish, rice and beans, macaroni and cheese, caramelized plantains, figs (green bananas), breadfruit balls, purple yams, salad, and more. **Known for:** plantation-to-plate Creole cuisine; natural environment; plantation tours before or after your meal. $ *Average main: US$25* ✉ *Fond Doux Plantation & Resort, West Coast Rd., Château Belair* ☎ *758/459–7545* 🌐 *www.fonddouxresort.com/dining.*

$$$$ 🍴 **Boucan.** *Caribbean.* Aah ... chocolate! Here on the Rabot Estate, a working cocoa plantation, that heavenly flavor is infused into just about every dish—cacao gazpacho or citrus salad with white chocolate dressing for starters. **Known for:** "pioneering" cacao cuisine; open-air dining room with Piton view; sunset at the bar with a cacao Bellini. $ *Average main: US$32* ✉ *Boucan by Hotel Chocolat, Rabot Estate, West Coast Rd., Soufrière* ✥ *3 miles (5 km) south of Soufrière* ☎ *758/572–9600* 🌐 *www.hotelchocolat.com.*

★ $$$ Fodor's Choice 🍴 **Dasheene at Ladera.** *Caribbean.* The terrace restaurant at Ladera Resort has breathtaking, close-up views of the Pitons and the sea between them, especially beautiful at sunset. The atmosphere is casual by day and magical at night. **Known for:** fresh, stylish island cuisine; Piton view; live local music every evening. $ *Average main: US$30* ✉ *Ladera Resort, Soufrière* ✥ *2 miles (3 km) south of Soufrière* ☎ *758/459–6623* 🌐 *www.ladera.com.*

$$$ 🍴 **The Hummingbird.** *Caribbean.* The cheerful restaurant-bar in the Hummingbird Beach Resort specializes in French Creole cuisine. Try fresh seafood or chicken seasoned with local herbs and accompanied by fresh-picked vegetables from the Hummingbird's garden. **Known for:** authentic Caribbean food; great in-town, on-the-beach location; a favorite for three decades. $ *Average main: US$25* ✉ *Hummingbird Beach Resort, Anse Chastanet Rd., Soufrière* ☎ *758/459–7232* 🌐 *www.istlucia.co.uk.*

$$$$ 🍴 **Orlando's.** *Caribbean.* A man on a mission, chef Orlando Satchell opened his restaurant in downtown Soufrière to present his "Share the Love" (or STL) style of Caribbean

cooking. Portions are small, but the flavors and richness of the food make it perfectly filling. **Known for:** "star" chef yet always accommodating; exquisite "small plates" and excellent wine; fine dining in a casual courtyard atmosphere. $ *Average main: US$38* ⊠ *Bridge St., Soufrière* ☎ *758/459–5955* ⊕ *www.orlandosrestaurantstl.com* ☾ *Closed Mon. and Tues.*

WHERE TO STAY

Most people—particularly honeymooners—choose to stay in one of St. Lucia's many grand beach resorts, most of which are upscale and pricey. Several are all-inclusive, including the three Sandals resorts, two resorts owned or managed by Sunswept (BodyHoliday St. Lucia and Rendezvous), St. James's Club Morgan Bay Resort & Spa, East Winds Inn, Coconut Bay Beach Resort & Spa, Serenity at Coconut Bay, and Royalton St. Lucia.

If you're looking for lodgings that are smaller and less expensive, St. Lucia has dozens of small inns and hotels that are primarily locally owned and frequently quite charming. They may or may not be directly on the beach. Luxury villa communities and independent private villas are another alternative in St. Lucia. Most of the villa communities are in the north near Cap Estate.

Hotel reviews have been shortened. For full information, visit Fodors.com.

PRIVATE VILLAS AND CONDOS

Luxury villa and condo communities are an important part of the accommodations mix on St. Lucia, as they can be an economical option for families, other groups, or couples vacationing together. Several communities have opened in recent years, and more are on the way. The villa units themselves are privately owned, but nonowners can rent individual units directly from the property managers for a vacation or short-term stay, much like reserving hotel accommodations. Units with fully equipped kitchens, up to three bedrooms, and as many baths run $200 to $2,500 per night, depending on the size and the season.

Local real-estate agencies will arrange vacation rentals of privately owned villas and condos that are fully equipped. Most private villas are in the hills of Cap Estate in the very north of the island, at Rodney Bay or Bois d'Orange, or

Cap Maison's Spanish Caribbean architecture features terra-cotta roof tiles and large private balconies.

in Soufrière among St. Lucia's natural treasures. Some are within walking distance of a beach.

All rental villas are staffed with a cook who specializes in local cuisine and a housekeeper; in some cases, a caretaker lives on the property and a gardener and night watchman are on staff. All properties have telephones, and some have Internet access and fax machines. Telephones may be barred against outgoing overseas calls; plan to use a phone card or calling card. Most villas have TVs, DVDs, and CD players. All private villas have a swimming pool; condos share a community pool. Vehicles are generally not included in the rates, but rental cars can be arranged for and delivered to the villa upon request. Linens and basic supplies (such as bath soap, toilet tissue, and dishwashing detergent) are included. Pre-arrival grocery stocking can be arranged.

Units with one to nine bedrooms and the same number of baths run $200 to $2,000 per night, depending on the size of the villa, the amenities, the number of guests, and the season. Rates include utilities and government taxes. Your only additional cost will be for groceries and staff gratuities. A security deposit is required upon booking and refunded after departure less any damages or unpaid miscellaneous charges.

Rental Contacts **Discover Villas of St. Lucia.** ☎ 758/484–3066, 758/450–0002 ⊕ discovervillasstlucia.com. **Tropical Villas.** ☎ 758/450–8240 ⊕ www.tropicalvillas.net.

BEST BETS FOR LODGING

Fodor's offers a selective listing of quality lodging experiences, from the island's best boutique hotels to its most luxurious beach resorts. Here, we've compiled our top recommendations based on the different types of lodging found on the island. The very best properties—in other words, those that provide a particularly remarkable experience—are designated in the listings with the Fodor's Choice logo.

FODOR'S CHOICE

Bay Gardens Beach Resort & Spa, BodyHoliday Saint Lucia, Boucan by Hotel Chocolat, Calabash Cove Resort & Spa, Cap Maison, Fond Doux Plantation & Resort, Jade Mountain, Ladera, Landings Resort & Spa, Marigot Bay Resort & Marina, Sugar Beach, A Viceroy Resort, Ti Kaye Resort & Spa

BEST BEACH RESORTS

Bay Gardens Beach Resort & Spa, BodyHoliday Saint Lucia, Royal St. Lucia Resort and Spa, Sugar Beach, A Viceroy Resort

BEST FOR HONEYMOONERS

Calabash Cove Resort & Spa, Jade Mountain, Ladera, Rendezvous, Sandals Grande St. Lucian, Sugar Beach, A Viceroy Resort

BEST FOR FAMILIES

Bay Gardens Beach Resort & Spa, Coconut Bay Beach Resort & Spa, St. James's Club Morgan Bay, Windjammer Landing Villa Beach Resort

3

VIGIE TO CAP ESTATE

★ $$$$ FodorsChoice **BodyHoliday Saint Lucia.** *Resort.* At this adults-only spa resort on picturesque Cariblue Beach—where daily treatments are included in the rates—you can customize your own "body holiday" online even before you leave home. **Pros:** special rates for solo travelers; fabulous spa treatments, all included; interesting activities, such as archery, include free instruction. **Cons:** expensive (but includes a lot of amenities!); lots of steps to the spa, though you can get a lift; small bathrooms in some rooms. $ *Rooms from: US$1,088* ✉ *Cariblue Beach, Cap Estate* ☎ *758/457–7800, 800/544–2883* 🌐 *www.thebodyholiday.com* 🛏 *155 rooms* 🍴 *All-inclusive.*

★ $$$ FodorsChoice **Calabash Cove Resort & Spa.** *Resort.* The luxurious suites and Balinese-inspired cottages at this inviting boutique resort spill gently down a tropical hillside to a secluded beach on Bonaire Bay, just south of Rodney Bay. The private cottages, constructed of mahogany, stone, and other natural materials, all face the sea to take advantage of the sunset. **Pros:** stylish, sophisticated, and friendly atmosphere; great food served in lovely alfresco setting; wedding parties can reserve the entire resort. **Cons:** the long, bone-crunching dirt road to the entrance; steps to the cottages and beach may be difficult for those with physical challenges; few on-site "activities". [$] *Rooms from: US$435* ✉ *Bonaire Estate, Off Castries–Gros Islet Hwy., south of Rodney Bay, Marisule Estate* ☎ *758/456–3500, 800/917–2683 in U.S.* 🌐 *www.calabashcove.com* 🛏 *26 rooms* 🍴 *Breakfast.*

★ Fodor'sChoice **Cap Maison.** *Resort.* Prepare to be spoiled by the doting staffers at this intimate villa resort—the luxurious service includes unpacking (if you wish) and a personal butler for any little needs that arise. **Pros:** private and elegant with outstanding service; cocktails with a view at Cliff Bar or surf side at Rock Maison; rooftop plunge pools in most suites. **Cons:** air-conditioning in bedrooms only; 92 steps to the beach; meals are expensive (but delicious) with few nearby options. [$] *Rooms from: US$438* ✉ *Smuggler's Cove Dr., Cap Estate* ☎ *758/457–8670, 888/765–4985 in U.S.* 🌐 *www.capmaison.com* 🛏 *49 rooms* 🍴 *Breakfast.*
$$$
FAMILY

$$$$ **East Winds Inn.** *Resort.* Guests keep returning to this small all-inclusive resort on a secluded beach halfway between Castries and Rodney Bay, where 7 acres of botanical gardens surround 13 duplex gingerbread-style cottages, three ocean-view rooms, and a suite. **Pros:** lovely beach; excellent dining; peaceful and quiet. **Cons:** not best choice for families, though children welcome; very expensive; six-night minimum. [$] *Rooms from: US$955* ✉ *La Brelotte Bay, Gros Islet* ☎ *758/452–8212* 🌐 *www.eastwinds.com* 🛏 *30 suites* 🍴 *All-inclusive.*

★ Fodor'sChoice **The Landings Resort & Spa.** *Resort.* On 19 acres along the Pigeon Point Causeway at the northern edge of Rodney Bay, this villa resort surrounds a private, 17-slip harbor where guests can dock their own yachts, literally, at their doorstep. **Pros:** spacious, beautifully appointed units; perfect for yachties, couples, families, even business travelers; kids club and playground. **Cons:** condo atmosphere; little hike to beach from some rooms; all-inclusive option carries surcharges for some menu items and premium drinks. [$] *Rooms from: US$467* ✉ *Pigeon Island Causeway, Gros Islet* ☎ *758/458–7300, 844/886–3762 in U.S.* 🌐 *www.landingsstlucia.com* 🛏 *188 rooms* 🍴 *Breakfast.*
$$$
FAMILY

$$$$ 🏨 **Sandals Grande St. Lucian.** *Resort.* Perched on the narrow Pigeon Island Causeway at St. Lucia's northern tip, Sandals Grande offers panoramic views of Rodney Bay on one side and the Atlantic Ocean on the other. **Pros:** grand accommodations, especially the over-the-water bungalow suites; 12 restaurants and countless activities; free scuba for certified divers. **Cons:** really long ride (at least 90 minutes) from/to Hewanorra, but transfers are complimentary; beach can be crowded; while romantic, it's not peaceful or quiet. [$] *Rooms from: US$711* ✉ *Pigeon Island Causeway, Pigeon Island* ☎ *758/455–2000* 🌐 *www.sandals.com* 🛏 *301 rooms* 🍴 *All-inclusive.*

$$$$ 🏨 **Sandals Halcyon Beach Resort & Spa.** *Resort.* This is the most intimate and low-key of the three Sandals resorts on St. Lucia; like the others, it's beachfront, all-inclusive, for couples only, and loaded with amenities and activities—including personalized butler service in some suites. **Pros:** all the Sandals amenities in a more intimate setting; lots of dining and activity choices; exchange privileges (including golf) at other Sandals properties. **Cons:** it's Sandals, so it's a theme property that's not for everyone; it's small and popular, so book well in advance; rooms at back of property, nearest the main road, can be noisy at night. [$] *Rooms from: US$652* ✉ *Choc Bay, Choc* ☎ *758/453–0222, 888/726–3257* 🌐 *www.sandals.com* 🛏 *169 rooms* 🍴 *All-inclusive.*

$$$$ FAMILY 🏨 **St. James's Club Morgan Bay.** *Resort.* Singles, couples, and families enjoy tons of sports and activities at this all-inclusive resort on 22 secluded acres surrounding a stretch of white-sand beach. **Pros:** six restaurants, six bars, four pools, four tennis courts, and more; children's club with organized activities; free waterskiing, sailing, and tennis lessons. **Cons:** huge resort can be very busy, especially when full; relatively small beach given resort's size; Wi-Fi only in some rooms and for a fee. [$] *Rooms from: US$515* ✉ *Choc Bay, Choc* ☎ *758/457–3700, 866/830–1617* 🌐 *www.morganbayresort.com* 🛏 *335 rooms* 🍴 *All-inclusive.*

$ 🏨 **Villa Beach Cottages.** *Hotel.* Tidy housekeeping cottages with gingerbread-laced facades are steps from the beach at this family-run establishment 3 miles (5 km) north of the airport in Castries. **Pros:** just feet from the water; beautiful sunsets from your balcony; peaceful and quiet environment. **Cons:** close quarters; rent a car, as you'll go out for meals (or groceries); beach is quite narrow and pools are small. [$] *Rooms from: US$265* ✉ *John Compton (Castries-Gros Islet) Hwy., Choc* ☎ *758/450–2884, 866/542–1991 in U.S.* 🌐 *www.villabeachcottages.com* 🛏 *20 rooms* 🍴 *No meals.*

$$ [🏨] **Windjammer Landing Villa Beach Resort.** *Resort.* Mediterranean-style villas—which are as appropriate for a family or group vacation as for a romantic getaway—climb the hillside on one of St. Lucia's prettiest bays. **Pros:** lovely, spacious units with seating areas and kitchenettes; amazing sunset views from every villa; five restaurants, four bars, in-villa dining, room service ... you choose. **Cons:** far from main road, so you'll need a car if you plan to leave the property often; meal and bar costs add up fast unless you choose the all-inclusive option; some villa sitting rooms are open-air, meaning no air-conditioning and occasional insects. [$] *Rooms from: US$320* ✉ *Trouya Point Rd., La Brellotte Bay, Bois d'Orange* ☎ *758/456–9000, 877/522–0722 in the U.S.* 🌐 *www.windjammer-landing.com* 🛏 *331 units* 🍴 *No meals.*

FAMILY

RODNEY BAY VILLAGE

★ **Fodor's Choice** [🏨] **Bay Gardens Beach Resort & Spa.** *Resort.* One of three Bay Gardens properties in Rodney Bay Village, this family-friendly resort has a prime location on beautiful Reduit Beach. **Pros:** families love the kitchenettes ... and the pool; complimentary passes to Splash Island Water Park just offshore; good value for families. **Cons:** accommodations are large but fairly basic; plan to eat elsewhere; time for some room renovations. [$] *Rooms from: US$230* ✉ *Reduit Beach Ave., Rodney Bay* ☎ *758/457–8006, 877/620–3200 in U.S.* 🌐 *www.baygardensbeachresort.com* 🛏 *75 rooms* 🍴 *No meals.*

$ **FAMILY**

$ [🏨] **Bay Gardens Hotel.** *Hotel.* Independent travelers and regional businesspeople swear by this cheerful, well-run boutique hotel in Rodney Bay Village. **Pros:** terrific value; Croton suites are best bet; close to nightspots and shopping. **Cons:** not beachfront, although there's a beach shuttle; heavy focus on business travelers; on the main road, so noise can be an issue for some rooms. [$] *Rooms from: US$155* ✉ *Castries–Gros Islet Hwy., Rodney Bay* ☎ *758/457–8006, 877/620–3200* 🌐 *www.baygardenshotel.com* 🛏 *71 rooms* 🍴 *No meals.*

$ [🏨] **blu St. Lucia.** *Resort.* Singles, couples, families, and business travelers all find this a good base in Rodney Bay Village—right across from Reduit Beach—and a reasonably priced one, too. **Pros:** close to the Rodney Bay restaurants and action; 100 yards from Reduit Beach; coffee and homemade cake bar in lobby. **Cons:** not beachfront, although pretty close; bathrooms have showers only—and could use upgrading; service and housekeeping need attention.

FAMILY

[$] *Rooms from: US$267* ✉ *Reduit Beach Ave., Rodney Bay* ☎ *758/456–9800, 877/502–2022 in U.S.* 🌐 *www.harlequin-blu.com* 🛏 *72 rooms* 🍴 *Breakfast.*

$ 🏨 **Coco Palm.** *Hotel.* This popular hotel in Rodney Bay Village
FAMILY overlooks an inviting pool and a separate cozy guesthouse, Kreole Village, at the edge of the property. **Pros:** love those swim-up rooms; nightly poolside entertainment; walk to all the Rodney Bay Village action. **Cons:** not directly on the beach; skip the all-inclusive package, as good restaurants are nearby; nightly music can be loud (until 10). [$] *Rooms from: US$169* ✉ *Rodney Bay* ☎ *758/456–2800, 877/655–2626 in U.S.* 🌐 *www.coco-resorts.com* 🛏 *103 rooms* 🍴 *Breakfast.*

$$$$ 🏨 **Royal St. Lucia Resort and Spa.** *Resort.* This luxurious
FAMILY all-suites resort on St. Lucia's best beach caters to every whim—for the whole family. **Pros:** great location on Reduit Beach; two suites equipped for disabled guests; convenient to Rodney Bay restaurants, clubs, and shops. **Cons:** don't expect all-day dining—get snacks at the nearby supermarket; rooms ready for a little TLC; food and extras are pricey. [$] *Rooms from: US$568* ✉ *Reduit Beach Ave., Rodney Bay* ☎ *758/452–9999* 🌐 *rexresorts.com/st-lucia/royal/* 🛏 *96 rooms* 🍴 *Breakfast.*

GREATER CASTRIES

$ 🏨 **Auberge Seraphine.** *Hotel.* This small inn is a good choice for those looking for convenient accommodations and who don't require a beachfront location, activities, or special amenities. **Pros:** close to Vigie airport, the marina and Castries; nice view of the harbor activity from rooms and the pool deck; simple but comfortable rooms at a can't-be-beat price. **Cons:** rooms are fairly basic and could use a face-lift; rather isolated in terms of walking anywhere; no on-site activities other than a swim in the pool. [$] *Rooms from: US$125* ✉ *Vielle Bay, Vigie* ☎ *758/453–2073* 🌐 *www.aubergeseraphine.com* 🛏 *24 rooms* 🍴 *No meals.*

$$$$ 🏨 **Rendezvous.** *Resort.* Romance is alive and well at this easy-going, all-inclusive, boutique resort (for couples only) that stretches along the dreamy white sand of Malabar Beach at the end of the George F. L. Charles Airport runway. **Pros:** very convenient to Castries and Vigie Airport; romance is always in the air—popular wedding venue; attentive, accommodating staff. **Cons:** no room TVs, if that matters; occasional flyover noise from nearby airport; limited dining choices—and it's all-inclusive. [$] *Rooms from: US$875* ✉ *Malabar Beach, Vigie* ☎ *758/457–7900, 800/544–2883 in U.S.* 🌐 *www.theromanticholiday.com* 🛏 *100 rooms* 🍴 *All-inclusive.*

$$$$ **Sandals Regency La Toc.** *Resort.* The second largest of the three Sandals on St. Lucia, this resort distinguishes itself with a 9-hole golf course (for guests only); like the others, though, this Sandals is all-inclusive and for couples only. **Pros:** lots to do—never a dull moment; complimentary airport shuttle; on-site 9-hole golf course. **Cons:** somewhat isolated location on a bluff west of Castries; expert golfers will prefer the St. Lucia Golf & Country Club; lots of hills and steps. [$] *Rooms from: US$609* ✉ *La Toc Rd., Castries* ☎ *758/452–3081, 888/726–3257* 🌐 *www.sandals.com* ⛳ *9-hole, 3,141-yard, resort-style course on the property* 🛏 *331 rooms* 🍴 *All-inclusive.*

MARIGOT BAY TO ANSE LA RAYE

$ **Inn on the Bay.** *B&B/Inn.* Renting just five rooms, Normand Viau and Louise Boucher—owners (since 1995) of this delightful inn high on the southern hillside overlooking the entrance to Marigot Bay—treat you as their personal guests (adults only). **Pros:** the view overlooking lovely Marigot Bay; spacious rooms and large modern bathrooms; personal (yet unobtrusive) attention. **Cons:** few, if any, amenities besides peace, quiet, and nature; no TV in guest rooms; no direct beach access. [$] *Rooms from: US$265* ✉ *Marigot Bay* ☎ *758/451–4260, 514/907–1027 in U.S.* 🌐 *www.saint-lucia.com* 🛏 *5 rooms* 🍴 *Breakfast.*

$ **Mango Beach Inn.** *B&B/Inn.* When the Marigot Bay ferry delivers you to the dock across the bay, a small gate opens to a stone staircase that leads through a jungle of trees and flowers to this delightful, tidy little B&B. **Pros:** spectacular views of Marigot Bay; beach, restaurants, and activities nearby; lovely hosts and personalized service. **Cons:** tiny rooms; showers only in the bathrooms; steps to the inn may be difficult for anyone with physical challenges. [$] *Rooms from: US$200* ✉ *North side of the bay, Marigot Bay* ☎ *758/458–3188* 🌐 *www.mangobeachmarigot.com* 🛏 *3 rooms* 🍴 *Breakfast.*

★ Fodor's Choice **Marigot Bay Resort & Marina by Capella.** *Resort.*
$$ Five miles (8 km) south of Castries, this ultrachic—yet
FAMILY laid-back—villa resort climbs the hillside overlooking what author James Michener called "the most beautiful bay in the Caribbean." Bedrooms are exquisitely decorated in a contemporary style with dark Balinese furniture, creamy upholstery accented with colorful cushions, a comfy bed with pillow-top mattress, and dark hardwood flooring. **Pros:** ground-level units good for those with difficulty nego-

DID YOU KNOW?

Many people consider Reduit Beach (pronounced red-wee) in Rodney Bay to be the best beach in St. Lucia.

tiating stairs; complimentary hourly treats at the pool; oversize villa accommodations. **Cons:** car recommended to explore beyond Marigot Bay; nearby beach is tiny, so head to Anse Cochon (complimentary transfers); while meals are good, a la carte dining is pricey. ⑤ *Rooms from: US$342* ⊠ *Marigot Bay* ⊹ *South side of the bay, overlooking the marina* ☎ *758/458–5300, 877/384–8037 in U.S.* ⊕ *www. capellahotels.com/saintlucia* ⟿ *124 rooms* ⓞ *No meals.*

$ ⵏ **Marigot Beach Club & Dive Resort.** *Resort.* Divers love this place, and everyone loves the location facing the little palm-studded beach at Marigot Bay. Some accommodations are right on the beachfront; others are on the hillside with a sweeping view of the bay. **Pros:** deeply discounted rates off-season; beautiful views of Marigot Bay from every room; good casual dining with live entertainment on Saturday nights. **Cons:** adjacent beach is tiny; hillside rooms require a trek; general maintenance issues are problematic. ⑤ *Rooms from: US$156* ⊠ *Marigot Bay* ☎ *758/451–4974* ⊕ *www.marigotbeachclub.com* ⟿ *36 rooms* ⓞ *No meals.*

★ Fodor'sChoice ⵏ **Ti Kaye Resort & Spa.** *Resort.* Rustic elegance
$$ is not an oxymoron at this upscale cottage community that spills down a hillside above fabulous Anse Cochon beach. **Pros:** great for a wedding, honeymoon, or getaway (adults only); excellent dining at Kai Manje; on-site dive shop. **Cons:** those 166 steps down to (and up from) the beach; room TV costs extra; location is far from anywhere—rent a car to get around. ⑤ *Rooms from: US$336* ⊠ *Anse Cochon, off the West Coast Rd., Anse La Raye* ⊹ *Halfway between Anse la Raye and Canaries* ☎ *758/456–8101, 888/300-7026 in the U.S.* ⊕ *www.tikaye.com* ⟿ *33 rooms* ⓞ *No meals.*

SOUFRIÈRE

$$$$ ⵏ **Anse Chastanet Resort.** *Resort.* Spectacular, individually designed rooms—some with fourth walls open to the stunning Pitons view—peek out of the thick rain forest that cascades down a steep hillside to the beach. **Pros:** great location for divers; the open-wall Piton views; attractive room furnishings and artwork. **Cons:** no pool; no in-room TVs or phones and air-conditioning only in beachfront rooms; steep hillside not conducive to strolling or to guests with walking or cardiac issues. ⑤ *Rooms from: US$600* ⊠ *1000 Anse Chastanet Rd., Soufrière* ☎ *758/459–7000, 800/223–1108 in U.S.* ⊕ *www.ansechastanet.com* ⟿ *49 rooms* ⓞ *No meals.*

★ Fodor'sChoice ⵏ **Boucan by Hotel Chocolat.** *Hotel.* Anyone who
$$$$ loves chocolate will love this themed boutique hotel just

CLOSE UP

Bananas

More than 10,000 St. Lucian banana farmers produced 134,000 tons of the familiar fruit in the early 1990s, most of which were exported to Europe. By 2005, when the Caribbean nations had lost their preferential treatment in the European market, fewer than 2,000 banana farmers were producing about 30,000 tons. Nevertheless, you'll still see bananas growing throughout St. Lucia, especially in the rural areas around Babonneau in the northeast and south of Castries near Marigot Bay. As you pass by the banana fields, you'll notice that the fruit is wrapped in blue plastic. That's to protect it from birds and insects—because there's no market for an imperfect banana.

south of Soufrière and within shouting distance of the Pitons. **Pros:** daily beach shuttle service; chocolate lover's dream; self-guided trail walks and cocoa tours throughout the estate. **Cons:** no air-conditioning, but naturally breezy; no TV, but a preloaded iPod and free Wi-Fi; no children 18 or under. [$] *Rooms from: US$525* ✉ *Rabot Estate, West Coast Rd., Soufrière* ✣ *2 miles (3 km) south of Soufrière* ☎ *758/724-6183, 800/757–7132 in the U.S.* 🌐 *www.thehotelchocolat.com* ⇨ *14 rooms* 🍴 *Breakfast.*

★ **Fodor'sChoice** 🏨 **Fond Doux Plantation & Resort.** *Resort.* Here at
$$ one of Soufrière's most active agricultural plantations, nine
FAMILY historic homes salvaged from all around the island have been rebuilt on the 135-acre estate and refurbished as guest accommodations. **Pros:** an exotic, eco-friendly experience; striking location on an 18th-century plantation; free beach shuttle. **Cons:** no room TVs; no air-conditioning; a car is advised, as local sights are a few miles away. [$] *Rooms from: US$300* ✉ *Fond Doux Estate, Soufrière* ✣ *4 miles (7 km) south of Soufrière* ☎ *758/459–7545* 🌐 *www.fonddouxestate.com* ⇨ *15 rooms* 🍴 *Breakfast.*

$ 🏨 **Hummingbird Beach Resort.** *B&B/Inn.* Unpretentious and welcoming, this delightful little inn on Soufrière Harbour has simply furnished rooms—a traditional motif emphasized by four-poster beds and African wood sculptures—in small seaside cabins. **Pros:** local island hospitality; small and quiet; good food. **Cons:** few amenities—but that's part of the charm; most rooms have no air-conditioning; beach out front is rather narrow. [$] *Rooms from: US$90* ✉ *Anse*

Chastanet Rd., Soufrière 758/459–7232 *www.istlucia.
co.uk* 10 rooms Breakfast.

★ Fodor'sChoice **Jade Mountain.** *Resort.* This premium-class,
$$$$ premium-priced, adults-only hotel is an architectural wonder perched on a picturesque mountainside overlooking the
Pitons and the Caribbean. **Pros:** amazing accommodations;
huge in-room pools; incredible Pitons view from every
"sanctuary." **Cons:** sky-high rates; no air-conditioning
(except in one "sky suite"); not a good choice for anyone
with disabilities. *Rooms from: US$1,480* *Anse Chasta-
net, Anse Chastanet Rd., Soufrière* 758/459–4000 *www.
jademountainstlucia.com* 28 rooms No meals.

$ **La Haut Resort.** *B&B/Inn.* It's all about the view—the
FAMILY Pitons, of course—and the appeal of staying in an intimate
and affordable family-run inn. **Pros:** lovely for weddings
and honeymoons but also for families; stunning Piton views;
complimentary fresh fruit daily. **Cons:** no air-conditioning
in some rooms; spotty Wi-Fi access; vehicle recommended.
Rooms from: US$200 *West Coast Rd., Soufrière* Just
north of Soufrière 758/459–7008, 866/773–4321 *in the
U.S.* *www.lahaut.com* 17 rooms No meals.

★ Fodor'sChoice **Ladera.** *B&B/Inn.* The elegantly rustic Ladera,
$$$$ perched 1,100 feet above the sea directly between the two
Pitons, is one of the most sophisticated small inns in the
Caribbean but, at the same time, takes a local, eco-friendly
approach to furnishings, food, and service. **Pros:** excellent
cuisine at Dasheene; hand-hewn furniture makes each room
unique; open fourth walls and private plunge pools provide breathtaking views. **Cons:** communal infinity pool is
small; steep drops make this the wrong choice for people
with disabilities; no air-conditioning (but breezy, so no real
need). *Rooms from: US$770* *Rabot Estate, Soufrière–
Vieux Fort Hwy., Soufrière* 3 miles (5 km) south of town
758/459–6600, 866/290–0978 in the U.S. *www.ladera.
com* 37 rooms No meals.

$$ **Stonefield Villa Resort.** *Resort.* The 18th-century plantation
house and cottage-style villas that dot this 26-acre fami-
ly-owned estate, a former lime and cocoa plantation that
spills down a tropical hillside, afford eye-popping views
of Petit Piton. **Pros:** very private, very quiet, very natural
setting; beautiful pool; great sunset views from villa decks.
Cons: adults only, no kids under 17; fitness facility could
use air-conditioning; no room TVs. *Rooms from: US$332*
West Coast Rd., Soufrière 1 mile (1½ km) south of
Soufrière 758/459–7037, 800/420–5731 in U.S. *www.
stonefieldresort.com* 16 villas Breakfast.

A private in-suite plunge pool at Ladera Resort

★ Fodor's Choice 🏨 **Sugar Beach, A Viceroy Resort.** *Resort.* Located in Val des Pitons, the steep valley between the Pitons and the most dramatic 192 acres in St. Lucia, magnificent private villas are tucked into the dense tropical foliage that covers the hillside and reaches down to the sea. **Pros:** exquisite accommodations, scenery, service, and amenities; huge infinity pool; complimentary Wi-Fi and use of iPad during stay. **Cons:** very expensive; fairly isolated, so a meal plan makes sense; rental car advised. [$] *Rooms from: US$867* ✉ *Val des Pitons, Soufrière* ✣ *2 miles (3 km) south of town* ☎ *800/235–4300 in U.S., 758/456–8000* 🌐 *www.viceroyhotelsandresorts.com/sugarbeach* 🛏 *78 rooms* 🍴 *Breakfast.*

$$$$

FAMILY

VIEUX FORT

$$$ 🏨 **Coconut Bay Beach Resort & Spa.** *Resort.* Coconut Bay is a sprawling (85 acres), family-friendly, seaside retreat minutes from Hewanorra International Airport. **Pros:** great for families or couples; excellent kitesurfing; five minutes from the airport. **Cons:** bathrooms have showers only; rough surf beyond the reef; disappointing restaurants, and this is an all-inclusive with nothing else nearby. [$] *Rooms from: US$426* ✉ *Off Micoud Hwy., Vieux Fort* ☎ *758/459–6000, 877/352–8898 in U.S.* 🌐 *www.cbayresort.com* 🛏 *250 rooms* 🍴 *All-inclusive.*

FAMILY

$$$$ 🏨 **Serenity at Coconut Bay.** *All-Inclusive.* This upscale yet casual, private yet social, adults-only enclave is tucked into a corner of the expansive oceanfront gardens sur-

rounding sister property, Coconut Bay Beach Resort. **Pros:** perfect choice for a romantic interlude, honeymoon, or anniversary; five minutes from Hewanorra International Airport; full access to all of Coconut Bay Beach Resort's restaurants/activities. **Cons:** remote location vis-à-vis island sights/outside activities; long walk or shuttle to the resort's beach; very expensive even with special offers. $ *Rooms from: US$1,000* ✉ *Eau Piquant, Vieux Fort* ✣ *Adjacent to Coconut Bay Beach Resort & Spa* ☎ *758/459–6068, 877/252–0304 in the U.S.* 🌐 *serenityatcoconutbay.com* 🛏 *36 rooms* 🍴 *All-inclusive.*

NIGHTLIFE AND PERFORMING ARTS

PERFORMING ARTS

St. Lucia Jazz. This popular music festival, held in May for more than 25 years, became part of Soleil, St. Lucia Summer Festival, in 2017. Caribbean and international jazz musicians participate in events throughout the island for four days, culminating on the last day in a major concert at Pigeon Island National Landmark. ✉ *Pigeon Island* 🌐 *www.stlucia.org/jazzfestival.*

NIGHTLIFE

Most resort hotels have entertainment—island music, calypso singers, and steel bands, as well as disco, karaoke, and talent shows—every night in high season and a couple of nights per week in the off-season. Otherwise, Rodney Bay is the best bet for nightlife. The restaurants and bars there attract a crowd nearly every night.

BEER GARDENS

Antillia Brewing Company. Antillia brews handcrafted wheat beers, stout, and specialty ales in its brewery at Odsan Industrial Park. You can take a tour of the brewery, but it's easier (and more fun) to enjoy a pint or two—or a flight—at the company's Antillia Beer Garden, adjacent to the cruise terminal at Pointe Seraphine. ✉ *Pointe Seraphine, Castries* ☎ *758/458–0844.*

CASINOS

Treasure Bay Casino. St. Lucia's first (and only, so far) casino has more than 200 slot machines, 22 gaming tables (poker, blackjack, roulette, and craps), and a sports bar with 28 screens. ✉ *Baywalk Mall, Reduit Beach Ave., Rodney*

Cocoa Tea

The homemade chocolate balls or sticks that vendors sell in the market are formed from locally grown and processed cocoa beans. St. Lucians use the chocolate to make cocoa tea—a beverage that actually originated in Soufrière but has since become a popular drink wherever cocoa is grown throughout the Caribbean. The chocolate is grated and steeped in boiling water, along with a bay leaf and cinnamon stick.

Sugar is added, along with a little milk or cream and some vanilla. Some people add nutmeg, as well, and some cornstarch to make it thicker and more filling. Cocoa tea began as a breakfast treat but is now enjoyed with a slice of bread as a snack or even as a dessert. Be sure to bring some chocolate sticks or balls home with you. One sniff and you won't be able to resist buying a few.

Bay ✢ Just off Castries–Gros Islet Hwy. ☎ 758/459–2901 ⊕ *www.treasurebaystlucia.com.*

STREET PARTIES

FAMILY **Anse la Raye Seafood Friday.** For a taste of St. Lucian village life, head for this street festival, held every Friday night beginning at 6:30. The main street in this tiny fishing village—about halfway between Castries and Soufrière—is closed to vehicles, and residents prepare what they know best: fish cakes, grilled or stewed fish, hot bakes (biscuits), roasted corn, boiled crayfish, and lobster (grilled before your eyes). Prices range from a few cents for a fish cake or bake to $10 or $15 for a whole lobster. Walk around, eat, chat with locals, and listen to live music until the wee hours. ⊠ *Main St., Anse La Raye ✢ Off West Coast Rd.*

★ Fodor'sChoice **Gros Islet Jump-Up.** The island's largest street party is a Friday-night ritual. Huge speakers set up on the street blast Caribbean music all night long. Sometimes there are live bands. When you take a break from dancing, you can buy barbecue fish or chicken, rotis (turnovers filled with meat and/or vegetables), beer, and soda from villagers who set up grills along the roadside. It's the ultimate carnival fete. ⊠ *Dauphin St., Gros Islet ✢ Off Castries–Gros Islet Hwy.*

SHOPPING

The island's best-known products are wood carvings, straw mats, clay pottery, and clothing and household articles made from batik and silk-screened fabrics that are designed and produced in island workshops. You can also take home straw hats and baskets and locally grown cocoa, coffee, spices, sauces, and flavorings.

AREAS AND MALLS

Baywalk Mall, at Rodney Bay, is a large complex of boutiques, restaurants, banks, a beauty salon, jewelry and souvenir stores, and the island's first (and only, so far) casino.

Along the harbor in Castries, rambling structures with bright-orange roofs house markets that are open from 6 am to 5 pm Monday through Saturday. Saturday morning is the busiest and most colorful time to shop. For more than a century, farmers' wives have gathered at the **Castries Market** to sell produce—which, alas, you can't import to the United States. But you can bring back spices (such as cocoa, turmeric, cloves, bay leaves, ginger, peppercorns, cinnamon sticks, nutmeg, and mace), as well as bottled hot-pepper sauces—all of which cost a fraction of what you'd pay back home. The **Craft Market**, adjacent to the produce market, has aisles and aisles of baskets and other handmade straw work, rustic brooms made from palm fronds, wood carvings, leather work, clay pottery, and souvenirs—all at affordable prices. The **Vendors' Arcade**, across the street from the Craft Market, is a maze of stalls and booths where you can find handicrafts among the T-shirts and costume jewelry.

Gablewoods Mall, on the Gros Islet Highway in Choc Bay, a couple of miles north of downtown Castries, has shops that sell groceries, wines and spirits, jewelry, fashions, crafts, books and overseas newspapers, music, souvenirs, household goods, and snacks.

Along with the boutiques, restaurants, and other businesses that sell services and supplies, a large supermarket is the focal point of each **J.Q.'s Shopping Mall**; one is at Rodney Bay, and another is at Vieux Fort.

Marigot Marina Village in Marigot Bay has shops and services for boaters and landlubbers alike, including a bank, grocery store, business center, art gallery, assortment of boutiques, and a café.

Duty-free shopping areas are at **Pointe Seraphine,** an attractive Spanish-motif complex on Castries Harbour with a dozen shops, and **La Place Carenage,** an inviting three-story complex on the opposite side of the harbor. You can also find duty-free items at Baywalk Mall, in a few small shops at the arcade at the Royal St. Lucia hotel in Rodney Bay, and, of course, in the departure lounge at Hewanorra International Airport. You must present your passport and airline ticket to purchase items at the duty-free price.

Vieux Fort Plaza, near Hewanorra International Airport in Vieux Fort, is the main shopping center in the southern part of St. Lucia. You'll find a bank, supermarket, bookstore, and clothing stores.

SPECIALTY ITEMS

BOOKS AND MAGAZINES

Sunshine Bookshop. In addition to newspapers and magazines, this shop carries novels and titles of regional interest, including books by the St. Lucian Nobel laureate Derek Walcott and other Caribbean authors. ⊠ *Gablewoods Mall, Castries-Gros Islet Hwy., Choc* ☎ *758/458-0633.*

CLOTHES AND TEXTILES

The Bagshaws of St. Lucia. Using Sydney Bagshaw's original designs, this shop in La Toc sells clothing and table linens in colorful tropical patterns. The fabrics are silk-screened by hand in an adjacent workroom. You can also find Bagshaw boutiques at Pointe Seraphine and La Place Carenage, as well as a selection of items in gift shops at Hewanorra Airport. Visit the workshop to see how the designs are turned into colorful silk-screened fabrics, which are then fashioned into clothing and household articles. ⊠ *La Toc Rd., Castries* ☎ *758/451–9249* ⊙ *Closed weekends.*

The Batik Studio. The superb batik sarongs, scarves, and wall panels sold here are designed and created on-site by the shop's proprietor, Joan Alexander Stowe. ⊠ *Hummingbird Beach Resort, Anse Chastanet Rd., Soufrière* ☎ *758/459–7985.*

Caribelle Batik. Craftspeople demonstrate the art of batik and silk-screen printing while seamstresses use the batik fabric to make clothing and wall hangings, which you can buy in the shop. The studio is in an old Victorian mansion, high atop Morne Fortuné and a 10-minute drive south of Castries. There's a terrace where you can have a cool drink

and a garden full of tropical orchids and lilies. Caribelle Batik creations are also available in gift shops throughout St. Lucia. ⊠ *Howelton House, Old Victoria Rd., Morne Fortuné* ☎ *758/452–3785.*

Sea Island Cotton Shop. High-quality T-shirts, Caribelle Batik clothing and other resort wear, and colorful souvenirs are sold at attractive prices. ⊠ *Baywalk Mall, Reduit Beach Ave., Rodney Bay* ⊹ *Off Castries–Gros Islet Hwy.* ☎ *758/458–4220.*

HANDICRAFTS

Choiseul Arts & Crafts Centre. A project of the Ministry of Education to encourage skill development and local crafts, this center carries handmade furniture, clay pots, wood carvings, and straw items. Many of St. Lucia's artisans come from the area—on the southwest coast, halfway between Soufrière and Vieux Fort. It's closed Sunday. ⊠ *South Coast Hwy., La Fargue* ⊹ *5 miles (8 km) south of Choiseul Village* ☎ *758/454–3226.*

Eudovic's Art Studio. This workshop, studio, and art gallery has wall plaques, masks, and abstract figures hand-carved by sculptor Vincent Joseph Eudovic from local mahogany, red cedar, and eucalyptus wood. ⊠ *West Coast Rd., Goodlands, The Morne, Morne Fortuné* ☎ *758/452–2747* ⊕ *www.eudovicart.com.*

★ **Fodor'sChoice Zaka.** You may get a chance to talk with artist and craftsman Simon Gajhadhar, who fashions totems and masks from driftwood, branches, and other environmentally friendly wood sources—taking advantage of the natural nibs and knots that distinguish each piece. Once the "face" is carved, it is painted in vivid colors to highlight the exaggerated features and provide expression. ⊠ *Jalousie Rd., Malgretoute* ⊹ *Off Soufrière–Vieux Fort Rd.* ☎ *758/457–1504* ⊕ *www.zaka-art.com.*

SPORTS AND ACTIVITIES

BIKING

Although the terrain is pretty rugged, a tour operator has put together a fascinating bicycle tour that appeals to novice riders as well as those who enjoy a good workout. The bike tour costs $60 per person.

Bike St. Lucia. Small groups of bikers are accompanied on jungle biking tours along 8 miles (13 km) of groomed trails—with naturally occurring challenges (such as rocks and roots) and a few mud holes to challenge purists—that meander through the remnants of the 18th-century Anse Mamin Plantation, part of the 600-acre Anse Chastanet Estate in Soufrière. Stops are made to explore the French colonial ruins, study the beautiful tropical plants and fruit trees, have a picnic lunch, and take a dip in a river swimming hole or at the beach. There's an orientation loop for learning or brushing up on off-road riding skills, and there are beginner, intermediate, and advanced tracks. If you're staying in the north, you can arrange a tour that includes transportation to the Soufrière area and lunch at Anse Chastanet Resort. ⊠ *Anse Mamin Plantation, Anse Chastanet Adventure Center, Soufrière* ☎ *758/459–7755* ⊕ *www.bikestlucia.com.*

BOATING AND SAILING

Rodney Bay and Marigot Bay are centers for bareboat and crewed yacht charters. Their marinas offer safe anchorage, shower facilities, restaurants, groceries, and maintenance for yachts sailing the waters of the eastern Caribbean. Charter prices range from $1,900 to $10,000 or more per week, depending on the season and the type and size of vessel, plus about $400 more per day if you want a skipper and cook. Some boat charter companies do not operate in August and September—the height of the hurricane season.

Bateau Mygo. Choose a monohull or catamaran for your half-, full-, or two-day cruise along the west coast, or charter by the week and explore neighboring islands. ⊠ *Chateau Mygo, Marigot Bay ✛ Adjacent to the Marina Village* ☎ *758/721–7007* ⊕ *www.sailsaintlucia.com.*

Destination St. Lucia Ltd. (*DSL*). For its bareboat yacht charters, DSL's vessels include two catamarans (42 and 44 feet) and several monohulls ranging in length from 32 to 46 feet. ⊠ *Rodney Bay Marina, Rodney Bay* ☎ *758/452–8531* ⊕ *www.dsl-yachting.com.*

Moorings Yacht Charters. Bareboat and crewed catamarans and monohulls are available for charter. You can also plan a one-way sail through the Grenadines, either picking up or dropping off at the company's facility in Grenada. ⊠ *Rodney Bay Marina, Rodney Bay* ☎ *758/451–4357, 888/952–8420 in U.S.* ⊕ *www.moorings.com.*

DIVING AND SNORKELING

★ Fodor'sChoice You'll find on-site dive shops at several resorts, including BodyHoliday St. Lucia, Sandals Grande, Royal St. Lucia, and Rendezvous in the north; Marigot Bay Beach Resort and Ti Kaye farther south; and Anse Chastanet and Sugar Beach, A Viceroy Resort, in Soufrière. Nearly all dive operators, regardless of their own location, provide transportation from Rodney Bay, Castries, Marigot Bay, or Soufrière. Depending on the season and the particular trip, prices range from about $40 for a one-tank shore dive or $90 for a one-tank boat dive to $225 to $320 for a 6-dive package over three days and $350 to $500 for a 10-dive package over five days—plus a Marine Reserve permit fee of $5 to $15, depending on the number of days. Dive shops provide instruction for all levels (beginner, intermediate, and advanced). For beginners, a resort course (pool training), followed by one open-water dive, runs from about $100 to $130, depending on the number of days and dives included. Snorkelers are generally welcome on dive trips and usually pay $50 to $75. All prices generally include taxi/boat transfers, lunch, and equipment.

Anse Chastanet, near the Pitons on the southwest coast, is the best beach-entry dive site. The underwater reef drops from 20 feet to nearly 140 feet in a stunning coral wall.

A 165-foot freighter, *Lesleen M,* was deliberately sunk in 60 feet of water near **Anse Cochon** to create an artificial reef; divers can explore the ship in its entirety and view huge gorgonians, black coral trees, gigantic barrel sponges, lace corals, schooling fish, angelfish, sea horses, spotted eels, stingrays, nurse sharks, and sea turtles.

Anse La Raye, midway up the west coast, is one of St. Lucia's finest wall and drift dives and a great place for snorkeling.

At the **Pinnacles,** four coral-encrusted stone piers rise to within 10 feet of the surface.

Superman's Flight is a dramatic drift dive along the steep walls beneath the Pitons. At the base of **Petit Piton** a spectacular wall drops to 200 feet, where you can view an impressive collection of huge barrel sponges and black coral trees; strong currents ensure good visibility.

A large brain coral off the coast of St. Lucia

DIVE OPERATORS

Dive Fair Helen. In operation since 1992 and owned by a St. Lucian environmentalist, this PADI center offers half- and full-day excursions on two custom-built dive boats to wreck, wall, and marine reserve areas, as well as night dives and instruction. ✉ *Marina Village, Marigot Bay* ☎ *758/451–7716* ⊕ *www.divefairhelen.com.*

★ Fodor'sChoice **Dive Saint Lucia.** Operating out of a LEED Platinum-certified building at Rodney Bay Marina, St. Lucia's state-of-the-art dive center has a purpose-built training pool, fully equipped classrooms for adult and junior instruction, fully equipped compressors, a PADI 5-star Instructor Development Center (IDC), equipment rental and storage, guided dives, and two specialized dive boats (46-foot *Newton*)—each with a 30-diver capacity. Handicap-accessible facilities include a motorized lift chair. Dive trips include lunch, drinks, and hotel transfers (north of Castries). ✉ *Rodney Bay Marina, Castries-Gros Islet Hwy., Rodney Bay* ☎ *758/451–3483* ⊕ *www.divesaintlucia.com.*

Island Divers. At the edge of the National Marine Park, with two reefs and an offshore wreck accessible from shore, this dive shop at Ti Kaye Resort & Spa offers shore dives, boat dives, PADI certification, equipment rental, and an extensive list of specialty courses. Hotel transfers available. ✉ *Ti Kaye Resort & Spa, off West Coast Rd., Anse La Raye*

⊹ *Between Anse la Raye and Canaries* ☎ *758/456–8110* ⊕ *www.tikaye.com/diving.*

Scuba St. Lucia. Daily (and nightly) beach and boat dives and resort and certification courses are available from this PADI 5-star facility located on Anse Chastanet Beach, and so is underwater photography and snorkeling equipment. Transportation from the north of the island can be arranged. ⊠ *Anse Chastanet Resort, Anse Chastanet Rd., Soufrière* ☎ *758/459–7755, 800/223–1108 in U.S.* ⊕ *www.scubastlucia.com.*

FISHING

Among the deep-sea creatures you can find in St. Lucia's waters are dolphin (the fish, also called dorado or mahi-mahi), barracuda, mackerel, wahoo, kingfish, sailfish, and white and blue marlin. Sportfishing is generally done on a catch-and-release basis, but the captain may permit you to take a fish back to your hotel to be prepared for your dinner. Neither spearfishing nor collecting live fish in coastal waters is permitted. Half- and full-day deep-sea fishing excursions can be arranged at Vigie Marina. A half day of fishing runs about $85 to $90 per person to join a scheduled party; a private charter will cost $400 to $1,500 for up to six or eight people, depending on the size of the boat and the length of time. Beginners are welcome.

Captain Mike's. Named for Captain Mike Hackshaw and run by his family, Bruce and Andrew, this operation has a fleet of Bertram powerboats (31 to 46 feet) that accommodate up to eight passengers for half- or full-day sportfishing charters; tackle and cold drinks are supplied. Customized sightseeing or whale/dolphin-watching trips ($50 per person) can also be arranged for four to six people. ⊠ *Vigie Marina, Vigie* ☎ *758/452–7044* ⊕ *www.captmikes.com.*

Hackshaw's Boat Charters. In business since 1953, this company runs charters on *Blue Boy,* a 31-foot Bertram; *Limited Edition,* a 47-foot custom-built Buddy Davis; and *Party Hack,* a 64-foot double-deck power catamaran also used for snorkeling, whale-watching, and party cruises. ⊠ *Vigie Marina, Seraphine Rd., Vigie* ☎ *758/453–0553* ⊕ *www.hackshaws.com.*

GOLF

St. Lucia has only one 18-hole championship course: **St. Lucia Golf Resort & Country Club**, which is in Cap Estate. **Sandals Regency La Toc Golf Resort and Spa** has a 9-hole course for its guests.

St. Lucia Golf Resort & Country Club. St. Lucia's only public course is at the island's northern tip and features broad views of both the Atlantic and the Caribbean, as well as many spots adorned with orchids and bromeliads. Wind and the demanding layout present challenges. The Cap Grill serves breakfast, lunch, and light meals until 7 pm; the Sports Bar is a convivial meeting place all day long. You can arrange lessons at the pro shop and perfect your swing at the 350-yard driving range. Fees include carts, which are required; club and shoe rentals are available. Reservations are essential. Complimentary transportation from your hotel (north of Castries) is available for parties of three or more. ✉ *Cap Estate* ☎ *758/450–8523* ⊕ *www.stluciagolf.com* 🖅 *$120 for 18 holes, $90 for 9 holes* ⚲ *18 holes, 6829 yards, par 71.*

GUIDED TOURS

Taxi drivers are well informed and can give you a full tour and often an excellent one, thanks to government-sponsored training programs. Full-day island tours cost $140 for up to four people, depending on the route and whether entrance fees and lunch are included; half-day tours, $100. If you plan your own day, expect to pay the driver $40 per hour plus tip.

Island Routes. This Sandals partner offers dozens of adventure tours, including guided, drive-it-yourself dune buggy safaris of Soufrière's natural sites and attractions (six hours, $175). A longer version includes a cruise down the west coast from Rodney Bay. Drivers must be at least 23, have a valid driver's license, and be able to operate a manual transmission. Other tours include hiking, biking, and zip-lining adventures; a guided historical tour; and many, many more. ✉ *Castries* ☎ *877/768–8370 in U.S., 758/455–2000* ⊕ *www.islandroutes.com.*

Jungle Tours. This company specializes in rain-forest hiking tours in small groups and for all ability levels. You're required only to bring hiking shoes or sneakers and have a willingness to get wet and have fun. The cost is $95 per person and includes lunch, fees, and transportation via an open Land Rover truck. ✉ *Cas en Bas* ☎ *758/715–3438* ⊕ *www.jungletoursstlucia.com.*

St. Lucia Helicopters. How about a bird's-eye view of the island? A 10-minute North Island tour ($108 per person) leaves from the hangar in Castries, continues up the west coast to Pigeon Island, then flies along the rugged Atlantic coastline before returning inland over Castries. The 20-minute South Island tour ($176 per person) starts at Pointe Seraphine and follows the western coastline, circling beautiful Marigot Bay, Soufrière, and the majestic Pitons before returning inland over the volcanic hot springs and tropical rain forest. A complete island tour combines the two and lasts 30 minutes ($220 per person). All tours require a minimum of four passengers. ⊠ *George F. L. Charles Airport, Island Flyers Hangar, Vigie* ☏ *758/453–6950* ⊕ *www. stluciahelicopters.com.*

St. Lucia National Trust. Among the trust's fascinating ecotours are a hike through a mangrove forest, a boat trip and trek to Maria Islands Nature Reserve, a native fishing tour on a traditional pirogue, handicraft production, horseback riding, or sea moss harvesting. ⊠ *Pigeon Island National Landmark, Pigeon Island, Pigeon Island* ☏ *758/454–5014 Maria Islands Interpretation Centre, Vieux Fort, 758/453– 7656* ⊕ *www.slunatrust.org.*

HIKING

The island is laced with trails, but you shouldn't attempt the more challenging ones—especially those that are deep in the rain forest—on your own.

St. Lucia Forestry Department. Trails under this department's jurisdiction include the Barre de L'Isle Trail (just off the highway, halfway between Castries and Dennery), the Forestiere Trail (20 minutes east of Castries), the Des Cartiers Rain Forest Trail (west of Micoud), the Edmund Rain Forest Trail and Enbas Saut Waterfalls (east of Soufrière), the Millet Bird Sanctuary Trail (east of Marigot Bay), and the Union Nature Trail (north of Castries). Most are two-hour hikes on 2-mile (3-km) loop trails; the bird-watching tour lasts four hours. The Forestry Department charges $25 for access to the hiking trails ($10 for nature trails), and provides guides ($2–$30, depending on the hike) who explain the plants and trees that you'll encounter and keep you on the right track. Seasoned hikers climb the Pitons, the two volcanic cones rising 2,461 feet and 2,619 feet from the ocean floor just south of Soufrière. Hiking is recommended only on Gros Piton, which offers a steep but safe trail to the top. The first half of the hike is moderately difficult; reaching the summit is challenging and should be attempted only by those who are physically fit. The view from the top is spectacular. Tourists are also permitted to hike Petit Piton, but the second half of the hike requires a good deal of rock climbing, and you'll need to provide your own safety equipment. Hiking either Piton requires permission from the Forestry Department and a knowledgeable guide. ⊠ *Gabriel Charles Forestry Complex, Union, Castries* ☎ *758/468–5645, 758/489–0136 for Piton permission.*

Tet Paul Nature Trail. Climb the natural "stairway" for a stunning 360° view of St. Lucia including the entire southern coast (and neighboring St. Vincent in the distance), Mt. Gimie in the island's center, the Pitons on the nearby west coast, and as far north as Martinique on a clear day. This St. Lucia Heritage Site, just 10 minutes from downtown Soufrière, is an easy-to-moderate, 45-minute hike, with stops along the way to observe the scenery and a picnic area. ⊠ *West Coast Rd., Soufrière ✛ 3 miles (5 km) south of town behind Fond Doux Plantation* ☎ *758/723–2930* ⊕ *www.tetpaulnaturetrail.com.*

HORSEBACK RIDING

Creole horses, a breed native to South America and popular on St. Lucia, are fairly small, fast, sturdy, and even-tempered animals suitable for beginners. Established stables can accommodate all skill levels. They offer countryside trail rides, beach rides with picnic lunches, plantation tours, carriage rides, and lengthy treks. Prices run about $40 for a one-hour guided ride, $65 for two hours, and $75 for a three-hour beach ride with swimming (with the horses). Local people sometimes appear on beaches with their steeds and offer 30-minute rides for $15 to $20; ride at your own risk.

FAMILY **Atlantic Shores Riding Stables.** Two-hour trail rides roam along the beach, three-hour treks roam the countryside, and private rides can be arranged. Beginners and children are welcome. ⊠ *Micoud Hwy., Savannes Bay, Vieux Fort* ☎ *758/285–1090* ⊕ *www.atlanticridingstables.com.*

FAMILY **HoofPrint Horse Riding Ranch.** First-timers and "old hands" alike enjoy riding through the Roseau Valley's endless banana plantations, especially when the ride includes a swim (with or without your horse) at remote Roseau Beach. An extended excursion includes a barbecue on the beach.

The Des Cartiers Rain Forest Trail is a 1-mile (2-km) loop.

✉ *Morne D'Or, Roseau Valley, Roseau* ☎ *758/520–5102* ⊕ *www.hoofprintranch.com.*

Morne Coubaril Estate. Horseback riding is just one of the many activities at Morne Coubaril Estate, a historic plantation in Soufrière. Tour the estate atop your steed, noting the views of Soufrière Bay and Petit Piton, or take the longer tour through the rain forest to the volcano and sulphur springs. ✉ *West Coast Rd., Malgretoute* ✛ *2 miles (3 km) south of town* ☎ *758/459–7340* ⊕ *www.mornecoubarilestate.com.*

SEA EXCURSIONS

A day sail or sea cruise from Rodney Bay or Vigie Cove to Soufrière and the Pitons is a wonderful way to see St. Lucia and a great way to get to the island's distinctive natural sites. Prices for a full-day sailing excursion to Soufrière run about $110 per person and include a land tour to the Diamond Botanical Gardens, lunch, a stop for swimming and snorkeling, and a visit to pretty Marigot Bay. Add zip-lining, if you wish! Half-day cruises to the Pitons, three-hour whale-watching tours, and two-hour sunset cruises along the northwest coast will cost $50 to per person.

FAMILY **Captain Mike's Whale/Dolphin Watching Tours.** With 20 species of whales and dolphins living in Caribbean waters, your chances of sighting some are very good on these three-hour trips ($50 per person) aboard *Free Willie*, a

60-foot Defender. ⊠ *Vigie Marina, Ganthers Bay, Castries* ☎ *758/452–7044* ⊕ *www.captmikes.com.*

★ Fodor'sChoice **Endless Summer Cruises.** Endless Summer Cruises
FAMILY has three party catamarans (46 to 62 feet long) and runs day trips along the coast to Soufrière—tours, entrance fees, lunch, and drinks included—for $110 per person. The trips operate on Tuesday and Friday; get to the dock by 7:45 am! ⊠ *Reduit Beach Ave., Rodney Bay* ☎ *758/450–8651* ⊕ *www.stluciaboattours.com.*

Mystic Man Tours. Glass-bottom boat, sailing, catamaran, deep-sea fishing, snorkeling, and/or whale- and dolphin-watching tours are all great family excursions; there's also a sunset cruise. Most trips depart from Soufrière. ⊠ *Maurice Mason St., Soufrière* ✛ *On the bay front* ☎ *758/459–7783, 800/401–9804* ⊕ *www.mysticmantours.com.*

FAMILY **Sea Spray Cruises.** Sail down the west coast from Rodney Bay to Soufrière on *Mango Tango* (a 52-foot catamaran), *Tango Too* (an 80-foot catamaran), *Jus Tango* (a 65-foot catamaran)—or the tall ship *Black Magic*, which is all decked out as a pirate ship. The all-day Tout Bagay (a little bit of everything) tour includes a visit to the sulphur springs, drive-in volcano, and Morne Coubaril Estate. The view of the Pitons from the water is majestic. You'll have lunch and drinks on board, plenty of music, and an opportunity to swim at a remote beach. Tout Bagay operates Monday, Wednesday, and Saturday. Sea Spray operates several other boat tours, including a sunset cruise, on other days. ⊠ *Rodney Bay Marina, Rodney Bay* ☎ *758/458–0123, 321/220–9423 in U.S.* ⊕ *www.seaspraycruises.com.*

WINDSURFING AND KITEBOARDING

Windsurfers and kiteboarders congregate at Anse de Sables Beach in Vieux Fort, at the southeastern tip of St. Lucia, and at Cotton Bay, at the island's northeastern tip, to take advantage of the blue-water and high-wind conditions that the Atlantic Ocean provides.

Aquaholics. There's no better place to kitesurf—or learn to kitesurf—than on a beautiful, crescent-shaped bay at the northeastern tip of St. Lucia, where the Atlantic Ocean meets the Caribbean Sea, and the trade winds are consistent from November to June. ⊠ *Cas-En-Bas Beach, Cotton Bay, Cap Estate* ☎ *758/726–0600* ⊕ *www.aquaholicsstlucia.com.*

TRAVEL SMART BARBADOS AND ST. LUCIA

GETTING HERE AND AROUND

Barbados and St. Lucia are two popular resort destinations in the eastern Caribbean's southern arc. St. Lucia is situated between Martinique to the north and St. Vincent to the south. Barbados is about 100 miles (160 km) east of St. Lucia. The two islands are about 20 or 30 minutes apart by air.

▌AIR TRAVEL

BARBADOS

You can fly nonstop to Barbados from Miami (American) and Boston, Fort Lauderdale, and New York–JFK (JetBlue).

Caribbean Airlines offers connecting service from Fort Lauderdale, Miami, Orlando, and New York–JFK via Port of Spain, Trinidad, but this adds at least two hours to your flight time even in the best of circumstances and may not be the best option for most Americans. Barbados is also well connected to other Caribbean islands via LIAT. Grenadines Air Alliance (Mustique Airways and SVG Air) connects Barbados with St. Vincent and with Bequia, Canouan, Mustique, and Union Island in the Grenadines. Many passengers use Barbados as a transit hub, often spending the night each way. Not all airlines flying into Barbados have local numbers. If your airline doesn't have a local contact number on the island, you may have to pay for the call.

Airline Contacts American Airlines. ☎ 246/428–4170, 800/744–0006 in Barbados, 800/433–7300 in U.S. ⊕ www.aa.com. **Caribbean Airlines.** ☎ 246/528–1950, 800/744–2225 in the Caribbean ⊕ www.caribbean-airlines.com. **Grenadine Air Alliance.** ☎ 246/228–5544 ⊕ www.grenadine-air.com. **JetBlue.** ☎ 246/418–4174, 800/538–2583 in U.S. ⊕ www.jetblue.com. **LIAT.** ☎ 246/428–0986, 888/844–5428 in the Caribbean, 866/549–5428 in U.S. ⊕ www.liat.com.

AIRPORTS AND TRANSFERS

Grantley Adams International Airport (BGI) is a stunning, modern facility located in Christ Church Parish, on the south coast. The airport is about 15 minutes from hotels situated along the south or east coast, 45 minutes from the west coast, and about 30 minutes from Bridgetown. If your hotel does not offer airport transfers, you can take a taxi or a shared van service to your resort.

Airports Contacts Grantley Adams International Airport (*BGI*). ☎ 246/418–4242 ⊕ www.gaia.bb.

ST. LUCIA

American Airlines flies nonstop from Charlotte and Miami to Hewanorra (UVF) in Vieux Fort, with connecting service from New York and other major cities. Delta flies nonstop from Atlanta to UVF. JetBlue flies nonstop to UVF from Boston and New York (JFK). United flies nonstop to

UVF from New York (Newark). LIAT flies to George F. L. Charles Airport (SLU) in Castries from several neighboring islands.

Airline Contacts American Airlines. ☏ 800/744-0006 in Barbados, 800/433-7300 in U.S. ⊕ www.aa.com. Delta. ☏ 800/221-1212 in St. Lucia, 800/241-4141 in U.S. ⊕ www.delta. com. JetBlue. ☏ 877/766-9614 in St. Lucia, 800/538-2583 in U.S. ⊕ www. jetblue.com. LIAT. ☏ 758/452-2348, 888/844-5428 in the Caribbean, 866/549-5428 in U.S. ⊕ www.liat. com. United. ☏ 800/864-8331 in St. Lucia and the U.S. ⊕ www.united.com.

AIRPORTS AND TRANSFERS

St. Lucia has two airports. Hewanorra International Airport (UVF), which accommodates large jet aircraft, is at the southeastern tip of the island in Vieux Fort. George F. L. Charles Airport (SLU), also referred to as Vigie Airport, is at Vigie Point in Castries in the northwestern part of the island and accommodates only small prop aircraft due to its location and runway limitations.

Some large resorts—particularly the all-inclusive ones—and package tour operators provide roundtrip airport transfers. That's a significant amenity if you're landing at Hewanorra, as the one-way taxi fare is expensive: about $80 to $100 for four passengers for the 90-minute ride to Castries and the north; about $75–$80 for the 45-minute ride to Soufrière. Taxis are always available at the airports.

If you land at George F. L. Charles Airport, it's a short drive to resorts in the north and about 20 minutes

to Marigot Bay but more than an hour on a winding road to Soufrière.

Some people opt for a helicopter transfer between Hewanorra and Castries, a quick 12-minute ride with a beautiful view at a one-way cost of $165 per passenger. Helicopters operate in daylight hours only and carry up to six passengers; luggage usually follows by ground transportation.

Airport Contacts George F. L. Charles Airport (SLU). ☏ 758/457-6149 ⊕ www.georgeflcharlesairport. com. Hewanorra International Airport (UVF). ☏ 758/457-6160 ⊕ www.hewanorrainternationalair-port.com. St. Lucia Helicopters. ☏ 758/453-6950 ⊕ www.stluciaheli-copters.com.

▌BOAT AND FERRY TRAVEL

BARBADOS

No ferries provide interisland service to or from Barbados at this writing.

ST. LUCIA

Visitors combining a visit to St. Lucia with a visit to Martinique, Dominica, or Guadeloupe may opt for the L'Express des Iles fast ferry, a modern, high-speed catamaran that calls in Castries four days a week. The trip between St. Lucia and Fort de France, Martinique, takes 1½ hours; Roseau, Dominica, 3½ hours; and Point à Pitre, Guadeloupe, 5½ hours.

Water taxis are available to shuttle passengers between Soufrière and Marigot Bay or Castries. When cruise ships are in port in Castries, a water taxi shuttles back and forth between Pointe Seraphine on the north side of the harbor and La Place Carenage on the south side of the harbor for $2 per person each way.

Ferry Contacts Feel Good Water Taxi & Tours. ⊠ *Bay front, Soufrière* ☎ *758/721–2174* ⊕ *www.feelgood-watertaxiandtours.com.* **Israel King Water Taxi & Tours.** ⊠ *Rodney Bay Marina, Rodney Bay* ☎ *758/717–3301* ⊕ *israelkingwatertaxi.com.* **L'Express des Iles.** ⊠ *Castries Ferry Terminal* ☎ *758/456–5022* ⊕ *www.express-des-iles.com.* **Solomon Water Taxi & Tours.** ☎ *758/717–5643* ⊕ *www.solomon-saintlucia.com.*

▌BUS TRAVEL

BARBADOS

Bus service is efficient and inexpensive. Public buses are blue with a yellow stripe; yellow buses with a blue stripe are privately owned and operated; and private "Zed-R" vans (so called for their ZR license plate designation) are white with a maroon stripe and also privately owned and operated. All buses travel frequently along Highway 1 (between Bridgetown and Speightstown) and Highway 7 (along the south coast), as well as inland routes. The fare is Bds$2 for any one destination; exact change in either local or U.S. currency ($1) is appreciated. Buses run about every 20 minutes. Small signs on roadside poles that say "To City" or "Out of City," meaning the direction relative to Bridgetown, mark the bus stops. Flag down the bus with your hand, even if you're standing at the stop. Bridgetown terminals are at Fairchild Street for buses to the south and east and at Lower Green for buses to Speightstown via the west coast.

ST. LUCIA

Privately owned and operated minivans constitute St. Lucia's bus system, an inexpensive and efficient means of transportation used primarily by local people. Minivan routes cover the entire island and run from early morning until approximately 10 pm. You may find this method of getting around most useful for short distances—between Castries and the Rodney Bay area, for example; longer hauls can be uncomfortable. The fare between Castries and Gablewoods Mall is EC$1.25; Castries and Rodney Bay, EC$2; Castries and Gros Islet, EC$2.25; Castries and Vieux Fort (a trip that takes more than two hours), EC$10; Castries and Soufrière (a bone-crushing journey that takes even longer), EC$10. Minivans follow designated routes (signs are displayed on the front window) and have green number plates beginning with the letter *M*; ask at your hotel for the appropriate route number for your destination. Wait at a marked bus stop or hail a passing minivan from the roadside. In Castries, minivans depart from the corner of Micoud and Bridge streets, behind the markets.

In addition to the driver, each minivan usually has a conductor, a young man whose job it is to collect fares, open and close the door, and generally take charge of the passenger area. If you're sure of where you're going, simply knock twice on the metal window frame to signal that you want to get off at the next stop. Otherwise, just let the conductor or driver know where you're going, and he'll stop at the appropriate place.

CAR TRAVEL

BARBADOS

Barbados has good roads, but traffic can be heavy on the highways, particularly around Bridgetown. Be sure to keep a map handy, as the road system in the countryside can be very confusing—although the friendly Bajans are always happy to help you find your way. Drive on the left, British-style. When someone flashes headlights at you at an intersection, it means "after you." Be especially careful negotiating roundabouts (traffic circles). The speed limit is 30 mph (50 kph) in the country, 20 mph (30 kph) in town. Bridgetown actually has rush hours: 7 to 9 am and 4 to 6 pm. Park only in approved parking areas; downtown parking costs Bds75¢ to Bds$1 per hour.

CAR RENTALS

Most car-rental agencies require renters to be between 21 and either 70 or 75 years of age and have a valid driver's license and major credit card. Dozens of agencies rent cars, jeeps, or minimokes (small, open-sided vehicles). Rates range from about $50 per day for a minimoke to $65 or more per day for a four-wheel-drive vehicle and $85 or more for a luxury car (or $225 to $400 or more per week) in high season. Most firms also offer discounted three-day rates, and many require at least a two-day rental in high season.

A local driver's permit, which costs $5 (valid for two months), is obtained through the rental agency. The rental generally includes insurance, pickup and delivery service, maps, 24-hour emergency service, and unlimited mileage.

Car-Rental Contacts Coconut Car Rentals. ⊠ *Dayrell's Rd., Rockley* ☎ *246/437–0297* ⊕ *www.coconut-cars.com.* **Courtesy Rent-A-Car.** ⊠ *Grantley Adams International Airport* ☎ *246/431–4133* ⊕ *www.courtesyrentacar.com.* **Drive-a-Matic Car Rental.** ⊠ *CWTS Complex, Lower Estate, Warrens* ☎ *246/434–8440, 800/581–8773* ⊕ *www.carhire.tv.*

ST. LUCIA

Roads in St. Lucia are winding and mountainous, except north of Castries, making driving a challenge for timid or apprehensive drivers and exhausting for everyone else. Between Castries and Rodney Bay, traffic jams are not uncommon, particularly during rush hours. You drive on the left, British-style. Seat belts are required, and speed limits (32 mph/51 kmh in urban areas) are enforced, especially in and around Castries.

CAR RENTALS

To rent a car you must be at least 25 years old and provide a valid driver's license and a credit card. If you don't have an international driver's license, you must buy a temporary St. Lucia driving permit at the car-rental office for $20 (EC$54), which is valid for three months. Car-rental rates are usually quoted in U.S. dollars and start at $50 per day or $300 per week.

Car-Rental Contacts Avis.
✉ *Hewanorra International Airport, Vieux Fort* ☎ *758/454–6325, 758/452–2046 George F. L. Charles Airport* ⊕ *www.avis.com.* **Cool Breeze Jeep/Car Rental.** ☎ *758/459–7729* ⊕ *www.coolbreezecarrental.com.* **Cost-Less Rent-a-Car.** ✉ *Harmony Suites, Rodney Bay* ☎ *758/450–3416, 908/818–8506 in the U.S.* ⊕ *www.costless-rentacar.com.* **Courtesy Car Rentals.** ☎ *758/452–8140, 315/519–7684 in the U.S.* ⊕ *courtesycarrentals.com.* **Hertz.** ✉ *Hewanorra International Airport, Vieux Fort* ☎ *758/454–9636* ⊕ *www.hertz.com.*

▌CRUISE SHIP TRAVEL

BARBADOS

Up to eight ships at a time can dock at Bridgetown's Deep Water Harbour, on the northwest side of Carlisle Bay. The cruise-ship terminal has duty-free shops, handicraft vendors, a post office, a telephone station, a tourist information desk, and a taxi stand. To get to downtown Bridgetown, follow the shoreline to The Careenage. It's a 15-minute walk or a $4 taxi ride.

Taxis await ships at the pier. Drivers accept U.S. dollars and appreciate a 10% tip. Taxis are unmetered and operate at an hourly rate of $35 to $40 per carload (up to three passengers) plus a 10% tip. Most drivers will cheerfully narrate an island tour.

ST. LUCIA

Most cruise ships dock at the capital city of Castries, on the island's northwest coast, at either of two docking areas: Pointe Seraphine, a port of entry and duty-free shopping complex, or Port Castries (Place Carenage), a commercial wharf across the harbor. Ferry service connects the two piers. Smaller vessels occasionally call at Soufrière, on the island's southwest coast. Ships calling at Soufrière must anchor offshore and bring passengers ashore via tender. Tourist information booths are at Pointe Seraphine and at Place Carenage. Downtown Castries is within walking distance of the pier, and the produce market and adjacent crafts and vendors' markets are the main attractions. Soufrière is a sleepy West Indian town, but it's worth a short walk around the central square to view the French Colonial architecture; many of the island's spectacular natural sights are in or near Soufrière.

Taxis are available at the docks in Castries. Although they are unmetered, the standard fares are posted at the entrance to Pointe Seraphine. Taxi drivers are well informed and can give you a full tour—often an excellent one—thanks to government-sponsored training programs. From the Castries area, full-day island tours for up to four people cost $40 to $75 per person, depending on the route and whether entrance fees and lunch are included; full-day sightseeing trips to Soufrière cost around $140 for up to four people. If you plan your own day, expect to pay the driver at least $40 per hour plus a 10% tip. Whatever your destination, negotiate the price with the driver before you depart—and be sure that you both understand whether the rate is quoted in EC or U.S. dollars.

TAXI TRAVEL

BARBADOS

Taxis operate 24 hours a day. They aren't metered but rates are fixed by the government. Taxis carry up to three passengers, and the fare may be shared. Sample one-way fares from Bridgetown are $20 to Holetown, $25 to Speightstown, $20 to St. Lawrence Gap, and $30 to Bathsheba. Always ask the driver to quote the price before you get in, and be sure that you both understand whether it's quoted in Bds or U.S. dollars. Drivers can also be hired for an hourly rate of about $35–$40 for up to three people.

ST. LUCIA

Taxis are unmetered, although fares are fairly standard. Sample fares for up to four passengers are Castries to Rodney Bay, $25; Rodney Bay to Cap Estate, $12; Castries to Cap Estate, $25; Castries to Marigot Bay, $30; Castries to Anse La Raye, $40; Castries to Soufrière, $80–$100; and Castries to Vieux Fort, $80. Always ask the driver to quote the price before you get in, and be sure that you both understand whether it's quoted in EC or U.S. dollars. Drivers are generally careful, knowledgeable, and courteous. Drivers can also be hired for an hourly rate of about $40 per hour for up to three people.

ESSENTIALS

ACCOMMODATIONS

BARBADOS

Most visitors stay either in luxurious beachfront enclaves on the fashionable west coast—in St. James and St. Peter parishes, north of Bridgetown—or on the action-packed south coast with easy access to small, independent restaurants, bars, and nightclubs in and around St. Lawrence Gap. A few inns on the remote southeast and east coasts offer spectacular ocean views and tranquillity, but those on the east coast don't have swimming beaches nearby.

In keeping with the smoke-free policy enforced throughout Barbados, smoking is restricted to open outdoor areas such as the beach. It is not permitted in hotels (neither rooms nor public areas) or in restaurants.

Prices in Barbados may be twice as high in season (December 15–April 15) as during the quieter months, although special promotions and vacation packages are often available throughout the year. Most hotels include no meals in their rates; some include breakfast, many offer a meal plan, others require you to purchase the meal plan in the high season, and a few offer all-inclusive packages.

Resorts run the gamut—from unpretentious to knock-your-socks-off—in terms of size, intimacy, amenities, and price. Many are well suited to families. A few small, cozy inns are in the east and southeast regions of the island. Families and long-term visitors may also choose from a wide variety of condos (everything from busy time-share resorts to more sedate vacation complexes). Villas and villa complexes can be luxurious, simple, or something in between. And apartments are available for vacation rentals in buildings or complexes with as few as three or four units or as many as 30 to 40 units—or even more.

ST. LUCIA

Nearly all resorts and small inns are tucked into lush surroundings on secluded coves, unspoiled beaches, or forested hillsides in three locations along the calm Caribbean (western) coast: in the greater Castries area between Marigot Bay, a few miles south of the city, and Labrelotte Bay in the north; in and around Rodney Bay and north to Cap Estate; and in and around Soufrière on the southwest coast near the Pitons. There's only one pair of resorts in Vieux Fort, near Hewanorra. The advantage of being in the north is that you have access to a wider range of restaurants and nightlife; in the south you may be limited to hotel dining rooms—albeit some of the best—and a few other dining options in and around Soufrière.

Most people—particularly honeymooners— choose to stay in one of St. Lucia's many grand beach resorts, most of which are upscale and fairly pricey. Several are all-inclusive, including three Sandals resorts, two Sunswept resorts (BodyHoliday Saint Lucia and Rendezvous), St. James's Club Morgan Bay, East Winds Inn, Coconut Bay Beach Resort & Spa and Serenity at Coconut Bay, and Royalton St. Lucia Resort & Spa. Others may offer an all-inclusive option. If you are looking for something more intimate and perhaps less expensive, a locally owned inn or small hotel is a good option; it may or may not be directly on the beach. Luxury villa communities that operate like hotels are a good alternative for families. Several are in the north in or near Cap Estate.

▐ COMMUNICATIONS

INTERNET

BARBADOS

Barbados began an initiative in November 2011 to provide free Wi-Fi access hotspots throughout the island. Most hotels and resorts provide free Wi-Fi and one or more Internet terminals for guest use.

ST. LUCIA

Most hotels and resorts in St. Lucia offer Wi-Fi and Internet terminals, often at no charge to guests. Wi-Fi hotspots are located in several bars and restaurants and at Marina Village at Marigot Bay.

PHONES

BARBADOS

The area code for Barbados is 246. Local calls from private phones are free; some hotels charge a small fee. For directory assistance, dial 411. Prepaid phone cards, which can be used throughout Barbados and other Caribbean islands, are sold at shops, attractions, transportation centers, and other convenient outlets.

Most U.S. cell phones will work in Barbados, though roaming charges can be expensive. Buying a local SIM card for your own unlocked phone may be a less expensive alternative if you're planning an extended stay or expect to make a lot of local calls. Top-off services are available at several locations throughout the island.

Contacts Digicel. ✉ *Williams Tower, Williams Industries Complex, 2nd fl.* ☎ *246/467-7000* ⊕ *www. digicelbarbados.com.* **FLOW.** ✉ *Windsor Lodge, Government Hill, Bridgetown* ☎ *800/804-2994* ⊕ *discoverflow.co/barbados.*

ST. LUCIA

The area code for St. Lucia is 758. Some hotels charge a small fee (usually about EC$1) for local calls. Many retail outlets sell phone cards to use for either local or international calls from any telephone in St. Lucia.

Most U.S. cell phones will work in St. Lucia, though roaming charges can be expensive. Buying a local SIM card for your own unlocked phone may be a less expensive alternative if you're planning an extended stay or expect to make a lot of local calls. Top-off services are available at several locations throughout the island.

Contacts Digicel. ☎ 758/728–3400 ⊕ www.digicelstlucia.com. FLOW. ☎ 800/804–2994 ⊕ discoverflow.co/stlucia.

▌ EATING OUT

BARBADOS

Barbados prides itself on its many wonderful restaurants, many of which can compete with top-notch dining experiences anywhere in the world. On the west coast, excellent restaurants are concentrated in St. James Parish along Highway 1, particularly in and around Holetown. Restaurants on 1st Street and 2nd Street in Holetown, for example, offer a variety of cuisines and prices that range from inexpensive to plan ahead! On the south coast, St. Lawrence Gap is the mother lode of Barbados activity, with a number of dining choices lining both sides of the street (or "gap").

ST. LUCIA

The bulk of St. Lucia's restaurants—both casual and classy—are concentrated in Rodney Bay Village, although you'll find excellent dining in the Vigie area of Castries and in pretty Marigot Bay. In Soufrière, the best dining is in small hotels and inns, which always welcome nonguests for both lunch and dinner.

MEALS AND MEAL TIMES

Resort breakfasts are frequently lavish buffets that offer tropical fruits and fruit juices, cereal, fresh rolls and pastries, hot dishes (such as codfish, corned-beef hash, and potatoes), and prepared-to-order eggs, pancakes, and French toast.

Lunch could be a sit-down meal at a beachfront café or a picnic at a secluded cove. But dinner is the highlight, often combining the expertise of internationally trained chefs with local know-how and ingredients.

Of course, you'll want to take advantage of the weekend evening street parties in both Barbados (Oistins) and St. Lucia (Gros Islet and Anse La Raye), where you can buy and try local food barbecued right before your eyes and accompanied by music and conviviality— a wonderful experience for the whole family.

Expect breakfast to be served from 7:30 am to 10 am; lunch from noon to 2 pm or so; and dinner from 7 pm to about 10 pm. Some restaurants have specific mealtimes; others serve continuously all day long.

Unless otherwise noted, the restaurants listed in this guide are open daily for lunch and dinner.

PAYING

Major credit cards (American Express, MasterCard, and Visa) are accepted in most Caribbean restaurants. We note in reviews when credit cards are not accepted. Price charts for restaurants are included in each island's Planner.

RESERVATIONS AND DRESS

It's always a good idea to make a reservation if you can. In some small or pricey restaurants, it's required. For very popular restaurants, book as far ahead as you can (often 30 days) and reconfirm as soon as you arrive. Large parties should always call ahead to check the reservations policy. Very few, if any, restaurants require men to wear a jacket or a jacket and tie. Shorts and T-shirts at dinner and beach attire or bare feet anytime are universally frowned upon in restaurants throughout the Caribbean.

WINES, BEERS, AND SPIRITS

Mount Gay, Cockspur, and Malibu are the most popular local rum brands in Barbados, "the birthplace of rum"; Bounty and Chairman's Reserve, in St. Lucia. Some distilleries are open to the public for tours, tastings, and duty-free shopping.

Both islands also have their own breweries—Banks in Barbados and Piton in St. Lucia. Both are light, refreshing beers—perfect for hot summer afternoons at the beach.

Those who prefer a nonalcoholic drink will love the fresh fruit punch, a lime squash, or a bottle of Ting—a carbonated grapefruit drink from Jamaica that's often available in Barbados and St. Lucia. For something unusual and purely local, try mauby, a strong, dark, rather bitter beverage made from the bark of a tree; ginger beer; sea moss, a reputed aphrodisiac made from a combination of seaweed, sweetener, milk, and spices; and coconut water, the liquid inside a green "jelly coconut" often sold on the street by a "jellyman" who, for $1 or so, will nip off the top of the coconut with his sharp machete so you can drink the coconut water inside.

▌ ELECTRICITY

BARBADOS

The electric current throughout Barbados is 110 volts, 50 cycles (U.S. standard).

ST. LUCIA

The electric current on St. Lucia is 220 volts, 50 cycles, with a square, three-pin plug (U.K. standard). Dual-voltage computer and phone chargers or other appliances require a plug adapter, which you can often borrow from the hotel. For North American appliances that are not dual-voltage, you'll also need a transformer to convert the voltage. More and more hotels and resorts have added 110-volt outlets for general use but sometimes only for electric razors. Many hotels and resorts also provide iPod docking stations.

▌ HEALTH

Tap water in both Barbados and St. Lucia is generally safe to drink, although bottled water is always available if you prefer.

The major health risk in the Caribbean is sunburn or sunstroke. Protect your skin, wear a hat, and use sunscreen

Swimming on the windward (Atlantic Ocean) side of either island is unsafe—even for experienced swimmers. Tricky currents, powerful waves, strong undertows, and rocky bottoms can be extremely dangerous—and lifeguards are nonexistent.

Watch out for black, spiny sea urchins that live on the rocky sea floor in both shallow and deep waters. Stepping on one is guaranteed to be painful for quite some time, as the urchin releases its spikes into the offending body. To remove a spike, simply pull it out and apply an antiseptic. To remove an embedded spike, first apply some warm oil (preferably olive oil) to soften and dilate the skin and then remove the spike with a sterile needle.

Dengue fever is one of the common viral diseases transmitted to humans by the bite of mosquitoes, and the Caribbean—including the islands of Barbados and St. Lucia—is one of the regions of the world that is considered a "risk area" by the CDC. No vaccine is available to prevent dengue fever, but travelers are advised to protect against mosquito bites by using insect repellent and protective clothing when in swampy or forested areas.

The worst insect problem may well be the tiny "no-see-ums" (sand flies) that appear after a rain, near swampy ground, and at the beach around sunset. If you're hiking through the rain forest in St. Lucia, however, wear long pants and a shirt with long sleeves—just in case.

On the west coast of Barbados in particular, beware of the manchineel tree, which grows near the beach, looks like a beautiful shade tree, and has fruit that looks like little green apples—but are poisonous—and bark and leaves that can burn the skin if you touch them; even the droplets of water that might reach your skin can burn you if you seek protection under the tree during a shower.

HIV is a problem throughout the Caribbean, and visitors to the region should take appropriate precautions to prevent contracting the virus.

Do not fly within 24 hours of scuba diving.

MEDICAL INSURANCE AND ASSISTANCE

Consider buying trip insurance with medical-only coverage. Neither Medicare nor some private insurers cover medical expenses outside the United States. Medical-only policies typically reimburse you for medical care (excluding care related to pre-existing conditions) and hospitalization abroad, as well as medical evacuation.

Another option is to sign up with a medical-evacuation assistance company. A membership in one of these companies provides doctor referrals, emergency evacuation or repatriation, 24-hour hotlines for medical consultation, and other assistance. International SOS Assistance Emergency and AirMed International provide evacuation services and medical referrals. MedjetAssist offers medical evacuation.

Medical Assistance Companies AirMed International. ☎ 800/356–2161, 205/443–4840 ⊕ www.airmed.com. **International SOS.** ☎ 215/942–8226 ⊕ www.internationalsos.com.

Medical-Only Insurers International Medical Group. ☎ 800/628–4664, 317/655–4500 ⊕ www.imglobal.com.

▌ HOURS OF OPERATION

BARBADOS

Banks are open Monday through Thursday 8–3, Friday 8–5 (some branches in supermarkets are open Saturday morning 9–noon). At the airport, the Barbados National Bank is open from 8 am until the last plane leaves or arrives, seven days a week (including holidays). Most stores in Bridgetown are open weekdays from 8:30 or 9 to 4:30 or 5, Saturday from 8:30 to 1 or 2. Stores in shopping malls outside Bridgetown may stay open later. Some supermarkets are open daily 8–6 or later.

ST. LUCIA

Banks are open Monday through Thursday 8–2, Friday 8–5; a few branches in Rodney Bay are also open Saturday 9–noon. Most stores are open weekdays 8:30–4:30, Saturday 8–12:30; stores in shopping malls are open Monday through Saturday 9–7; Pointe Seraphine and Place Carenage shops are open weekdays 9–5, Saturday 9–2. Some hotel gift shops may be open on Sunday.

▌ MAIL

BARBADOS

An airmail letter from Barbados to the United States or Canada costs Bds$2.80 for a half ounce, Bds$3.80 for one ounce; an airmail postcard costs Bds$2.80. When sending mail to Barbados, be sure to include the parish name in the address. The General Post Office in Cheapside, Bridgetown, is open weekdays 7:30–5; branches in each parish are open weekdays 8–3; the Sherbourne Conference Center branch is open weekdays 8:15–4:30 during conferences.

ST. LUCIA

The General Post Office is on Bridge Street in Castries and is open weekdays 8:30–4:30; all towns and villages have branches. Post offices are open weekdays 8:30–4:30. Postage for airmail letters to the United States, Canada, and the United Kingdom is EC$1.50 per ½ ounce; postcards are EC80¢.

▌ MONEY

BARBADOS

The Barbados dollar is pegged to the U.S. dollar at the rate of Bds$1.98 to $1. U.S. paper currency (not coins) is widely accepted, although you are likely to get your change in local currency. Major credit cards and traveler's checks are also widely accepted. ATMs are available 24 hours a day throughout the island and dispense local currency. All prices quoted in this book are in U.S. dollars unless indicated as Bds$.

ST. LUCIA

The official currency in St. Lucia is the Eastern Caribbean dollar (EC$) at the exchange rate of EC$2.67 to $1. U.S. paper currency (not coins) is accepted nearly everywhere— although you are likely to get your change in local currency. Major credit cards and traveler's checks are also widely accepted. ATMs dispense local currency. All prices quoted in this book are in U.S. dollars unless indicated as EC$.

▌ PASSPORTS AND VISAS

To enter either Barbados or St. Lucia, all visitors must produce a valid passport and have a return or ongoing ticket.

▌ SAFETY

Although crime isn't a significant problem in either Barbados or St. Lucia, take the same precautions that you would at home—lock your door, secure your valuables, and don't carry too much money or flaunt expensive jewelry on the street or beach.

▌ TAXES AND SERVICE CHARGES

BARBADOS

A 7.75% government tax is added to all hotel bills. A 7.5% V.A.T. is imposed on restaurant meals, admissions to attractions, and merchandise sales (other than those that are duty-free). Prices are often tax-inclusive; if not, the V.A.T. will be added to your bill. A 10% service charge is often added to hotel bills and restaurant checks.

ST. LUCIA

A V.A.T. (value-added tax) of 10% is added to all hotel and restaurant bills. Most restaurants and some hotels also add a service charge of 10% in lieu of tipping.

▌ TIME

Barbados and St. Lucia are both in the Atlantic Standard Time zone, which is one hour later than Eastern Standard Time and four hours earlier than GMT. As is true throughout the Caribbean, neither island observes daylight saving time, so Atlantic Standard Time is the same time as Eastern Daylight Time during that period (March through October).

▌ TIPPING

BARBADOS

If no service charge is added to your bill, tip waiters 10% to 15% and maids $2 per room per day. Tip bellhops and airport porters $1 per bag. Taxi drivers and tour guides appreciate a 10% tip.

ST. LUCIA

If no service charge is added to your bill, tip waiters 10%–15%. Tip porters and bellhops $1 per bag and hotel maids $2 per night, although many of the all-inclusive resorts have a no-tipping policy. Taxi drivers and tour guides also appreciate a 10% tip.

▌ TRIP INSURANCE

Comprehensive trip insurance policies typically cover trip cancellation and interruption, letting you cancel or cut your trip short due to illness. Such policies might also cover evacuation and medical care. (For trips abroad you should have at least medical-only coverage. See Medical Insurance and Assistance under Health.) Some policies also cover you for trip delays due to bad weather or mechanical problems, as well as for lost or delayed luggage.

Another type of coverage to consider is financial default—that is, when your trip is disrupted because a tour operator, airline, or cruise line goes out of business. Generally, you must buy this when you book your trip or shortly thereafter; also, it's available only if your operator doesn't appear on a list of excluded companies.

Always read the fine print of your policy to make sure that you're covered for the risks that most concern you. Compare several policies to be sure you're getting the best price and range of coverage available.

Insurance Comparison Site SquareMouth. ☎ 800/240-0369 ⊕ www.squaremouth.com.

Comprehensive Travel Insurance Allianz Travel Insurance. ☎ 866/884-3556 ⊕ www.allianztravelinsurance.com. **CSA Travel Protection.** ☎ 877/243-4135, 240/330-1529 call collect ⊕ www.csatravelprotection.com. **Travel Insured International.** ☎ 800/243-3174 ⊕ www.travelinsured.com.

▌ VISITOR INFORMATION

BARBADOS
Barbados Tourism Authority Barbados Tourism Marketing, Inc. ✉ Warrens Office Complex, 1st fl., West Wing, Warrens ☎ 246/535-3700, 800/221-9831 in U.S. ⊕ www.visitbarbados.org ✉ Grantley Adams International Airport, Arrivals Lounge ☎ 246/428-5570 ✉ Cruise-ship terminal, Deep Water Harbour, Bridgetown ☎ 246/426-1718.

ST. LUCIA
St. Lucia Tourist Board St. Lucia Tourist Board. ☎ 212/867-2950, 800/456-3984 in U.S. ⊕ www.stlucianow.com.

▌ WEDDINGS

BARBADOS
Barbados makes weddings relatively simple for nonresidents, as there are no minimum residency requirements. Most resorts—and many smaller hotels and inns—offer wedding packages and have on-site wedding coordinators to help you secure a marriage license and plan a personalized ceremony and reception. Alternatively, you may wish to have your wedding at a scenic historic site or botanical garden, on the grounds of a restored great house, or at sunset on a quiet beach.

To obtain a marriage license, which often can be completed in less than a half hour, both partners must apply in person and present valid passports to the Ministry of Home Affairs (located in the General Post Office building, Cheapside, Bridgetown, 246/621–0227, and open 8:15–4:30 weekdays). If either party was previously married and widowed, you need to present a certified copy of the marriage certificate and a death certificate for the deceased spouse; if either party is divorced, you need a certified copy of the official divorce decree. The license fee is $100 plus $13 for a stamp. For a civil marriage, a separate fee of $125 is payable to the Court; for an alternative venue, $175. All fees must be paid in cash. A notarized parental consent is required if either party is under the age of 18. Finally, you must make arrangements for an authorized marriage officer (a magistrate or minister) to perform the ceremony.

ST. LUCIA

St. Lucia may be the most popular island in all of the Caribbean for weddings and honeymoons. Nearly all of St. Lucia's resort hotels and most of the small inns offer attractive wedding-honeymoon packages, along with coordinators to handle the legalities and help plan a memorable event. Several resorts, including the three Sandals resorts on St. Lucia, offer complimentary weddings to couples booking a minimum-stay honeymoon. The most striking setting, though, may be between the Pitons at Ladera or Sugar Beach, A Viceroy Resort—or at one of the nearby resorts that also offer spectacular Piton views, such as Jade Mountain, Anse Chastanet, Ladera, or several smaller properties. Alternatively, botanical gardens, historical sites, waterfalls, or breezy boat trips are all romantic settings for the special event.

There is no waiting period to get married in St. Lucia. You can marry on the same day that you arrive if you apply for a "special" marriage license, pay a $200 special marriage license fee, and have all the necessary documents mailed in advance. You must present valid passports, birth certificates, a divorce decree if either party is divorced, an appropriate death certificate if either party is widowed, and a notarized parental consent if either party is under the age of 18. Most couples opt for the standard marriage license, which costs $125 and requires three days of residence on the island prior to the wedding ceremony. In either case, special or standard, you can expect additional registrar and certificate fees amounting to about $60.

INDEX

A

Accommodations, *176–177*

Accra Beach, *54*

Accra Beach Hotel and Spa 🏨, *74–75*

Air travel, *170–171*

Airports, *18, 171*

Andromeda Botanic Gardens, *43*

Animal Flower Cave, *43–44*

Anse Chastanet, *128, 161*

Anse Chastanet Resort 🏨, *150*

Anse Cochon, *129, 161*

Anse des Pitons, *132*

Anse La Raye, *161*

Anse La Raye "Seafood Friday", *155*

Antillia Brewing Company, *154*

Apartment rentals, *71*

Apsara ✕, *139–140*

Aquariums
Barbados, 28, 48–49

Arlington House Museum, *28, 48*

Art, shopping for, *94–95*

Atlantic Rally for Cruisers, *108*

Atlantis, The ✕, *61, 64–65*

Atlantis Hotel, The 🏨, *20, 80*

ATMs, *17, 181*

Auberge Seraphine 🏨, *147*

B

Bamboo and Cocoa Pod at Fond Doux Estate ✕, *140*

Bananas, *151*

Barbados, *8, 29–104*
beaches, 14, 16–17, 21, 52–56, 59

Bridgetown, 16, 35–38, 60–61, 89, 92–93
Central Barbados, 50–52
East Coast, 42–46, 58, 64–65, 80–81
exploring, 35–38, 44–46, 48–53
festivals and seasonal events, 23
history, 30
Holetown, 65–67, 81, 84–86, 91
hotels, 17, 20, 32–33, 69–71, 73–77, 80–81, 84–87
nightlife, 87, 89–91
prices, 17, 33
restaurants, 20, 59–61, 63–68, 178
St. Lawrence Gap, 61, 71, 73–74, 90
shopping, 22, 91–95
South Coast, 38, 40–42, 54–56, 63–64, 74–77, 80, 91, 93–94
sports, 16, 21, 22, 95–104
timing the visit, 23, 32
transportation, 16, 31, 32, 170–175
West Coast, 48–50, 58–59, 67–68, 86–87, 94–95

Barbados Beach Club 🏨, *75*

Barbados Concorde Experience, *38*

Barbados Military Cemetery, *41–42*

Barbados Museum & Historical Society, *38, 40*

Barbados Sea Turtle Project, *73*

Barbados Wildlife Reserve, *28, 43*

Barclays Park, *44*

Barre de l'Isle Forest Reserve, *126*

Barrow, Errol, *41*

Bars
Barbados, 89–91
St. Lucia, 154

Barson's Cave, *28*

Bathsheba Beach, *58*

Baxter's Road, *89–90*

Bay Gardens Beach Resort & Spa 🏨, *28, 146*

Bay Gardens Hotel 🏨, *146*

Baywalk Mall, *156*

Beaches
Barbados, 16, 21, 52–56, 58–59
St. Lucia, 18, 22, 128–129, 132–133

Big Chef Steakhouse ✕, *137*

Biking
St. Lucia, 159–160

blu St. Lucia 🏨, *146–147*

Blue Olive Restaurant & Wine Bar ✕, *137*

Boat travel, *171–172*

Boating & sailing
Barbados, 21, 103–104
St. Lucia, 18, 22, 28, 160

BodyHoliday Saint Lucia 🏨, *143*

Bottom Bay Beach, *54–55*

Boucan ✕, *21, 140*

Boucan by Hotel Chocolat 🏨, *150–151*

Bougainvillea Beach Resort 🏨, *28, 71*

Breweries, *154*

Bridgetown, Barbados, *16, 35–38, 60–61, 89, 92–93*

Brighton Beach, *59*

Broad Street, *92*

Brown Sugar ✕, *61, 63, 136*

Bubba's Sports Bar, *91*

Bus travel, *172–173*

Business hours, *181*

Buzz Seafood & Grill ✕, 137

C

Café Luna ✕, 63
Café Sol ✕, 61
Calabash Cove Resort & Spa ☆, 143–144
Cap Grill ✕, 134
Cap Maison ☆, 144
Car rentals
Barbados, 32, 38, 173
St. Lucia, 108, 173–174
Car travel, 173–174
Careenage, The, 35–36
Carnival, 107
Casinos, 154–155
Castries, St. Lucia, 112–115, 116–119, 136–137, 147–148
Castries Market, 115, 156
Cathedral of the Immaculate Conception, 115
Cattlewash Beach, 58
Caves, 28, 43–44, 51
Cell phones, 177–178
Cemeteries, 41–42
Chalky Mount, 44
Champers ✕, 61, 63
Chateau Mygo House of Seafood ✕, 21, 138
Chefette ✕, 64
Cherry Tree Hill, 46
Children, attractions
Barbados, 28, 37, 38, 40–41, 42, 43–44, 45, 48–49, 50–51, 54, 56, 59, 91, 102, 103, 104
St. Lucia, 28, 113, 114, 115, 122, 124–125, 126, 132–133, 155, 166–167, 168
Children, dining
Barbados, 60–61, 63, 64–65, 68
St. Lucia, 28, 134, 138, 139, 140
Children, lodging
Barbados, 71, 73, 74, 75–76, 77, 80, 84, 85, 86, 87

St. Lucia, 28, 143, 144, 145, 146–147, 148, 150, 151, 152, 153
Choiseul Arts & Crafts Centre, 159
Churches
Barbados, 37, 45–46
St. Lucia, 115
Cliff at Cap, The ✕, 21, 61, 65, 135
Cliff Beach Club, The ✕, 65
Climate, 23
Club, Barbados Resort & Spa, The ☆, 81
Coal Pot, The ✕, 21, 135
Cobblers Cove Hotel ☆, 20, 86–87
Coco Palm ☆, 147
Cocoa Tea, 155
Coconut Bay Beach Resort & Spa ☆, 28, 153
Coconut Court Beach Hotel ☆, 75
Codrington Theological College, 44
Colleges and universities, 44
Colonnade Mall, 92
Colony Club Hotel ☆, 81
Communications, 177–178
Condominium rentals, 141–142
Coral Reef Club ☆, 81, 84
Country Club at Sandy Lane, 99–100
Courtyard Bridgetown by Marriott ☆, 75
Craft Market, 156
Crane, The ☆, 20, 75–76
Crane Beach, 55–56
Credit cards, 11, 176, 181
Cruise ship travel, 174–175

Crystal Cove Hotel ☆, 26, 84
Cuban Monument, 49

D

Dance clubs
Barbados, 89, 90
Daphne's ✕, 21, 61, 65–66
Dasheene Restaurant and Bar ✕, 21, 140
Derek Walcott Square, 115
Diamond Falls Botanical Gardens and Mineral Baths, 121–122, 123
Dining, 11, 178. ⇨ see also Restaurants
Discovery Bay ☆, 84
Distilleries, 22, 119
Dive Saint Lucia (dive center), 162
Divi Southwinds Beach Resort ☆, 28
Diving and snorkeling
Barbados, 21, 95–98
St. Lucia, 18, 22, 161–163
Doolittle's ✕, 139
Dover Beach, 53–54
Drift Ocean Terrace Lounge, 91
Duke's Night Lounge, 91
Duty-free shopping, 92, 93

E

Earthworks Pottery (shop), 94
East Winds Inn ☆, 144
Edmund Forest Reserve, 122
Electricity, 17, 19, 170
Emancipation Statue, 42
Endless Summer Cruises, 168
Eudovic's Art Studio, 159

F

Fairmont Royal Pavilion
🏨, 84
Farley Hill National
Park, 44
Ferry travel, 113,
171–172
Festivals
Barbados, 23
St. Lucia, 23, 108, 154,
155
Fish Pot, The ✕, 21, 61,
67–68
Fisherman's Pub ✕, 68
Fishing
Barbados, 16, 22, 98
St. Lucia, 18, 22, 107,
163
Flower Forest, 50
Folkestone Marine Park
& Visitor Centre, 28,
48–49
Fond Doux Estate, 122,
124
Fond Doux Plantation &
Resort 🏨, 151
Fort Charlotte, 118

G

Gablewoods Mall, 156
Gardens
Barbados, 37, 43, 50,
51–52
St. Lucia, 121–122,
126–127
George Washington
House, 28, 40
Golf
Barbados, 99–100
St. Lucia, 164
Government House,
119–120
Groceries, 92
Gros Islet Jump-Up, 155
Guides
Barbados, 100
St. Lucia, 164–165
Gun Hill Signal Station,
50–51

H

Handicrafts, shopping
for, 159
Harbour Lights (club),
89
Harrison's Cave, 28, 51
Harry Bailey
Observatory, 42
Health issues, 179–180
Helicopter tours, 165
Hiking
Barbados, 100–101
St. Lucia, 165–166
Hilton Barbados Resort
🏨, 76
Holetown, 65–67, 81,
84–86, 91
Holetown Landing, 46
Horse racing, 102
Horseback riding, 28,
166–167
Hotels, 11
Barbados, 17, 20, 32–33,
69–71, 73–77, 80–81,
84–87
prices, 11, 17, 19, 33,
110
St. Lucia, 19, 110,
141–148, 150–154
House, The 🏨, 20,
84–85
Hummingbird, The ✕,
140
Hummingbird Beach
Resort 🏨, 151–152
Hunt's Gardens, 51–52
Hurricane Hole Bar &
Restaurant ✕, 139

I

Inn on the Bay 🏨, 148
Insurance, 180
International Creole
Day, 108
Internet, 177
Island Inn Hotel 🏨, 76
Itineraries, 24–25

J

J.Q.s Shopping Mall,
156

Jacques Waterfront
Dining ✕, 137–138
Jade Mountain 🏨, 20,
152
Jounen Kwéyòl Ente-
nasyonnal, 108
Juma's Restaurant ✕,
68
Jungle tours, 164

K

Kiteboarding, 104, 168
Kwéyòl, 129

L

La Haut Resort 🏨, 152
La Place Carenage, 119,
157
Ladera 🏨, 20, 152
Landings Resort & Spa,
The 🏨, 144
L'Azure at the Crane ✕,
61, 63
Lewis, Sir W. Arthur,
127
Lighthouses
Barbados, 42
Little Arches Hotel 🏨,
76
Little Good Harbour
🏨, 87
Lobster Pot, The ✕, 68
Lodging, 11. ⇨ see also
Hotels
apartment rentals, 71
condo rentals, 71
villa rentals, 33, 70
Lone Star ✕, 61, 66
Lone Star Hotel 🏨, 85

M

Mail, 181
Malls, 34, 92
Mamiku Gardens,
126–127
Manchineel trees, 59
Mango Bay 🏨, 85
Mango Beach Inn 🏨,
148
Maria Islands Nature
Reserve, 127–128

Marigot Bay, *113,*
138–139, 148, 149
Marigot Bay Resort &
Marina by Capella
🔲, *148, 150*
Marigot Beach, *132*
Marigot Beach Club &
Dive Resort 🔲, *150*
Marigot Marina Village,
156
Mews, The ✕, *61,*
66–67
Miami Beach, *56*
Money matters, *17,*
19, 181
Morgan Lewis Sugar
Mill, *45*
Morne Coubaril Histor-
ical Adventure Park,
124–125
Mount Gay Rum Visitors
Centre, *49*
Mullins Beach, *59*
Museums
Barbados, 28, 38, 40, 41,
45–46, 48–49, 50–51
St. Lucia, 113, 119, 122,
124

N
Naked Fisherman Beach
Bar & Grill ✕, *136*
National Heroes
Square, *37*
Nature preserves
Barbados, 28, 43
St. Lucia, 122, 126,
127–128
Nidhe Israel Syna-
gogue, *36*
Nightlife
Barbados, 87, 89–91
St. Lucia, 154–155

O
Ocean Two 🔲, *73*
Oistins Fish Fry ✕,
28, 91
Old Jam Inn, *90*
Orchid World & Tropical
Flower Garden, *52*
Orlando's ✕, *21,*
140–141

P
Parks
Barbados, 37, 44, 52
St. Lucia, 113, 124–125
Parliament Buildings, *37*
Passports, *182*
Paynes Bay Beach, *59*
Pebbles Beach, *56*
Pigeon Island National
Landmark, *28, 113*
Pigeon Point, *132*
Pink Plantation House,
The ✕, *136–137*
Pitons, The, *124*
Plantations, *44,*
136–137
Pointe Seraphine, *119,*
157
Prices
Barbados, 11, 17, 33
dining, 11, 19, 33, 110
lodging, 11, 19, 33, 110
St. Lucia, 11, 110
Primo Bar & Bistro
✕, *61*

Q
Queen's Park, *37*

R
Radisson Aquatica
Resort Barbados 🔲,
76–77
Ragamuffins ✕, *67*
Rain Forest Sky Rides,
114
Rainforest Adventures,
114
Red Door Lounge, *91*
Reduit Beach, *132–133*
Rendezvous 🔲, *20, 147*
Restaurants, *11, 178*
Barbados, 21, 59–61,
63–68, 178
prices, 11, 19, 33, 110
St. Lucia, 21, 133–141,
178
Rodney Bay, *113,*
137–138, 146–147
Rodney Bay Village,
115
Round House ✕, *65*

Round House Inn 🔲, *80*
Royal St. Lucia Resort
and Spa 🔲, *147*
Rum, *22, 49, 55, 119*

S
Safety, *34, 109*
Sailing. ➡ See Boating
and sailing
St James's Club Morgan
Bay 🔲, *28, 145*
St. Lawrence Gap,
53–54, 61, 71, 73–74,
90
St. Lucia, *14, 105–168*
beaches, 18, 22,
128–129, 132–133
Castries and the North,
112–115–119,
136–137, 147–148
exploring, 110,112–115,
118–119, 121–122,
124–128
festivals and seasonal
events, 23, 108, 154,
155
history, 107–108
hotels, 19, 21, 109–110,
141–148, 150–154
Marigot Bay, 113,
138–139, 148, 149
nightlife and the arts,
154–155
North: Rodney Bay to
Cap Estate, 137–138,
146–147
prices, 19, 110
restaurants, 133–141
shopping, 22, 156–157,
159
Soufrière, 121–122,
124–126, 139–141,
150–153
sports and activities, 18,
22, 159–168
timing the visit, 23,
107–108
transportation, 18, 108,
170–175
Vieux Fort and the East
Coast, 126–128,
134–136, 153–154

Vigie to Cap Estate,
134–136, 143–146
**St. Lucia Billfishing
Tournament,** 107
**St. Lucia Distillers Group
of Companies,** 119
St. Lucia Jazz Festival,
107, 154
St. Michael's Cathedral,
37
St. Nicholas Abbey,
45–46
St. Omar, Dunstan, 121
Sandals Barbados 🏨,
20, 73–74
**Sandals Grande St.
Lucian** 🏨, 145
**Sandals Halcyon Beach
St. Lucia** 🏨, 20, 145
Sandals Regency La Toc
🏨, 148
Sandals Royal Barbados
🏨, 74
Sandpiper, The 🏨, 85
Sandy Beach, 56
**Sandy Lane Hotel and
Golf Club** 🏨, 28, 85
Savannah Beach Hotel
🏨, 77
Scarlet ✕, 67
Scoopie's Jazz (club), 90
Scuba diving
Barbados, 21, 96–98
St. Lucia, 18, 22,
161–163
Sea Island Cotton Shop,
159
Sea-U Guest House
🏨, 81
Sea excursions
Barbados, 21, 102–103
St. Lucia, 167–168
Sea urchins, 103
Serenity at Coconut Bay
🏨, 20, 153–154
Shaker's ✕, 63–64
Shopping
areas & malls, 92,
156–157
Barbados, 22, 91–95
department stores, 93
duty-free, 92, 93, 119

St. Lucia, 22, 156–157,
159
Silver Point Hotel 🏨, 77
**Silver Sands-Silver Rock
Beach,** 56
**Sir Frank Hutson Sugar
Museum,** 49
Snake man, 119
Snorkeling
Barbados, 21, 96–97
St. Lucia, 22, 161–163
Sobers, Sir Garfield, 99
SoCo Hotel The 🏨,
77–78
Soufrière, St. Lucia,
121–122, 124–126,
139–141, 150–153
South Beach Hotel
🏨, 77
South Coast, 38, 40–42,
54–56, 63–64, 74–77,
80, 91, 93–94
South Point Light, 42
**Southern Palms Beach
Club** 🏨, 74
Sports and activities
Barbados, 16, 21, 22,
95–104
St. Lucia, 18, 22,
159–168
**Stonefield Estate Villa
Resort & Spa** 🏨, 152
Street parties, 155
Sugar, 45, 49, 5353
Sugar Bay Barbados 🏨,
28, 77, 80
**Sugar Beach, A Viceroy
Resort** 🏨, 20, 28, 153
Sulphur Springs Park,
124
**Sunbury Plantation
House & Museum,** 41
Surfing, 103–104
Sweetfield Manor 🏨,
28, 80
Symbols, 11
Synagogues, 36

T

Tamarind Cove Hotel
🏨, 28, 86
Tao ✕, 136

Tapas On The Bay ✕,
138
Taxes and charges, 17,
19, 182
Taxis, 175
Telephones, 177–178
Ti Bananne ✕, 138
Ti Kaye Resort & Spa
🏨, 20, 150
**Tiami Catamaran
Cruises,** 103
Tides, The ✕ 61, 67
Time zones, 182
Tipping, 182
**Toraille Waterfalls &
Gardens,** 126
Tours
Barbados, 28, 40, 49,
51, 100
St. Lucia, 114, 122, 124,
154, 164–165
Transportation, 170–175
Treasure Beach 🏨, 86
Trip insurance, 182–183
Turtle Beach, 54
Turtle Beach Resort 🏨,
28, 75
Turtles, 73
**Tyrol Cot Heritage
Village,** 50

V

Vendor's Arcade, 156
Vieux Fort, 126–128,
134–136, 153–154,
157
Vigie/Malabar Beach,
133
Villa Beach Cottages
🏨, 145
Villa rentals, 33, 70–71,
141–142
Visas, 182
Visitor Information, 183

W

Walcott, Sir Derek, 127
Waterfalls, 121–122,
123, 126
Waterfront Cafe ✕, 21,
60, 90

Waves Hotel and Spa
⬚ , 86
Weather, 23
Weddings
Barbados, 26–27, 34,
183
St. Lucia, 26–27, 110,
184
Welchman Hall Gully,
52
Windjammer Landing
Villa Beach Resort ⬚ ,
28, 146

Windsurfing
Barbados, 22, 104
St. Lucia, 168

Z
Zaka (shop), 159
Zen at the Crane ✕ , 64
Zip-line rides, 28, 114,
125

PHOTO CREDITS

Front cover: Alan Copson / AWL Images [Description: Soufriere Bay and Petit Piton, St. Lucia]. 1, Mrs. Joan Devaux/ Diamond Botanical Gardens and Waterfall. 2, Martin MoxterimageBROKER / age fotostock. 3 (top), Mikael Lamber. 3 (bottom), ben.ramirez/Flickr. 4 (top left and right), Saint Lucia Tourism Board. 4 (bottom), Heeb Christian / age fotostock. 5 (top), Eleanor Scriven / age fotostock. 5 (bottom), clarkography / Shutterstock. 6 (top), Ingolf Pompe / age fotostock. 6 (bottom), Sandy Lane Hotel. 7, M. Timothy O'Keefe / Alamy. 8 (top and bottom), Barbados Tourism Authority/Jim Smith. 10, Barbados Tourism Authority. **Chapter 1 Experience Barbados and St. Lucia:** 12-13, Benjamin Howell/ iStockphoto. **Chapter 2 Barbados:** 29, John Miller / age fotostock. 33, Barbados Tourism Authority/Andrew Hulsmeier. 35, Wollwerth | Dreamstime.com. 40, Barbados Concorde Experience. 45, St. Nicholas Abbey. 51, Shirley Kilpatrick/ Alamy. 57, Barbados Tourism Authority. 72, IngolfPompe / age fotostock. 78-79, Pete Phipp/Travelshots / age fotostock. 82-83, Barbados Tourism Authority/Mike Toy. 87, graham tomlin/Shutterstock. 88, World Pictures / age fotostock. 90, Roy Riley /Alamy. 95, Barbados Tourism Authority/Ronnie Carrington. 96, Kiera Bloom/Barbados Blue. 101, MAT/Shutterstock. **Chapter 3 St. Lucia:** 105, Colin Sinclair/age fotostock. 116-117, Ian Cumming / age fotostock. 120, Helene Rogers /age fotostock. 123, Ian Cumming / age fotostock. 130-131, Ian Cumming / age fotostock. 139, Ladera. 142, Mike Toy/Cap Maison. 149, Ian Cumming / age fotostock. 153, Ladera. 158, Gavin Hellier / age fotostock. 162, Stephen Frink Collection / Alamy. 167, M. Timothy O'Keefe/ Alamy. **Spine:** PHB.cz (Richard Semik)/Shutterstock. **About Our Writer:** Photo is courtesy of the writer.

Fodor's InFocus BARBADOS & ST. LUCIA

Editorial: Douglas Stallings, *Editorial Director*; Margaret Kelly, Jacinta O'Halloran, *Senior Editors*; Kayla Becker, Alexis Kelly, Amanda Sadlowski, *Editors*; Teddy Minford, *Content Editor*; Rachael Roth, *Content Manager*

Design: Tina Malaney, *Design and Production Director*; Jessica Gonzalez, *Production Designer*

Photography: Jennifer Arnow, *Senior Photo Editor*

Maps: Rebecca Baer, *Senior Map Editor*; Mark Stroud (Moon Street Cartography) and David Lindroth, *Cartographers*

Production: Jennifer DePrima, *Editorial Production Manager*; Carrie Parker, *Senior Production Editor*; Elyse Rozelle, *Production Editor*

Business & Operations: Chuck Hoover, *Chief Marketing Officer*; Joy Lai, *Vice President and General Manager*; Stephen Horowitz, *Director of Business Development and Revenue Operations*; Tara McCrillis, *Director of Publishing Operations*; Eliza D. Aceves, *Content Operations Manager and Strategist*

Public Relations and Marketing: Joe Ewaskiw, *Manager*; Esther Su, *Marketing Manager*

Writer: Jane E. Zarem

Editor: Alexis Kelly

Production Editor: Carrie Parker

5th Edition

ISBN 978-1-64097-040-3

ISSN 1941–0212

All details in this book are based on information supplied to us at press time. Always confirm information when it matters, especially if you're making a detour to visit a specific place. Fodor's expressly disclaims any liability, loss, or risk, personal or otherwise, that is incurred as a consequence of the use of any of the contents of this book.

SPECIAL SALES

This book is available at special discounts for bulk purchases for sales promotions or premiums. For more information, e-mail SpecialMarkets@fodors.com.

PRINTED IN THE UNITED STATES OF AMERICA

10 9 8 7 6 5 4 3 2 1

ABOUT OUR WRITER

Jane E. Zarem characterizes herself as a globe-trotting writer, intrepid researcher, fastidious editor, and curious soul with a positive outlook, mature view, and big-picture perspective. She loves the chance to kick back in the Caribbean each year on her updating missions to Barbados, St. Lucia, and several other islands for Fodor's *Caribbean*.

Jane's love affair with the Caribbean began several decades ago, when she joined a 10-day Windjammer cruise that called on islands that, at the time, she never knew existed: Tortola, Virgin Gorda, Nevis, St. Kitts, St. Maarten, Saba, St. Barth's. Tourism hadn't yet hit those island paradises, and most claimed more goats than people.

She has since made more than 80 trips to the Caribbean and has visited Barbados and St. Lucia more than a dozen times each. She has stared at the east coast of Barbados and swum between the Pitons in St. Lucia. She has visited historic great houses in Barbados and wandered through St. Lucia's Diamond Botanical Gardens. She has explored shops and markets in both Bridgetown and Castries, off-roaded along the northern tip of Barbados, and sailed along the west coast of St. Lucia. She has met wonderful people on both islands, who have welcomed her back with a big hug and a broad smile on each subsequent visit.

Jane has been a freelance travel writer for more than 25 years. Her very first travel-writing assignment involved updating the Connecticut chapter of Fodor's *New England* in the late 1970s. Since then, she has worked on many Fodor's guides, contributed travel articles to various newspapers and magazines, written travel and other business-related newsletters, and contributed numerous articles and research reports to trade magazines and other organizations. Most significantly, she has been a contributor to Fodor's *Caribbean* since 1994.

Acknowledgments

Writing this edition of *In Focus Barbados and St. Lucia* was a natural assignment for Jane and, she will tell you, "a labor of love." She could not have accomplished it without the assistance of the good people at the Barbados Tourism Authority and the St. Lucia Tourist Board, who have coordinated her trips to the respective islands over the many years.

EUGENE FODOR

Hungarian-born Eugene Fodor (1905–91) began his travel career as an interpreter on a French cruise ship. The experience inspired him to write *On the Continent* (1936), the first guidebook to receive annual updates and discuss a country's way of life as well as its sights. Fodor later joined the U.S. Army and worked for the OSS in World War II. After the war, he kept up his intelligence work while expanding his guidebook series. During the Cold War, many guides were written by fellow agents who understood the value of insider information. Today's guides continue Fodor's legacy by providing travelers with timely coverage, insider tips, and cultural context.